TITANIC
AND LIVERPOOL

For Angela, Stephanie and Benji
And the people of my home port, Liverpool

First published 2009 by
Liverpool University Press
4 Cambridge Street
Liverpool L69 7ZU
and
National Museums Liverpool
127 Dale Street
Liverpool L2 2JH

British Library Cataloguing-in-Publication data
A British Library CIP record is available

ISBN 978-184631-222-9 limp

Book design by March Graphic Design Studio, Liverpool
Printed and bound by Gutenberg Press, Malta

TITANIC
AND LIVERPOOL

ALAN SCARTH

CONTENTS

PREFACE AND ACKNOWLEDGEMENTS

Anyone writing a book today about *Titanic* has very many potential 'icebergs' to avoid. As any armchair Captain Smith will tell you, this is inevitable when you are trying to stay on course and on schedule in such dangerous waters. So much has been said and written about the ship since her disastrous maiden voyage in 1912 that it is now often very difficult to distinguish fact from fiction, reality from fantasy. *Titanic* and White Star Line author Paul Louden-Brown was recently quoted in the Dublin-based *Sunday Business Post* as saying: 'By now we know everything there is to know about the *Titanic*. Most of what you hear is repetition and with the centenary, there'll be more of that. But what we need to start asking is how we arrived at the *Titanic*. The real story here is not about a single sinking, but why such a ship existed in the first place.'[1] Having reached similar conclusions myself in recent years, I hope that this book will prove to be an original and enduring contribution to the subject.

I should like to thank National Museums Liverpool and Liverpool University Press for giving me the opportunity to write this book. At National Museums Liverpool, Dr. Jon Murden, Tony Tibbles and Rachel Mulhearn all read draft chapters and made helpful suggestions, as did Ian Murphy, Eleanor Moffat, Rebecca Watkin, Sally Berry and May Liu. Keith Sweeney took most of the photographs, especially those of items from the Museum's collection. Alison Stephens reformatted the text, while Bill Watson advised on the cover design. Sarah-Jane Farr of the Merseyside Archaeological Survey identified the site of Bruce Ismay's former home in south Liverpool. I am also grateful to the staff of the Maritime Archives and Library at Merseyside Maritime Museum for their assistance. At Liverpool University Press, I am indebted to Anthony Cond and his team for their enthusiasm, high standards and tight deadlines. Peter Bernie of Liverpool and London P. & I. Management Ltd graciously allowed me to consult his company's historic minute books relating to *Titanic*. Richard Bixter also assisted with the cover design. Above all, I must thank my wife Angela, daughter Stephanie and dog Benji for their constant support and encouragement, without which this book would not have been written.

PRIMARY SOURCES AND PHOTOGRAPHS

Most of the original archival material referred to in this book is held at the Maritime Archives and Library, Merseyside Maritime Museum, Albert Dock, Liverpool. Some of the contemporary newspaper sources used were viewed on microfilm at the Liverpool Record Office, Central Libraries, William Brown Street, Liverpool. Otherwise, the superb Encyclopedia Titanica website (http://www.encyclopedia-titanica.org) was a major source of biographical information. Another key source was the excellent website of the Titanic Inquiry Project (http://www.titanicinquiry.org), which provides online transcripts of both the United States Senate and British Board of Trade Inquiries, and the subsequent Limitation of Liability hearings in New York State. All other sources are duly acknowledged in the notes.

Unless otherwise stated all photographs used in this book are copyright of National Museums Liverpool. Special thanks are due to the Institute of Marine Engineering, Science and Technology (IMarEST), London, for providing images of Titanic engineers Joseph Bell and W.E. Farquharson from its Transactions of 1912. The Titanic Fund set up in that year for the widows and orphans of the *Titanic* engineers is now the Guild of Benevolence of the IMarEST and provides financial help to marine engineers and their dependants.

ABBREVIATIONS

British Inquiry	British Board of Trade (Wreck Commissioner's) Inquiry: http://www.titanicinquiry.org
ET	*Encyclopedia Titanica*: http://www.encyclopedia-titanica.org
IMM	International Mercantile Marine Company
JoC	*Journal of Commerce*
LDPM	*Liverpool Daily Post and Mercury*
MMM	Merseyside Maritime Museum
NML	National Museums Liverpool
TC	*The Titanic Commutator* (Journal of the Titanic Historical Society Inc.)
US Inquiry	United States Senate Inquiry: http://www.titanicinquiry.org

INTRODUCTION

It is an ancient Mariner,
And he stoppeth one of three.
'By thy long grey beard and glittering eye,
Now wherefore stopp'st thou me?'

Samuel Taylor Coleridge
The Rime of the Ancient Mariner
(1797-8)

Almost everyone has an opinion about *Titanic*. Her exceptionally dramatic and tragic story, still full of unresolved issues, has a powerful, worldwide appeal which seems to grow from generation to generation. Since the discovery of the wreck in 1985 by Dr. Robert Ballard, and James Cameron's blockbusting Hollywood film in 1997, her grip on the popular imagination has become stronger than ever. Today, constantly refuelled by fresh information, theories and controversies, the feverish international fascination with the ship continues to grow. As the one hundredth anniversary of her sinking approaches, the story of *Titanic* now belongs, not just to the British Isles, Europe and North America, but to the world.

It is noticeable that in recent years many researchers have focused on particular places which have connections with the ship, whether strong or weak. For example, the major roles played by Belfast, where *Titanic* was built, and Southampton, from which she embarked on her maiden voyage, have been increasingly explored and revealed. This also applies to Cherbourg, Queenstown, New York and Halifax, Nova Scotia, each of which, in their different ways, played significant parts in the story. Many other places around the world with rather less obvious *Titanic* links have similarly been spotlighted by researchers keen to find new, 'local' angles on this global story. It is, therefore, very surprising that so little attention has yet been paid to the very strong links between *Titanic* and the port of Liverpool.

It is well known that *Titanic* bore the name 'Liverpool' on her stern, since this is usually one of the last images of the ship shown in feature films as she slips beneath the waves. However, it seems to have been assumed by many *Titanic* authors and researchers that the relationship between the ship and her port of registration, or 'official home port', was indirect and weak. For example, in her recent book *Titanic: A Night Remembered*,[1] American historian Stephanie Barczewski explores the impact which *Titanic*'s loss had on Belfast, Southampton and Queenstown, but largely excludes Liverpool from her otherwise excellent and original study. In her introduction, she recalls a conversation on a train in which

> a man attempted to convince me that his relatives had owned a boarding
> house in Liverpool where many of *Titanic*'s passengers stayed the night
> before the ship sailed. My gentle protestations that the *Titanic* did not
> sail from Liverpool and in fact never visited that city at all were to no
> avail. Everyone, it seems, wants to claim a connection to the *Titanic*.[2]

Even if this gentleman's story is a complete myth, which, as Barczewski suggests, it may well be, it should not deflect our attention from a broader and deeper truth. As the author herself briefly acknowledges later in her book, Liverpool, like Belfast and Southampton, did have 'close connections to the [*Titanic*] disaster'.[3] While she rightly states that *Titanic* never visited Liverpool, there is absolutely no question that the great Atlantic port of north-west England and many of its people played key parts in the *Titanic* story. Indeed, far from being a minor player in the drama, as many accounts still appear to suggest, Liverpool was a protagonist.

The purpose of this book is not to retell every aspect of the *Titanic* story, but to reassess the ship's tragic history from the crucial Liverpool perspective. As the reader will soon realise, far from being a parochial excursion into local history, this approach transforms our understanding of the whole subject. The message on the great liner's stern was clear and direct: *Titanic* was a Liverpool ship.

CHAPTER 1

HOME PORT

I am the English sea-queen; I am she
Who made the English wealthy by the sea
The street of this my city is the tide
Where the world's ships, that bring my glory, ride …

John Masefield,
'*A Masque of Liverpool*' (1930)

LIVERPOOL

In late March 1912, as the final touches were being made to *Titanic* at the Harland and
Wolff shipyard in Belfast, the ship was registered in Liverpool for customs purposes.[1]
This was because her shipping company, the White Star Line, was based in the great
port of north-west England. So Liverpool became her official home port, as indeed it
had been for all previous White Star liners. *Titanic* would, therefore, carry the name
'Liverpool' on her stern, and not that of Southampton, the port from which she
would shortly sail on her tragic maiden voyage across the North Atlantic.

At this time Liverpool was the British Empire's foremost international
seaport and Europe's largest transatlantic port. From the 1860s it had expanded
far beyond its original Irish Sea and Atlantic trades to become the world's premier
liner port. The huge size of Liverpool's dock system and the range and quality of
its shipping services were internationally admired. The port was particularly well
known for its long-standing domination of the North Atlantic passenger trade,
involving the carriage of millions of European emigrants to the United States and
Canada. Indeed, it was due to its key role in this highly lucrative trade during the

nineteenth century that Liverpool had become the home port and headquarters of such famous North Atlantic shipping lines as Cunard, White Star, Allan, Dominion, Leyland and Canadian Pacific.[2] To one observer of the International Exhibition of Navigation, Commerce and Industry held in Liverpool in 1886, 'thanks to modern science and commercial enterprise, to the spirit and intelligence of the townsmen, and to the administration of the Mersey Docks and Harbour Board' the city had become a 'wonder of the world': 'It is the New York of Europe, a world-city rather than merely British provincial'.[3]

It is difficult today to grasp the full extent of Liverpool's prominence in international shipping and commerce at the beginning of the twentieth century. In his book *Liverpool: City of the Sea* (1997), Tony Lane commented: 'So many and so large were the fleets of passenger and cargo liners captained and crewed by Liverpudlians, swarmed over and serviced by tens of thousands of other citizens, that the scale and intensity of ocean-going and coastal traffic made Liverpool a city port like none had ever been before'.[4]

In 2004 'Liverpool – Maritime Mercantile City' was inscribed as a UNESCO World Heritage Site. The award was made on the basis that the site is 'the supreme example of a commercial port at a time of Britain's greatest global influence'.[5] A book produced by Liverpool City Council to celebrate this award states that '[by] the end of the nineteenth century a third of the total shipping in Britain was conducted through Liverpool and one seventh of the entire world's shipping was registered in Liverpool'.[6]

Not that the city's success was confined to shipping alone. The same source also emphasises that, at the same time, the city had become 'a world centre for underwriting, exchanges, insurance and banking, mostly under the control of Liverpool shipowners'.[7] In terms of commercial prestige and influence, Liverpool was at its peak. In 1907, Charles Hand, the local author of a book marking the 700th anniversary of Liverpool's grant of borough status from King John, expressed the confidence and optimism of Edwardian Liverpool when he wrote:

'Everything is bright and clear above the horizon; as yet no cloud is in the sky; all is fair, promising and hopeful …'.[8] As John Belchem remarks, this confidence was soon to be embodied 'in the imposing architecture (and attendant public sculpture) of the new Pier Head: the Mersey Docks and Harbour Building (1907), the Royal Liver Building (1911) and the Cunard Building (1913), the photogenic sea-facing skyline by which Liverpool remains instantly recognisable'.[9]

However, despite the 'blue sky thinking' of the city's leaders at the time, some aspects of Liverpool's exceptional commercial position were already under threat. In particular, the storm clouds were gathering over the port's formerly towering position in the Atlantic trades. Since the 1890s it had faced growing competition in the North Atlantic from Southampton on the English Channel coast and continental ports such as Hamburg, Bremen and Antwerp. A further threat to Liverpool's Atlantic dominance had emerged from the desire of certain American corporate interests to acquire a major stake in these trades. Between 1901 and 1902 the American industrial tycoon and financier John Pierpont Morgan and his associates had gained control of six North Atlantic shipping lines, three British and three American, to form his International Mercantile Marine Company (IMM). Morgan's main aim was to wrest control of the North Atlantic from European shipping lines by creating a huge, American-owned monopoly 'to remove harmful price competition'. The three British companies he acquired were the Liverpool-based Leyland, White Star and Dominion lines. Of these, the White Star Line, then the most successful passenger line on the Atlantic, was considered to be Morgan's greatest prize.[10] One eventual consequence of this controversial takeover would be the construction of the giant White Star liners *Olympic*, *Titanic* and *Britannic*.

WHITE STAR AND THE ISMAYS

The White Star Line, more formally known as the Oceanic Steam Navigation Company Limited, was founded in Liverpool in 1869 by 32-year-old Thomas Henry Ismay, who was soon joined as a partner by his friend William Imrie. The

Centrepiece of the Ismay
testimonial silver.

eldest son of shipbuilder Joseph Ismay of Maryport in Cumberland, Ismay had
travelled to Liverpool at the age of 16 to become an apprentice in the shipbroking
firm of Imrie and Tomlinson. After travelling to South America, he returned to
Liverpool and set up a business trading to Australia. In 1867 he bought the
bankrupt White Star Line of sailing clippers to Australia so that he could use its
name and flag for his new shipping company.[11] His venture into the North Atlantic
steamship business was first suggested to him 'over a game of billiards after
dinner' by Gustavus Schwabe, a prominent Liverpool-based merchant, who lived
at Broughton Hall, West Derby. Schwabe explained that his nephew, G. W. Wolff,
had recently gone into a shipbuilding partnership in Belfast with Mr. Edward
Harland.[12] Schwabe said that if Ismay would agree to have his steamers built by
Harland and Wolff he would support the scheme as much as he could, and would
persuade other Liverpool businessmen to do the same. The first list of
shareholders in Ismay's new company, formed on 6 September 1869, included
Edward James Harland and Gustav William Wolff. The company's first ship,
Oceanic, was completed in 1871 by Harland and Wolff Limited of Belfast, setting
new standards of naval architecture and passenger accommodation. Thus began the
exceptionally close business relationship between White Star and the Belfast
shipbuilders which would continue until the 1930s.[13]

Thomas Ismay was a no-nonsense, straight-talking, 'self-made' businessman.
Under his shrewd and forceful leadership White Star soon became the most
successful British transatlantic shipping line, despite the formidable rivalry of the
Cunard Line and several other Liverpool-based companies. At a time of fierce
competition and rapid technological change, the Line built a reputation for efficient
management and large, well-built steamships. Such was the esteem in which Ismay
was held by the White Star shareholders that, at a dinner on board RMS *Adriatic* in
Liverpool on 16 September 1885, they presented him with a magnificent silver gilt
dinner service by Messrs Hunt and Roskell of London, believed to be one of the
finest of its kind ever made. In the inscription engraved on this service, the

The White Star Line Head Office,
30 James Street, Liverpool.

shareholders acknowledged that it was to 'the sound judgement, untiring energy, and singleness of purpose he has displayed in the management of their affairs for the past fifteen years, [that] the prosperity of the Company is mainly due'.[14] They also presented Ismay with his portrait by John Everett Millais. In his introductory speech on this occasion, Mr. Thomas H. Jackson, Chairman of the Shareholders, remarked: 'we owe not a little to Mr. Ismay's coolness and good judgement into not being led into following in the wake of those who have rushed into large and costly steamers'. He then expressed his confidence that 'when he [Ismay] thinks the time has come to build larger and faster boats we, as Shareholders, shall be safe in his hands, for he will consider our interests before either the profit or fame of the managers'.[15] Reporting on these proceedings shortly afterwards, a writer for the *Liverpool Review* observed, in relation to the 'happy fate of the Shareholders of this Line', that '[they] have had, as it were, a mark placed on their portals, and the demon of ill luck has passed them over'.[16]

One of Thomas Ismay's most lasting legacies was the construction of the White Star Line building at 30 James Street, Liverpool. By the early 1890s the Company had outgrown its original, cramped offices at 10 Water Street, and needed new headquarters in keeping with its continuing success. Ismay had acquired a fine site near the waterfront, at the bottom of James Street, next to the Strand. In 1894 he asked the distinguished London architect Richard Norman Shaw to design the new building. Shaw, a younger brother of a founder of the Shaw Savill shipping line of London, had worked with Ismay twelve years earlier on a private commission to design and build 'Dawpool', a huge and eccentric mansion, for the shipping millionaire at Thurstaston on the Wirral. Working with Liverpool-based J.F. Doyle, his superintendent architect, Shaw reworked his earlier design for New Scotland Yard on London's Embankment for White Star's new offices on the Mersey. According to Andrew Saint, the architect's biographer, Shaw wanted 'a proud and hardy building with which to convey the mood of Merseyside'. He adds: 'New Scotland Yard's granite and brick, appropriate in London only for the police, fitted

J. Bruce Ismay in about 1900. (National Museums Liverpool, DX/1412).

the gritty independence of Liverpool's whole character'.[17]

The building was completed in 1898. Two years later the eighty staff based there were involved in the management of the entire White Star fleet and its worldwide services and connections. The James Street offices would be the headquarters of White Star until the late 1920s, when, having been acquired by the Royal Mail group, its head office was effectively transferred to London.[18]

When Thomas died in 1899, he was succeeded as chairman and managing director of the White Star Line by his eldest son, Joseph Bruce Ismay. Bruce was a very different character to his father, and was faced with very different challenges during his career. Born in 1862 at Enfield House, the family home in Great Crosby, north Liverpool, he began his schooling across the River Mersey at New Brighton. Later, he spent a few 'not very happy' years at fashionable Elstree preparatory school, near Reading, followed by a miserable eighteen-month period at Harrow public school in north London. A shy, rather introverted young man, he hated boarding school life, and his parents eventually sent him to Dinard in France to complete his formal education at a private school run by an English clergyman. In 1880, at the age of 18, he entered the firm of Ismay, Imrie and Company, managers of the Oceanic Steam Navigation Company, to serve a four-year apprenticeship. Six years later, shortly after returning from a long ocean trip to New Zealand, Australia, Japan and the United States, he was appointed Manager of the White Star Line Agency in New York.

It was in New York, well away from his father's intimidating shadow, that Bruce's life really changed for the better. Within a short time he had met and married Florence Schieffelin, the eldest daughter of a wealthy New York family. He had also become close friends with fellow Englishman Harold Arthur Sanderson, who was General Manager of Wilson and Sons of Hull, one of the largest private shipping companies in the world. Sanderson, born near Liverpool in Bebington, Cheshire, was three years older than Bruce and already had a fine reputation in the shipping world. Like Ismay, he had also married a New Yorker.

'Sandheys', Bruce Ismay's Georgian-style home in Mossley Hill Road, Liverpool (from Oldham, *Ismay Line*).

Map showing the site of Bruce Ismay's house 'Sandheys', Mossley Hill Road, Liverpool (O.S. 25" map, 1927, in black) in relation to more recent housing developments in the area (O.S. 25" map, 1939, in blue). © Crown Copyright and/or database right. All rights reserved. Licence number 100030424.

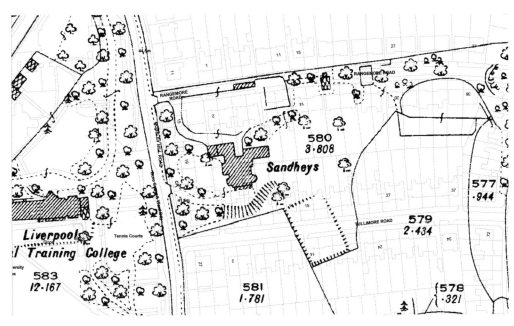

He had earlier succeeded his father as head of the shipping agents Sanderson & Son of State Street, New York. Through his friendship with Bruce Ismay, he would soon become General Manager for White Star in Liverpool and, like Ismay, would play an important part in the *Titanic* story.[19]

In 1891 Bruce Ismay returned to Liverpool to take up his partnership in the family firm. Although his father remained chairman, he increasingly left the day-to-day management of the White Star Line to his eldest son and the other partners. According to *The Times*, looking back at Bruce Ismay's career many years later: 'It has often been said that both Mr. Ismay and his father could get cargoes and make profits when their competitors were losing money'.[20]

The company remained privately owned, Thomas being the main shareholder, with most of the remaining shares being held by family members and personal friends. In June 1893 Bruce bought and moved into 'Sandheys', a large Georgian-style house situated in ten acres of land in Mossley Hill, a semi-rural suburb in south Liverpool.[21] This was to be his Liverpool home for almost thirty years. In 1911 his private telephone number was '31 Garston'.[22] In 1894 Harold Sanderson, having been appointed General Manager for White Star in Liverpool, became his neighbour when he moved with his family into Holmfield House, a fine property in an adjoining estate.[23]

After his father's death in December 1899, Bruce Ismay, at 37 years of age, became head of the family business. Figures published five years later by *The Times* revealed that he had inherited a very robust company indeed, which had, between 1897 and 1898, 'its share capital intact, a reserve fund as large as the share capital, and the whole valuable fleet paid for by means of past savings out of revenue'. Most unusually, the company was even owed money by its shipbuilders, Harland and Wolff Limited. Indeed, after credit and other adjustments were taken into account, the overall reserves of the company at that time were estimated to be in excess of £2.8 million.[24] Commenting on the exceptional results achieved over many years by White Star under Thomas Ismay's direction, a *Journal of*

Commerce columnist later observed that they were a tribute to Ismay's 'very sound principle' that in any business 'as much money as possible must be kept away from shareholders and devoted to depreciation or reserves'. Here, the same writer remarked, Ismay's policy of secrecy had been a distinct advantage, since it was probable that, had the majority of shareholders known fully what White Star was earning, they would have clamoured for higher dividends.[25]

One of Bruce Ismay's first decisions on becoming Chairman of White Star was to make Harold Sanderson a partner in the firm. The company continued to prosper, and in April 1901 the 21,000-ton passenger and cargo liner *Celtic*, the last ship ordered by Thomas Ismay, was launched by Harland and Wolff in Belfast. The immediate success of this ship, which eclipsed White Star's own *Oceanic* (II) by four thousand tons to become the largest ship in the world, reinforced Bruce's determination to continue his late father's policy of providing big ships with maximum passenger and cargo capacity but of only modest speed. *Celtic* was to be the first of the company's famous 'Big Four' liners, completed between 1901 and 1907 for service on the North Atlantic, namely *Celtic*, *Cedric*, *Baltic* and *Adriatic*. At the time of her maiden voyage each of these ships was the largest in service in the world. Over the next twenty years the 'Big Four' were widely admired for their steadiness in rough weather on their main route between Liverpool and New York. They were the immediate predecessors of White Star's '*Olympic* class' liners of 1911 to 1915, namely *Olympic*, *Titanic* and *Britannic*.[26]

MORGANISED

In April 1901 the American financier J.P. Morgan bought the Liverpool-based Leyland Line, Britain's major transatlantic cargo carrier, to add to the three American-owned lines already acquired for his proposed 'Atlantic Shipping Combine'. In the same month, probably encouraged by William James Pirrie, president of the British Chamber of Shipping and chairman of Harland and Wolff shipbuilders, 'acting as agent, self-appointed or otherwise',[27] Morgan's associates

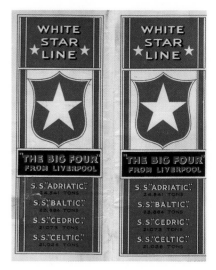

White Star Line advertising brochure for 'The Big Four From Liverpool', c.1922. (DX/2289)

also approached Bruce Ismay with a view to purchasing the White Star Line. Pirrie, himself a White Star shareholder, was known to have had much bolder and more ambitious plans than Ismay regarding the Line's future development, closely linked as it would undoubtedly be with that of his own shipbuilding firm.[28]

It had been a difficult year in the North Atlantic passenger trades due to a substantial fall in the number of emigrants to America and a fierce rates war among the shipping companies involved. Despite strong initial resistance by the Ismay family, the generous terms of Morgan's offer were eventually accepted and on 4 February 1902 the sale was provisionally agreed, before being formally ratified by White Star shareholders after a 'long and stormy' meeting on 17 May.[29] The final terms of the agreement were announced the following November. Each shareholder was to receive, 'in cash and shares', about fourteen times the value of their shares. Each was also to give the White Star staff £52 8s per share, totalling about £45,000 to be distributed among the 'jubilant' staff members.[30] The full purchase price of the White Star company was to be £10,699,436, of which £3,147,236 would be payable in cash, £5,034,800 in preference shares of the new combine, and £2,517,400 in the common stock of the company. The view of the British journal *Shipping World* was that 'a good bargain has been made on behalf of the shareholders of the great British line'.[31] In effect, Messrs J.P. Morgan & Company had paid ten times the net profits of the company in 1900, which had, unexpectedly, been 'one of the most profitable in the company's history'.[32] Morgan's purchase of the Dominion Line, another Liverpool-based transatlantic company, was agreed a few weeks later. Once again, Pirrie's influence is likely to have been behind this transaction, since Harland and Wolff had built the Dominion fleet and now, as Vale observes, 'held more of its paper (or credit) than it cared for'.[33] The formation of the new combine, to be named the International Mercantile Marine Company Incorporated (New Jersey), was announced by J.P. Morgan in London on 18 April.[34]

In Liverpool the startling news of the 'Morganeering' of three of the port's 'greatest and best known' shipping companies seems initially to have had a mixed and rather muted reaction. To a contributor to the 'Lancashire Today' section of the *Daily Dispatch* newspaper of 2 December, for example, since Liverpool was 'in a sense the next-door neighbour of New York', it was not surprising that American methods were 'to some extent in favour in Liverpool'. Citing the successful establishment in the city of the American-owned Diamond Match Company factory and the American purchase of Ogden's tobacco factory as 'practical examples of American tools and methods at work', he remarked that 'the tobacco and match trade alike remain in British hands'. In his view, as Liverpool had now 'received the honour of special attention on the part of Mr. Pierpont Morgan', there was little alarm about the American Combine in Liverpool, since there was 'no reason to suppose that it will have any evil effects upon the city as a seaport'.[35] A similar conclusion was reached by the *Liverpool Daily Courier* newspaper on 30 April 1902, which reported that despite some 'alarmist' opinion, the prevailing attitude was one of confidence in the port's established status and 'magnificent facilities'. However, in business circles the news clearly did cause some anxiety regarding the port's future prospects, particularly in the transatlantic passenger trade. As the same report continued, 'there are some misgivings, and it is quite realised that a keen fight will have to be had with Southampton'. With regard to the White Star Line, however, the general feeling in Liverpool was that the family ties of the Ismays with the Mersey seaport were so strong 'that to make any other place their headquarters would be an extreme step'.[36]

The reaction elsewhere in Britain, however, was rather less phlegmatic. Press and public opinion in Britain became increasingly hostile towards the Morgan scheme, seeing it as a serious threat to Britain's commercial and national interests. The government's apparent lack of a clear policy on this matter added to the anxiety. In March 1902 the New York *Mail and Express* reported that Morgan's purchase of White Star had been interrupted by the British Admiralty due to its agreement with White Star that several of the Line's biggest ships would be liable to be called upon for service as auxiliary cruisers in time of war.[37] It also emerged that, in February 1902, having failed to buy them, Morgan had signed a profit-sharing agreement with two major German lines operating on the North Atlantic, namely Hamburg America and North German Lloyd.[38] The fact that, in the *Deutschland* and the *Kronprinz Wilhelm* respectively, each of these companies had faster ships than any of their British rivals was a further cause for concern to the government, from both a naval and a commercial point of view.[39] As Gerald Balfour, President of the Board of Trade and brother of Conservative Prime Minister Arthur Balfour, commented in his major speech on 30 September 1902, the possession by the German companies of vessels of 'twenty three and a half knots' had been regarded as 'a reproach to our British companies'.[40] It was common knowledge that German passenger liners had held the unofficial North Atlantic speed record or 'Blue Riband' since 1897, when the North German Lloyd liner *Kaiser Wilhelm der Grosse* had relieved the Cunard Line's *Lucania* of this 'honour'.[41] It was also generally acknowledged that, in recent years, Germany had provided a growing threat to Britain's commercial and naval supremacy at sea.[42]

Matters eventually came to a head when, in 1902, the Morgan group approached the Cunard Line with a view to adding this, the last and most venerable British line on the North Atlantic, to its combine. However, deeply concerned by the strong public reaction against the White Star sale and its implications for national prestige and defence, the British government intervened and prohibited the sale. The new chairman of Cunard, James Burns, the second Lord Inverclyde, promptly took advantage of this situation by persuading the government to grant his company a low-interest loan of £2,600,000, repayable over twenty years. This would be used to build two passenger liners which would be the biggest, fastest and most luxurious in the world. They would be built to Admiralty standards for easy conversion into armed merchant cruisers if required, and be capable of unsurpassed speeds of 24–25 knots. The government would also provide an annual subsidy towards the operation of these ships. In return, the Cunard Line would remain wholly British and its fleet would be at the disposal of the British government in time of war.[43] The terms of this agreement were announced by Gerald Balfour, President of the Board of Trade, in a dramatic speech at the Cutlers' Feast in Sheffield on 30 September 1902. It would lead to the construction, from 1904 onwards, of the turbine-driven liners *Lusitania* and *Mauretania*. When completed in 1907, these magnificent ships would be the envy of the world.

In his Sheffield speech, having announced the ground-breaking Cunard deal, Balfour sensationally revealed that the government had also reached a twenty-year agreement with J.P. Morgan concerning the exact status of the British companies and ships which he had acquired. In effect, he said, only the share capital of White Star and the other British companies involved had been transferred to the Morgan combine, not the direct control of their ships. The ships of all these companies would continue to fly the British flag and employ British crews. The majority of directors in these companies were to be British subjects. The Admiralty would have the right to buy or hire any British ships in the combine, as and when required. The British companies concerned would continue to be treated equally with other companies when mail contracts were awarded. No British ship in the combination, or any ship built for a British company, was to be transferred to a foreign registry without the written consent of the President of the Board of Trade. Finally, at least one half of the shipping tonnage built in future years for the combine was to be for British companies in the group.[44]

In general, despite lingering doubts about the legality of the Morgan agreement, these two major and unexpected agreements were warmly applauded in the British press and shipping circles. On 2 October, for example, the *Liverpool Courier* revealed that the general trend of commercial opinion in the city was that 'the American multi-millionaire' had been 'outsailed' and that British shipping supremacy and Liverpool's pre-eminence as the Atlantic port had been 'completely secured for many years to come'.[45] A more measured view from Wall Street, as reported in the *Liverpool Daily Post* on 3 October, was that the agreement was 'a severe blow to the Morgan shipping trust', since without Cunard 'a monopoly of the Atlantic carrying trade is now impossible'. Another telling comment from the same source was that 'the Cunard Company, linked with Great Britain, may be regarded as a full-fledged rival of the Morgan trust'. The correspondent concluded by remarking that public opinion in the United States was increasingly opposed to such trust schemes and so it was very unlikely that Mr. Morgan would be able to secure a subsidy from the US government.[46]

On 1 October, the day after Balfour's speech, the incorporation of the International Maritime Company was announced in the office of J.P. Morgan and Company in New York. The colossal new company was to have eight American and five British directors, under the presidency of the American Clement A. Griscom. Among the five British directors were Bruce Ismay and William Pirrie, chairman of Harland and Wolff Limited, and also a director of the White Star Line. It was expected that Harland and Wolff Limited would build all of the new ships ordered for the British companies in the combine, and possibly others. The Executive and Finance Committee was to be composed entirely of American directors, but the subsidiary lines were to be permitted 'full liberty to manage their own affairs'. The new enterprise was to have a capital stock of $120,000,000. It had secured more than one hundred ships, representing one fifth of all transatlantic tonnage and a third of the North Atlantic passenger service.[47]

The momentum, however, had already been lost. The agreement between the British government and Cunard, in particular, had indeed been a major setback. The combine had also paid too much for the British companies concerned and soon became seriously short of money. Subsidies expected from the United States government did not materialise and many of the directors of the steamship companies concerned worked against each other rather than as a team. The IMM was unable to establish a monopoly on the North Atlantic and over the next few years was faced with a bitter price war with rival companies. On 11 June 1903 the British shipping journal *Fairplay* quoted a 'recent article' from the *New York World* which was headlined: 'J.P. Morgan's One Big Failure, The Ship Trust'. With an unusual and unfortunate choice of words, given the tragic event which it foreshadowed by several years, the article continued: 'The aim was Titantic [*sic*] – the control of an ocean'.[48]

In early 1904, Clement Griscom, in failing health, announced his intention to retire as president of the combine. At Morgan's request he approached Bruce Ismay to ask whether he would be willing to succeed him in this extremely demanding job. Ismay would be able to remain chairman of the White Star Line, but would need to divide his time between England and America. After much deliberation, Ismay reluctantly agreed to become president of the IMM. In his own words, expressed in a letter to Charles Steele, one of the American directors of the company, on 21 February 1904:

> I would like to say, had I consulted my own feelings in this matter I should, without the slightest hesitation, have declined the offer; and I have been very largely influenced in my decision by a desire to render any assistance I can to Mr. Morgan and yourself to place the I.M.M. Company in a satisfactory position.[49]

Three days later the terms of Ismay's acceptance of the post of President and Managing Director of the International Mercantile Marine Company were enshrined in a memorandum, previously agreed with Ismay and signed in New York by J. Pierpont Morgan, Charles Steele and P.A.B. Widener, another of the company's American directors. Unlike his predecessor, he would, according to the *New York Times*, have 'a free hand and unlimited power' to direct the combine.[50] To Britain's *Daily Dispatch*, he would be 'the unfettered autocrat of the destinies of the shipping trust. [...] Not only is the office business being done in Liverpool, but the steamers will be built in British shipping yards and repaired there as well.'[51] As Ismay himself 'genially' commented to the *Liverpool Courier* on 4 March

1904, 'wherever I happen to be in my official capacity as president, there the management will be for the time being and I shall, as occasion demands, be in attendance in Liverpool and New York'.[52]

In the *Manchester Guardian* of the following day, he was reported as saying: 'Somebody told me that the other day I said I was going to give up my house in Liverpool. It was very amusing. No, I am not going to move to New York.'[53] Significantly, however, while the memorandum did emphasise that Ismay's management of the business of the IMM Company would be 'unlimited and uncontrolled', it also included the crucial proviso that 'his decision on all points other than financial matters must be final'. In other words, the purse strings would not be entirely in his hands, but still, ultimately, under the control of the finance committee based in New York. Another important provision was that J.P. Morgan was prepared to underwrite the fixed charges of the IMM Company and subsidiary companies for just three years, until 1 January 1907. Any net earnings of the Company should be allocated first to pay such charges. Clearly this arrangement was intended to provide a time-limited safety net while Ismay concentrated on 'turning the company around'.

On 21 January a *Fairplay* journalist writing under the pen name 'The Look-Out Man' had commented, with some prescience, regarding rumours of Ismay's imminent new appointment, that '[the] White Star people know how to manage steamers, none better, and Mr. Bruce Ismay, as an independent manager, might perhaps be a very different man from Mr. Bruce Ismay as an official of the Combine'.[54] Six months later, in July 1904, the IMM published its first financial report during Bruce Ismay's presidency. This showed that in 1903 the whole of the IMM fleet, including White Star, made a net profit of just $4 million (£800,000), and a surplus after defraying all charges of just $335,000 (£67,000). As the White Star Line alone for the thirteen months to 31 December 1903 had earned a net profit of £642,151, a *Journal of Commerce* writer wondered what the IMM would have done 'had it not the White Star's bountiful earnings to make good the losses in other directions'. In his view, the figures explained 'the dominant position now held in the International Company by Mr. Bruce Ismay, the White Star's current chief, and the willingness of the American proprietors to place the management in his hands'. Clearly sensing difficult times ahead, the journalist then added the following prophetic note of caution: 'We are afraid, however, that, in his efforts to make the overcapitalised International Company pay, Mr. Bruce Ismay has a longer row to hoe than ever had his late father'.[55]

Yet more prophetic was Bruce Ismay's own comment in a letter written to Harold Sanderson from New York on 9 February 1904 regarding his agonising dilemma over whether to accept the position of IMM president. In words foreshadowing his controversial escape from *Titanic* several years later in one of the last lifeboats, he wrote: 'It would be easy to jump in, but it would be difficult, if not impossible, to climb out'.[56]

CHAPTER 2

THE SOUTHAMPTON SWITCH

Fare thee well to Princes Landing Stage,
River Mersey fare thee well ...

'The Leaving of Liverpool'
folk song, traditional

In his new role as President and Managing Director of the IMM, Bruce Ismay set about consolidating the combine's activities in Liverpool. By 1904 the White Star, Dominion, Leyland and American lines all had offices between 27 and 30 James Street. Their day-to-day business was largely managed by Liverpool-based directors, and they shared offices, engineering works and loading berths in the port. Ismay soon instructed the other lines in the combine to transfer their best ships and some of their more profitable routes to White Star.[1] This, together with agreements already in place since 1902 with Dutch and German lines, helped to offset the intense competition from non-IMM lines in the North Atlantic. Ironically, Ismay himself had originally regarded such schemes for the 'rationalisation of shipping deployment' with distaste until persuaded otherwise by Morgan and Pirrie.[2] A further irony was that White Star now faced its most formidable challenge on its own doorstep, from its old Liverpool-based rival, the Cunard Line.

On accepting the presidency of the IMM in February 1904, Ismay was already well aware of the serious threat which Cunard's new financial strength and proposed new ships would pose to both White Star's and the IMM's position in the North Atlantic. As the construction of the two Cunarders progressed he realised that, sooner or later, he would have to take decisive action to counteract their future success. He was also, no doubt, under growing pressure because Morgan's financial guarantees for the first three years of his presidency, although apparently not yet called upon in practice, would soon expire.[3]

Ismay finally took action on 7 January 1907, only weeks before *Lusitania* and *Mauretania* were due for completion. In a dramatic and largely unexpected press release, White Star announced that its express mail service to New York was being withdrawn from Liverpool. In future, its biggest and best ships would sail from Southampton, calling at Cherbourg and Queenstown on the outward voyage and at Plymouth and Cherbourg on the return. However, the company would continue to be based in Liverpool and run its traditional 'secondary service' from its home port each week to New York. According to the announcement, this decision was not due 'to any shortcomings in connection with Liverpool docks or approaches', but 'simply and solely' to meet the growing demand of first-class passengers to be able to embark and disembark at either a Continental or a British port. The move would enable White Star to compete in this 'growing section of the Western ocean business' with the New York steamers of the leading German lines, which had 'long recognised the desirability of meeting this demand'. The steamers allocated to the Southampton route were the *Oceanic*, *Majestic*, *Teutonic* and *Adriatic*.[4]

There had been much speculation in previous years that some, at least, of Liverpool's large Atlantic liners might eventually be transferred to Southampton to be much closer to London and Paris. Indeed, on 5 January 1907, just two days before White Star's announcement, *Lloyd's List and Shipping Gazette* wondered how long it would be before the Cunard Line would make Southampton the base for its fast transatlantic steamers, and how this would effect 'the monopoly of Liverpool as the home port of the cream of our Atlantic liners'.[5] For several years J.P. Morgan had also been known to have been seeking an alternative to Liverpool as Britain's main Atlantic port, mainly due to the cost of its railway connections.[6] Even so, the announcement of the transfer of White Star's express mail steamers to Southampton created something of a sensation in the shipping world and the popular press.

In Southampton the news was, understandably, greeted with great excitement and celebration. In Liverpool, on the other hand, some observers considered it to be a major blow to the port's pride and prestige which might well lead not only to a serious loss of business, but also to the loss of many seafaring and other shipping-related jobs. On 8 January, for example, the *Liverpool Courier* feared that about two thousand seafarers and their families and between six and eight thousand clerks 'would be forced to migrate from Liverpool'.[7] On the same day a *Liverpool Daily Post* writer considered that between fourteen and sixteen hundred seafaring personnel and their families, perhaps from four to five thousand persons in all, would be lost to the city, as well as other employees of the White Star company. The same writer also speculated that the Mersey Docks and Harbour Board would lose between £25,000 and £30,000 in tonnage dues each year. Big losses, he added, would be incurred by suppliers and handlers of coal, dock labourers dealing with cargoes, those repairing and painting ships, those involved in laundry work and tradesmen supplying fresh provisions, vegetables and fish to the liners. The city would also lose the money spent by passengers before embarking, and by the 'hundreds of people who travel to Liverpool to bid "Bon Voyage" to their relatives and friends'. Finally, there was the money paid for cabs to the landing stage or docks and that expended in railway fares to and from the city. In short, he concluded, Liverpool would sustain 'an enormous loss' by the removal of the four White Star steamers to Southampton.[8]

As for the national press, the summary verdict of the *Daily Express* on 7 January was that 'Southampton is the Liverpool of the future'.[9] *Lloyd's List and Shipping Gazette,* on the other hand, commented that White Star's proposed move to Southampton was intended to 'queer the pitch' before the new Cunarders could get to work. It suggested that this was a clever scheme intended 'to compel the Cunard Company to remain at Liverpool and thus leave the traffic of the Channel ports to the Combine companies'.[10] The shipping correspondent of the *Daily Telegraph* took a similar view, pointing out that the Morgan Combine,

NOT HEART-BROKEN.

SOUTHAMPTON: Not broken? Well, it's all the same to me one way or t'other!

"Enthusiasm runs high in Southampton over the prospects of the development of the port. . . . There is a disposition in some quarters in Liverpool to deny that the changes will permanently affect the prosperity of the port."—Daily Paper.

[With apologies to the proprietors of "Veritas" matches.]

'working in absolute unison, is strengthening its position against the Cunard Company'. He argued that Messrs Harland and Wolff, which had a 'large interest' in White Star, also built ships for the Hamburg America Line. So why, then, the writer asked, 'should the White Star seek to take bread out of the Hamburg-Amerika Company's mouth?'[11] In other words, there was no quarrel between the Combine and the German steamship companies which 'for years past' had been doing such good business at Southampton and Cherbourg. White Star had simply forestalled Cunard by 'slipping down first' to Southampton.

In view of such comments, on 9 January White Star was forced to issue a statement denying any hostility to any other company in diverting its steamers to Southampton and rejecting the view that competition in Liverpool 'is now, or is likely to become in future' too severe to enable the company to 'continue to employ so much of its tonnage profitably in the Liverpool and New York trade, &c'. The company insisted that the full reasons for the move had already been given.[12] This, no doubt, helped to reassure some observers. Meanwhile, in Liverpool, the commercial community was already beginning to recover its former confidence and optimism. One view reported in the *Liverpool Daily Post* on 8 January, for example, was that the loss caused by the transfer of four White Star steamers to Southampton would soon be made up by other ships. The same reporter added that the greatest shock to commercial men on the Exchange was sentimental. He quoted one 'commercial authority' as saying, 'We are sorry for this, but not pining. I am, of course, sorry that it is White Star because we are all very fond of the White Star in Liverpool.' The same gentleman commented that White Star was doing the right thing if it thought that 'its bread and butter' was at stake. [13]

Even *The Porcupine*, Liverpool's satirical magazine, widely read by the city's commercial classes, was fairly relaxed about the White Star move. In an article entitled 'White Star and White Feather', published on 12 January, for example, it made fun of some of the more extreme local criticisms aimed at Bruce Ismay and White Star for their actions. It began:

> Mr. Bruce Ismay, like the fat boy in *Pickwick*, seems fond of indulging an amiable propensity for making one's flesh 'creep'.

> Barely have we been persuaded to recover from the shock administered to our *amour propre* by the semi-Americanising of the White Star Line than there falls another bolt from the blue.

It then went on to ridicule the 'wailing and gnashing of teeth' on the part of a certain section of the press following White Star's decision to transfer its mail service to Southampton:

> The prestige of the city (avers the pessimist) has received a moral death blow. The defection of Messrs. Ismay, Imrie & Co.'s steamers will be followed by those of the Cunard Line. Grass will grow 'twixt the cobble

stones of the dock highway, and the green mould of stagnancy shall lie on the quays thereof. Then shall even the summer service of the Wallasey ferries be discontinued. Liverpool, like Pompeii, will be a buried city …

Later in the article, however, having 'set the spirit of levity on one side', the writer admitted that the situation was indeed 'alarming' for Liverpool in terms of the likely loss of jobs, business and people. He broadly supported White Star's decision because of its 'obvious advantage to the Company from a commercial and unsentimental standpoint', adding, pointedly, that 'our White Star friends said goodbye to sentiment some years ago'. Having rejected the 'absurd' idea that White Star intended to work with the German companies to 'crush' Cunard, he reserved judgement on whether White Star had indeed 'stolen a march' on its Cunard rivals. As regards the overall situation, however, he concluded that '[our] American Cousin almost invariably "finishes" his European tour in Paris. It has been a long-standing grievance of his that, in order to take ship home, he is compelled to re-cross [the] Channel and, via London, make his way to the Mersey'. He then admitted 'in all sorrow' that 'Liverpool, as a city, holds no attraction for our hustling friends "across the pond." Yet is every stone of the ancient City of Chester known to and beloved of them.'[14]

In the end, however, Bruce Ismay's decision to switch his prestige service to Southampton was bold and pragmatic. Most informed observers at the time realised that, sooner or later, one or both of Liverpool's largest Atlantic passenger lines would have to transfer their express mail steamers to the southern English port. Ismay, under pressure because of the imminent delivery of Cunard's two new leviathans, simply made the first move. Apart from the need to avoid the potentially crushing challenge of *Lusitania* and *Mauretania* in Liverpool, this was one way of preventing the German and other European lines from virtually monopolising the market in wealthy passengers wishing to travel via Southampton en route to London and Paris. Since the 1890s the southern port had gradually become more popular with wealthy American travellers in particular. By 1907, clearly resolved to tap into this increasingly lucrative market, several European lines, including Hamburg America and North German Lloyd, had already established regular calls at Southampton as part of their Atlantic services.[15] Ironically, in the early 1890s, following years of unscrupulous and bitter rate wars in the North Atlantic, White Star and Cunard had collaborated to induce two of its American-owned competitors on the Liverpool to New York route, namely the Inman and International Steamship Company and the American Line, to transfer their services to Southampton. In 1891 Thomas Ismay and John Burns, for White Star and Cunard respectively, persuaded Clement Griscom, President of Inman and International, to make Antwerp rather than Liverpool its European terminal and Southampton its British port of call. They then agreed to pay the American Line, of which Griscom was also head, compensation for moving to Southampton. White Star was to pay £20,000 and Cunard £30,000 per annum for five years. After further negotiations the American Line transferred its services to the Antwerp-Southampton-New York route in 1893.[16] Both Inman and International and the American Line were owned by the Philadelphia-based International Navigation Company, which in 1902, with the support of J.P. Morgan, would change its name to the International Mercantile Marine Company Limited of New Jersey. As we have seen, Clement Griscom was to be the first president of that huge American company, which would soon have such a major impact on the destinies of both the White Star and Cunard lines.

On Wednesday 22 May 1907 RMS *Adriatic*, the last of White Star's 'Big Four' and the largest ship in the world at the time, embarked on her maiden voyage from Liverpool to New York. A fortnight later, on 5 June, she inaugurated White Star's first regular express mail service from Southampton to New York, via Cherbourg and Queenstown. To mark this momentous occasion, Harold Sanderson, the company's General Manager, played host to guests including Mr. Richard Andrews, the Mayor of Southampton, Sir Charles Scotter, Chairman of the London and South Western Railway, and Lord Pirrie, Chairman of Harland and Wolff Limited, during the celebrations on board the ship at Southampton. *Adriatic*'s master on this epoch-making voyage was to be Captain Edward J. Smith, later of *Olympic* and *Titanic*.[17]

CHAPTER 3

THE BIG IDEA

She was the latest thing in the art of shipbuilding;
absolutely no money was spared in her construction.

J. Bruce Ismay
US Senate Inquiry, Day 1, 19 April 1912[1]

OLYMPIC AND TITANIC

On 7 September 1907 the Cunard Line's 31,550-ton, turbine-powered passenger
liner *Lusitania* began her maiden voyage from Liverpool to New York. She and her
near-sister *Mauretania*, whose maiden voyage began ten weeks later, immediately
outclassed every other vessel afloat, including White Star's new liner *Adriatic*.
Over the next few years, with these two magnificent vessels in service, Cunard
could rightly claim, as it did in its publicity of the time, to have the 'largest, finest
and fastest ships in the world'.[2]

By transferring White Star's express mail steamers to Southampton earlier in the
year, Bruce Ismay had already taken strong action aimed, at least in part, at
countering the impact of the new Cunarders on his own company's fortunes. Even
so, he knew that much more needed to be done. Indeed, he and his IMM colleagues,
including his old partner Lord Pirrie of Harland and Wolff, had been considering this
issue for some time. The construction of the 'Big Four', or '*Celtic* class', ships had
provided the means to maintain the traditional, highly successful Liverpool service
for many years to come. However, figures published by the *Liverpool Daily Post* on 10
January 1907 showed that, as regards the total number of passengers carried between
Liverpool and New York, White Star, having 'forged greatly ahead' until 1904, had

since been losing ground in relation to Cunard. In 1906, for example, Cunard had carried more than 120,000 passengers as opposed to White Star's 112,500. While both companies continued to maintain and develop Liverpool's share of the Atlantic passenger trade as a whole, it appeared that in recent years Cunard had begun to capture many of the First Class passengers who had previously travelled with White Star. According to the newspaper's analyst, '[in] first class traffic the upward movement of the White Star and the downward movement of the Cunard Line from 1899 till 1904 is as remarkable as the upward movement of the Cunard and the downward movement of the White Star has been during the past two years'. In his view, Cunard, with its new fast ships, 'may fairly hope to continue' the progress of the last two years with First Class passengers, which White Star was 'understood to be in quest of in going to Southampton'. White Star, he observed, were leaving large steamers in Liverpool to cater for Second and Third Class passengers, amongst whom they had since 1904 found more support than First Class.[3]

Given these circumstances, it is not surprising that Bruce Ismay and his associates now began to consider ordering an even more impressive class of ships than the 'Big Four', one that would be able to compete with all its rivals for wealthy passengers on the Southampton–New York route. On their regular trips to London, Ismay and Pirrie sometimes met at their respective residences in the city, where they were near-neighbours. On one such occasion, probably in July 1907, Pirrie invited Ismay and his wife to dinner at his home in Downshire House, Belgrave Square. After dinner, the two men discussed the possibility of building two new liners of unprecedented size and luxury, but of moderate speed, for White Star's weekly Southampton express mail service. The two ships concerned would later be named *Olympic* and *Titanic*.[4] These plans were, presumably, intended to supersede those announced by the IMM the previous month to build nine new steamers, including a 'fast steamer for the North Atlantic trade' which would 'surpass anything hitherto attempted, both as regards size and luxury of Appointments'.[5] Continuing the White Star tradition, therefore, the idea was to

combine great size, safety and comfort with economy of operation. This, they felt, would prove more attractive to First and Third Class passengers than by making speed the top priority. By the end of the evening, they had agreed on the general appearance and specifications of the vessels concerned.

The initial ideas for the 'Olympic class' liners, as they eventually became known, were 'enthusiastically endorsed' by John Pierpont Morgan.[6] On 11 September, while Lusitania was on her maiden voyage to New York, Harland and Wolff 'officially admitted' that they were working on plans for a new White Star liner which would be bigger than Cunard's 'wonder ship'. The keel for the new liner would be laid 'in a few months'.[7] Later, a third liner, Britannic, was added to the two originally proposed. However, it was relatively easy to produce the basic ideas for these enormous and luxurious new ships. As each ship would cost over £1.5 million ($7.5m), it was not so easy to find the money with which to build them. Ever since its inception in 1902, the IMM's serious shortage of working capital had caused major problems in financing the construction of new ships for its constituent companies. White Star was the only company in the

Modern Liverpool, oil painting by Walter Richards, 1907. This scene illustrates the confidence of the booming port in its 700th Anniversary year. The four-funnelled Cunard liner *Lusitania* (or *Mauretania*) is moored at the Landing Stage (left). (MMM.2007.31)

Unpublished (draft) poster for Cunard Line by the Liverpool-based artist Odin Rosenvinge, c. 1907–12. (MMM.2007.31)

group which had been consistently profitable, partly because some of the newest and best ships of its partners had been transferred to its fleet.[8] In return, especially under Ismay's presidency of the combine, White Star's profits had been used to support IMM purposes in general. Indeed, according to F.E. Hyde, between September 1903 and December 1907 the flow of White Star resources to the IMM had made it necessary for the Liverpool line to seek overdrafts from its bankers, Glyn, Mills and Company of London, in order to finance 'certain shipbuilding requirements'.[9]

Matters were made worse in 1907 by the serious economic recession in the United States. Under these circumstances, it is not surprising that in early 1908, to help raise the money needed to build the *Olympic* class ships, the White Star Line had to issue additional shares worth £2.5 million. These were soon bought by eager investors.[10] In spite of this, and despite the company's continuing success in its shipping operations, it still urgently needed to find major new sources of investment. Hence, from late 1908 onwards, White Star entered into a series of mortgage agreements involving its existing ships, using the ships themselves as security or guarantees for the loans. Although such arrangements had become standard practice among British shipowners due to the ever-increasing costs of shipbuilding, the sheer scale of White Star's borrowing at this time was extraordinary. In each case, the specified lenders or joint mortgagees were the same three individuals, namely, The Honourable Algernon Henry Mills, The Right Honourable Alfred Lyttleton and Francis Chatillon Danson, Esq. Mills, the second son of the first Baron Hillingdon, was a managing partner of White Star's bank Glyn, Mills, Currie and Company of London.[11] Lyttleton, a Liberal Unionist politician and former Secretary of State for the Colonies under Prime Minister Balfour, was related to Mills, and also had offices in the city of London.[12] Danson belonged to a prominent Merseyside family and was the very able and energetic senior partner of F.C. Danson and Company of 301–302 Tower Building, Liverpool, the city's leading firm of average adjusters.[13]

As the sole Liverpool-based mortgagee concerned, Francis Chatillon Danson is of particular interest. Born in 1855, he was the son of John Towne Danson, sometime journalist, farmer, barrister and marine insurance underwriter who became founder and secretary of the Thames and Mersey Marine Insurance Company. After being educated at Liverpool College and in Paris, Francis was articled by his father to the well-known Liverpool firm of average adjusters Baily, Lowndes and Stockley. In 1879 he established his own firm of average adjusters at 22B Liverpool and London Chambers, High Street, Exchange, Liverpool. The business prospered and eventually Danson acquired the work of most of the leading Liverpool liner companies, including White Star, Leyland, Bibby, Harrison, the African Steam Navigation Company, Lamport and Holt, and Booth.

Sir F.C. Danson, c. 1920. (NML)

Following White Star's purchase by the International Mercantile Marine Company in 1902, Danson was informed that the adjustments or assessments of marine loss claims relating to White Star would have to be prepared in London in future, and so he opened an office there in order to retain the business.[14] However, in March 1904, shortly after Bruce Ismay was appointed as President of the IMM, Danson received a letter from Mr. Stephen Loinch of Johnson and Higgins, Average Adjusters of 49 and 51 Wall Street, New York. Loinch, who had only recently met his British associate in Liverpool, expressed the view that Ismay's new position would 'certainly be favourable' to Danson's interests, and 'very satisfactory to ourselves'.[15] In April he wrote a further letter in which he was able to confirm that his personal friend, Mr. Philip A.S. Franklin, formerly Manager of the Atlantic Transport Line and now Vice-President of the IMM, would be 'in entire charge of the business of the new Company, under Mr. Ismay'. He concluded by assuring Danson that he would shortly be able to get Franklin 'to issue general instructions to have all matters of G/A [General Adjustment] on your side, placed in your hands'. This meant that the average adjustment business of the IMM would be entrusted to Danson in the United Kingdom and to Loinch's firm in the United States.[16] He later sent Danson a copy of a letter he had written to Franklin strongly recommending his British counterpart for this work. This began with the statement: 'Mr. F.C. Danson of Liverpool has been the average adjuster for the White Star and American Lines for many years past and is, in our opinion, by far the most able and capable party to have charge of your adjustments in Great Britain'.[17]

It would seem reasonable to assume that this recommendation was accepted by Franklin and his IMM colleagues. In the event, despite Danson's establishment of an office in London, the White Star Line's claims continued to be adjusted in his firm's Liverpool offices until the 1930s.[18] The long-standing connection of F.C. Danson with White Star certainly helps to explain why he became one of the three joint mortgagees for the Line's fleet from 1908 onwards. He was, in effect, investing in a company which was one of his oldest and most valued customers. Danson, who lived across the River Mersey from Liverpool at 'Rosewarne', 74 Bidston Road, Oxton, Wirral, Cheshire, was a man of wide interests and influence. Among the high-profile organisations with which he was involved were Liverpool University, Liverpool School of Tropical Medicine, Liverpool Chamber of Commerce, and the Mersey Docks and Harbour Board. He was knighted in 1920 for his work as a member of the Admiralty Transport Arbitration Board during the First World War.[19]

To return to the financing of White Star's *Olympic* class liners, *Olympic*'s registration certificate, originally dated 25 May 1911, shows that on 19 September of that year, in order 'to secure an account current', White Star transferred all 64 shares of the ship to the usual three joint mortgagees, namely 'The Honourable Algernon Henry Mills of 67 Lombard Street, in the city of London, The Right Honourable Alfred Lyttleton of 3 Papers Buildings, Temple, in the city of London and Francis Chatillon Danson, of Tower Building, Liverpool, Esquire'.[20] Although *Titanic*'s registration certificate, dated 25 March 1912, records no mortgage arrangement, this is probably because the ship sank before such a deal could be finalised.[21] As regards *Britannic*, the third of the *Olympic* class ships, in December 1915 White Star did arrange another mortgage, involving all 64 shares in the ship, with Mills and Danson, the only two surviving joint mortgagees for *Olympic*.[22]

This evidence certainly appears to support Paul Louden-Brown's view that J.P. Morgan did not finance the construction of the *Olympic* class liners.[23] Even so, it is likely that Morgan's advice and influence was behind Ismay's exceptionally bold financial dealings at this time. No doubt Lord Pirrie also had a significant part in them, given his own considerable experience of major financial deals.[24] Louden-Brown further asserts that the Oceanic Steam Navigation Company (White Star) 'mortgaged its entire fleet in order to finance the construction of the "*Olympic*" class liners'. The registration records for White Star ships show that the company did indeed mortgage its entire fleet from late 1908 onwards.[25] In the absence of further major White Star construction projects over the next few years, most of the money raised may well have been used to pay Harland and Wolff, in instalments, for building the three *Olympic* class ships.[26] However, it remains unclear whether some of the money thus raised was also intended, and actually used, to support other White Star and IMM purposes.

In the meantime, Bruce Ismay began negotiations with the New York Harbor Board to construct a pier long enough to accommodate the huge new vessels. Due to the influence of J.P. Morgan, the City of New York agreed to pay for this work, despite the objections of many taxpayers.[27] Harland and Wolff's shipyard at Queen's Island, Belfast began the conversion of three slips into two, and the erection of a 220-foot Arrol gantry crane over both slips. Soon its architects and draughtsmen had completed the general arrangement plans for the first two ships of the class. On 29 July 1908 Bruce Ismay and Harold Sanderson, for the White Star Line, met Lord Pirrie and other representatives of Harland and Wolff at the shipyard to examine the plans. The owners having accepted the builders' proposals, two days later the order was confirmed and the construction of SS 400 (*Olympic*) and SS 401 (*Titanic*) could begin.

The construction of the two new ships was planned and supervised by a team led initially by Alexander Carlisle, General Manager and chief naval architect of the shipyard, who was Pirrie's cousin and brother-in-law. Bruce Ismay, Harold

Edward Wilding. (© Royal Geographical Society)

Sanderson and other White Star officials were regularly consulted as the work progressed.[28] Sometimes the meetings took place in Belfast, sometimes in Liverpool. In October 1909 and January 1910, for example, Carlisle and Pirrie took plans for the internal decorations and life-saving appliances on both ships to Liverpool for discussion with Ismay and Sanderson. The exact subject matter of each of these meetings, especially regarding lifeboat proposals, would later be closely scrutinised at both the American and British inquiries held shortly after the *Titanic* disaster. Merseyside Maritime Museum has an undated Harland and Wolff blueprint, apparently produced while *Olympic* and *Titanic* were still under construction, which illustrates a scheme to increase the lifeboat capacity of each ship from 16 to 32 boats.[29] This may well relate to Carlisle's proposal, rejected in May 1911 by the Board of Trade, to more than double the number of lifeboats which would initially be carried by each ship.[30] When Carlisle retired from Harland and Wolff in June 1910 he was succeeded as chief naval architect by his cousin, and Pirrie's nephew, Thomas Andrews, who completed the work on both *Olympic* and *Titanic*.

Another of the main naval architects involved in designing both *Olympic* and *Titanic* was Liverpool-born Edward Wilding. He was the eldest son of Henry Wilding, the recently retired Managing Director of the Leyland and Dominion lines of Liverpool, and former head of the British managers of the American Line, another subsidiary of the IMM.[31] Edward was Thomas Andrews' deputy in the Designing Department at Harland and Wolff. As well as being responsible for the general management of the various drawing offices, he held the key role of producing detailed design calculations for the new vessels, especially regarding stability, damage control and safety. As the chief witness called to represent Harland and Wolff at the British Board of Trade enquiry into the loss of *Titanic*, Wilding presented his evidence in a clear and concise manner, despite being under enormous pressure. The enquiry cleared Harland and Wolff of any blame for the loss of the vessel, and Wilding succeeded Andrews as the shipyard's chief naval architect. He soon implemented many of the lessons learned from the disaster.[32]

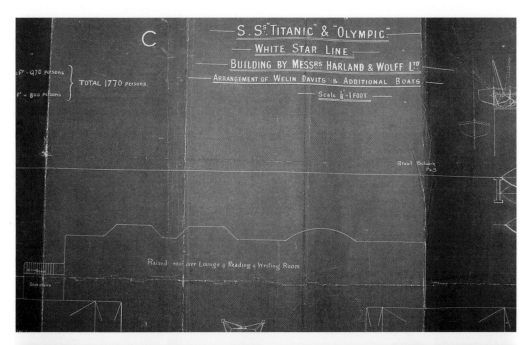

S. Ss "TITANIC" & "OLYMPIC."

WHITE STAR LINE

BUILDING BY MESSRS HARLAND & WOLFF LTD

ARRANGEMENT OF WELIN DAVITS & ADDITIONAL BOATS

Scale ⅛"-1 FOOT

Title from a Harland and Wolff blueprint showing a proposed arrangement of Welin davits and additional boats for RMS *Titanic* and *Olympic*. Undated, but probably c. 1911. (MMM ref. B/CUN)

Detail from the Harland and Wolff blueprint for RMS Titanic and Olympic, c. 1911, showing a proposal for 16 additional lifeboats to be added to the 14 lifeboats and 2 cutters originally planned. (MMM ref. B/CUN)

The above account illustrates just how close the working relationship was between the White Star Line's Liverpool managers and their Harland and Wolff counterparts in Belfast. It also shows that *Titanic* and her sisters, like all ships built for White Star since 1869, were very much the products or 'offspring' of the 'long and intimate relations'[33] between owner and builder.

GONE TO LAUNCH

Olympic's keel was laid on 16 December 1908 at slip no. 2 at Harland and Wolff's shipyard at Queen's Island, Belfast. She was launched 22 months later on 20 October 1910. *Titanic*'s keel was laid at slip no. 3 on 22 March 1909, and she was launched 26 months later on 31 May 1911. The two enormous hulls were

Olympic in Liverpool, 1 June 1911, from the Royal Liver Building clock tower. (Courtesy of Mark Chatterton)

Although this postcard, published soon after the *Titanic* disaster, is captioned 'Titanic', it actually shows *Olympic* in Liverpool, 1 June 1911.

49

built side by side, in adjacent slipways. On completion, *Titanic*, with an overall length of 882 feet 9 inches, was just three inches longer than *Olympic*. The keel of the third sister ship, *Britannic*, would be laid down on 30 November 1911 on the slip used for the building of *Olympic*.

After two days' sea trials, *Olympic* was handed over to White Star on 31 May 1911, the same day as *Titanic*'s launch.[34] The Liverpool tugs *Wallasey*, *Herculaneum*, *Hornby* and *Alexandra*, owned by the Alexandra Towing Company, were sent to Belfast to assist with both *Olympic*'s sea trials and *Titanic*'s launch.[35] Both *Herculaneum* and *Hornby* would return the following year with other Liverpool tugs, *Huskisson and Herald*, to stand by during *Titanic*'s sea trials.[36] To witness these major events in May 1911, a large party of distinguished guests, including John Pierpont Morgan, his business partner and IMM director Edward Grenfell, and Bruce Ismay and family, travelled from Fleetwood to Belfast via the cross-channel steamer *Duke of Argyll*. Among Liverpool area residents who later attended *Titanic*'s launch were White Star's General Manager Harold Sanderson, Assistant General Manager Henry Concanon, Publicity Manager R.J.A. Shelley, and George Melly, a senior manager of the Lamport and Holt Line.

Shortly after noon on a fine spring day, Lord Pirrie gave the signal to launch *Titanic*, rockets were fired, and the hydraulic launching triggers were released to commence the enormous ship's progress into the water. Less than an hour later, the huge crowds of spectators had dispersed and *Titanic*'s hull was towed to her wharf for fitting-out work to begin.

After the launch Lord and Lady Pirrie entertained their guests at luncheon at the Queen's Island shipyard. At about 2.30 pm Pirrie, Morgan, Ismay and a small party of other guests were ferried to *Olympic*, where they were welcomed by Captain Edward Smith. Two hours later, with her guests still on board, *Olympic* left Belfast for a courtesy visit to Liverpool, en route to Southampton to prepare for her maiden voyage to New York. Early the following morning she arrived at her port of registry, where, 'dressed overall' with flags, she was opened to the public.

Hundreds of people paid half a crown to tour the ship and marvel at her huge size and luxurious furnishings until 11.15 in the evening, when the liner left Liverpool for Southampton. Although she would make three commercial voyages from Liverpool to New York in late 1914, most of her sailings to and from the port in future years would be as a troopship during the First World War.[37]

FITTING OUT

The materials and fittings used in the construction of *Olympic* and *Titanic* were obtained from a vast range of sources and suppliers throughout Britain and beyond. In view of White Star's long presence in Liverpool, with its extensive port infrastructure, it is not surprising that many such items were provided by Liverpool firms. A number of such firms were regular contractors to the White Star Line. For example, Thomas Utley and Company, brass-founders of Silverdale Avenue, Tuebrook, made the three main bells and over twelve hundred portholes for each ship. The Merseyside Maritime Museum has some of the original casting patterns used in Utley's foundry to make these items, including that for the main

forecastle bell of both *Olympic* and *Titanic*.[38] The firm also made a novel range of Gothic-style windows, designed by Thomas himself, for the bars and dining-room of *Titanic*. Utley, a Liberal councillor and local magistrate, lived at Sefton House, Crosby Green, West Derby. He and his wife Jane were invited to sail on *Titanic*'s maiden voyage, but declined, apparently due to Jane's premonition that the ship would meet with disaster.[39]

The bridge and engine room telegraphs of *Olympic* and *Titanic* were designed by J. W. Ray and Company of 17 South Castle Street, Liverpool and manufactured by Chadburn's (Ship) Telegraph Company at their Cyprus Road works in Bootle, near Liverpool's north docks. Chadburn's long association with White Star began in the late nineteenth century, when William Chadburn lived at 15 Beach Lawn,

Mr. and Mrs. Thomas Utley. (courtesy of *Liverpool Daily Post and Echo*).

Crosby, two doors away from the home of Thomas Ismay.[40] The Willett-Bruce steam whistles fitted on the two foremost funnels of each ship and their electric control apparatus were designed by William Joseph Willett Bruce, Manager and Superintendent Engineer at the White Star Line's workshops at 27–29 Strand Road, Bootle.[41] Chadburn's made the steam whistles, while the 'automatic steamship whistle control' apparatus was made and supplied by Messrs T. Downie, consulting marine engineers, of 5 Castle Street, Liverpool.[42] The evaporating plant of both ships, capable of producing sixty tons of distilled water from sea water every twenty-four hours, mainly for use in the boilers, was supplied by the Liverpool Engineering and Condenser Company of Perry Street, Brunswick Dock. The main feed filters for condensed water, situated in the forward engine rooms, the firebars for the stokehold furnaces and the ash hoists were produced by Messrs Railton, Campbell and Crawford at the Washington Foundry, Cherry Lane, Walton. Aspinall's Patent Marine Engine Governor, 'fitted to over 2,000 Modern Steamers' and designed to 'prevent racing and broken shafts', was provided by Aspinall's Patent Governor Company of 7 Strand Street, Liverpool. The Metallic Valve Company of Colonial House, Water Street, Liverpool, provided 'a full

NEARLY ALL THE LEADING
BRITISH PASSENGER STEAMERS
ARE FITTED WITH
WILSON'S
COOKING APPARATUS.

Kitchen of a large Atlantic Liner fitted by Wilsons.

Please send Specifications to—

HENRY WILSON & CO. LTD.,
(T. MASSEY LYNCH, GEORGE E. FAIRBAIRN, HENRY KERR WILSON.)
CORNHILL WORKS.
Telephone Nos. 4790 & 4791, Bank.
Telegrams : " Wilson, Cornhill, Liverpool."
LIVERPOOL.

Advertisement for Henry Wilson & Company Ltd, Liverpool from *The Shipbuilder*, summer 1911.

First-class dinner plate, by Spode, in a pattern supplied to *Titanic* by Stoniers of Liverpool, possibly for use in the Café Parisien. (MMM.2002.42.4)

White Star Line 1st Class demi-tasse coffee cup and saucer, in a pattern supplied to *Titanic* by Stoniers of Liverpool. (MMM.1989.58.2.1)

equipment of valves' for both ships. Messrs Hutchison and Pollok Limited of Liverpool, whose ropeworks were at 182 Lodge Lane, supplied the 'White Star' brand of ropes and hawsers to both ships. J. Sanders and Company of Bridgewater Street, near Queen's Dock, Liverpool, 'Contractors to White Star Line and leading Steamship Companies', provided a range of paints for each ship. [43]

According to the souvenir edition of *The Shipbuilder*, published in the summer of 1911, the culinary departments of *Olympic* and *Titanic* were 'among the most complete in the world'. The two huge kitchen ranges installed on each ship, with a frontage of 96 feet and containing nineteen ovens, were then 'possibly the largest ever made'. These, together with a vast array of culinary equipment such as steam ovens, steam stockpots, hot closets and electric slicers, potato-peelers, mincers, whisks and freezers, were made and fitted by Henry Wilson and Company of Cornhill Works, Liverpool. [44] It is likely that a number of other firms and individuals from the Liverpool area were also involved in supplying and fitting out these vessels.

During the final preparations for *Titanic*'s departure from Belfast, the ship was provided with vast quantities of chinaware by Stonier and Company of

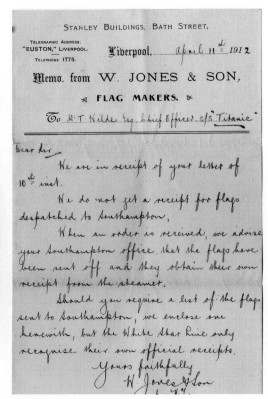

Titanic's Chief Officer, Henry Wilde, of Walton, Liverpool. (MMM ref. DX/2130)

Correspondence between W. Jones and Son, Flagmakers of Liverpool and *Titanic*'s Chief Officer, Henry Wilde, 11 April 1912. (Courtesy of Henry Aldridge and Son, Auctioneers, Wiltshire)

Liverpool. As with other White Star passenger liners, her stationery, blank menu cards and log cards were supplied by the Liverpool Printing and Stationery Company Limited. Her navigational charts and sailing directions were supplied by Philip, Son & Nephew Limited, 'booksellers, mercantile and export stationers, map, chart and educational publishers etc.' of 45–51 South Castle Street, Liverpool.[45] Shortly after the ship's departure from Belfast the flags for her maiden voyage, including one 'ice flag', large and small French ensigns, United States Mail and Royal Mail flags, various code and docking flags, a 'submarine flag' and 22 yards of assorted bunting, were sent directly to White Star's Sailing Department in Southampton by William Jones and Son, Flag Makers, of 14 Bath Street, Liverpool.[46]

CHAPTER 4

TRIED AND TESTED

In the *Titanic* we produced a ship which we believe
had only her sister vessel, the *Olympic*, for a peer,
and even this latter vessel was, in some important
respects, surpassed by her newer sister.

Harold Sanderson
22 April 1912[1]

There are two crew agreements for *Titanic*. One relates to her delivery trip from
Belfast to Southampton from 2 to 4 April 1912. The other concerns her maiden
voyage from Southampton to New York, via Cherbourg and Queenstown, which
began on Wednesday 10 April, and ended so tragically in the North Atlantic in the
early hours of Monday 15 April.

    Titanic was entered in the Liverpool customs register on 25 March 1912.[2] By
this date some officers and crew had already begun to assemble in Belfast to
prepare for her trials and delivery voyage. Among the first to arrive on the ship
were 'three very contented chaps' who had taken the midnight ferry from
Liverpool to Belfast on 20 March. These men, who had already been appointed as
senior officers for *Titanic*'s delivery voyage to Southampton, were Chief Officer
William McMaster Murdoch, First Officer Charles Herbert Lightoller, and Second
Officer David (Davy) Blair.[3]

    William McMaster Murdoch had previously been first officer of *Olympic*, which
had been dry-docked in Belfast for one week earlier that month for repairs to her
port propeller before returning to Southampton.[4] Indeed, he had been *Olympic*'s

Liverpool Customs Register entry for *Titanic*, 25 March 1912. (MMM ref. C/EX/L/4/105/123)

first officer on her delivery voyage from Belfast to Southampton the previous year. According to the crew agreement for *Titanic*'s delivery voyage, he signed on as chief officer on 24 March.[5] Originally from Dalbeattie in Scotland, Murdoch had joined White Star in 1899 and then sailed out of Liverpool for several years on the company's Australasian and New York services before moving to Southampton in 1907. He would be the highest ranking officer on *Titanic* until the arrival of Captain Herbert James Haddock from Southampton a few days later.[6]

58

NAME OF SHIP *Titanic*

Whether a Sailing or Steam Ship; if Steam how propelled.	Steamship Triple Screw	Where built	Belfast		When built	1912.	Name and Address of Builder

Number of Decks

123

Signal Letters :- H.V.M.P.

OFFICIAL NUMBER OF SHIP 131428

Number, Year, and Port of Registry	24/1912 Liverpool		Number, Year, and Port of previous Registry (if any)	new vessel	

PARTICULARS OF TONNAGE.

GROSS TONNAGE.		No. of Tons.	DEDUCTIONS ALLOWED.
Under Tonnage Deck ...		17870·66	On account of Space required for Propelling Power
Space or Spaces between Decks ... saloon upper & middle		14,142·81	On account of Spaces occupied by Seamen or Appre to their use, and kept free from Goods or Sto being the personal property of the Crew ...
Turret or Trunk ...			These Spaces are the following, viz. :—
Forecastle ...		270·29	In lower middle upper and saloon tw
Bridge Space ...		3633·45	poop forecastle bridge and round
Poop or Break ...		274·21	
Side Houses ...			
Deck Houses ...			
Chart House ...		3702·89	Deductions under s. 79 of the Merc 1894, and s. 54 of the Merchant
Spaces for Machinery, Light and Air, s. 78 (2) Merchant Shipping Act, 1894		1186·16	as follows :— Fore peak water ballast tank
Excess of Hatchways ...			Cubic Metres.

Murdoch's friend Charles Lightoller had formerly been first officer on *Oceanic*. Born in Chorley, Lancashire in 1874, he first went to sea in 1888 as a fourteen-year-old apprentice on the Liverpool sailing ship *Primrose Hill*. He sailed from Liverpool for most of the next twenty years, residing from 1904 until 1908 at 8 Cambridge Avenue, Crosby. Like Murdoch, he had moved to Southampton soon after the transfer of White Star's prestige mail service to the southern port.[7]

Thirty-seven-year-old David Blair, originally from the Isle of Wight, had been employed by White Star since 1902. His previous ship was *Teutonic*, but he had formerly been one of Lightoller's colleagues on *Oceanic*.[8]

Each of the four more junior deck officers for *Titanic*'s delivery voyage, namely Herbert Pitman, Joseph Boxhall, Harold Lowe and James Moody, received telegrams from Captain Charles Bartlett, White Star's marine superintendent in Liverpool, asking them to report to the company's Liverpool

Although supposedly showing Captain Edward Smith and the officers of RMS *Titanic*, this photograph actually shows Smith and the officers of *Olympic*, probably in 1911. Apart from Captain Smith (front row, with beard and medals), only Hugh McElroy (back row, far left) and William Murdoch (front row, far right) later served on *Titanic*. (© Museums and Galleries Northern Ireland, Ulster Folk and Transport Museum)

CAPTAIN SMITH AND OFFICERS S.S. TITANIC.
Lost on 15th April, 1912, after collision with Iceberg in North Atlantic.

office at 9 am on 26 March to collect their tickets for Belfast. Leaving Liverpool by ferry that night, they arrived in Belfast the following morning and reported to Murdoch on board *Titanic* at about noon.[9] According to the official crew list or 'Particulars of Engagement', all of these men signed on, with Murdoch, in Belfast on 24 March, even though none of them had, evidently, arrived there by that date. This presumably shows that the log was adjusted to ensure that, at least on paper, all the deck officers were in place before any of the crew were recruited. Also listed among the deck officers for the delivery voyage, but actually engaged as the ship's carpenter or joiner, was Liverpool-born John Maxwell. Twenty-nine-year-old Maxwell, most recently employed on the *Majestic*, signed on again for *Titanic*'s maiden voyage in Southampton on 6 April and died when she sank less than nine days later.[10]

Sixteen deck crew sailors and their temporary commanding officer, Captain H.J. Haddock, RNR, signed on for *Titanic* at Southampton on Monday 25 March with a view to boarding the ship the following Monday morning, 1 April.[11] Most

had transferred from either *Olympic* or *Oceanic*, the latter, Haddock's previous
ship, having been forced out of service due to the coal strike then in progress.
On Tuesday 26 March they all travelled together by train from Southampton to
Liverpool, before taking the ferry to Belfast to join *Titanic*. Among them were
two former *Oceanic* crew members with strong connections with the Liverpool
area, namely Frederick Fleet and Walter Wynn. Twenty-four-year-old Fleet would
soon become famous as the lookout in the crow's nest who first spotted the
iceberg which sank *Titanic*. Although born in Liverpool, he had been orphaned at
an early age and in about 1907 left his home city to pursue his seafaring career in
Southampton. Before signing on for *Titanic* he had spent four years as a lookout
on the *Oceanic*.[12] He survived *Titanic*'s sinking in lifeboat 6 and would be an
important witness at both the United States Senate and British Board of Trade
Inquiries. Chester-born Walter Wynn was a 41-year-old quartermaster. He also
survived the sinking (in lifeboat 9) and later testified at the Board of Trade
Inquiry (Day 11).[13]

As regards engineering staff, Joseph Bell, until recently *Olympic*'s chief engineer, had 'stood by' *Titanic* during the final stages of her construction to observe and advise. One of White Star's most experienced and respected engineer officers, Bell had supervised the installation of engines on several of White Star's latest liners, including *Titanic*, and sometimes served as chief engineer on their first few voyages.[14] Born in Maryport, Cumberland in 1861, he had begun his seafaring career in 1883 with the Lamport and Holt Line of Liverpool. He joined White Star in 1885 and served on many of the company's ships trading to New Zealand and New York before being promoted to chief engineer in 1891. A long-standing resident of the Liverpool area, in 1912 Bell lived with his wife and four children at 1 Belvidere Road, Great Crosby. At that date, in addition to his civilian post, he also held the rank of Lieutenant-Commander in the Royal Naval Reserve.[15] Although not officially signing on for *Titanic*'s delivery voyage until 2 April, he and a number of his colleagues took the opportunity to familiarise themselves with their new ship in the weeks leading up to her initial sailing.[16]

In all, 36 engineers and their support staff signed on in Belfast on 2 April 1912 for *Titanic*'s delivery voyage.[17] Of these, 19 transferred directly from *Olympic*, while most of the rest were from *Oceanic*, *Majestic* and other White Star liners taken out of service due to the coal strike. All of these men would later re-sign for *Titanic*'s maiden voyage in Southampton and none would survive her sinking. As well as Joseph Bell, almost all of the senior engineer officers on both the delivery and maiden voyages had strong Liverpool backgrounds. Six were born and raised in Liverpool, namely Second Engineer William Farquharson, Junior Second Engineers Norman Harrison and John Henry Hesketh, Senior Assistant Second Engineer Bertie Wilson, Senior Fourth Engineer Leonard Hodgkinson and Senior Electrician Peter Sloan. Although born in Manchester, Junior Electrician Alfred Allsop had lived in Liverpool and sailed from there for most of his working life. At least three other engineers on the delivery voyage,

William Farquharson, 2nd Chief Engineer (courtesy of the Institute of Marine Engineering, Science and Technology. (IMarEST), London)

Peter Sloan, *Titanic*'s Chief Electrician. (*Daily Sketch*, 23/4/1912)

namely George Hosking, Edward Dodd and George Chisnall, had obtained at least some of their seagoing experience on vessels sailing from Liverpool.[18]

On 29 March, 217 engine crew, including 92 who were transferring from *Olympic*, signed on for the delivery voyage. Most of these men did not re-sign in Southampton for *Titanic*'s maiden voyage. Over two hundred were from Belfast or other parts of Ulster.[19] However, there were three Liverpool-born men among the engine crew for *Titanic*'s delivery trip, namely Thomas Palles, William Swarbrick and Nicholas Holme. Palles, a 42-year-old single man living at 25 Upper Parliament Street, Liverpool, was a greaser whose previous ship had been the Cunard liner *Ivernia*. He did later re-sign for *Titanic*'s maiden voyage and died in the sinking. Swarbrick, a 24-year-old fireman, was one of four engine crew from White Star's *Heroic* who signed on for *Titanic*'s delivery trip but did not re-sign for her maiden voyage. Holme, a 36-year-old fireman, was equally fortunate, being one of two former crew members from the steamer *Kathleen* who also left *Titanic* at Southampton. Manchester-born Matthew Paton was a 26-year-old trimmer, previously employed on *Olympic*. Luckily for him, like Swarbrick and Holme, he left *Titanic* when she arrived at Southampton.[20]

On Monday 1 April, 120 male victualling or catering crew signed on.[21] All but two of these men transferred directly from *Olympic,* presumably to help ensure that all catering arrangements would go smoothly for both the delivery and maiden voyages of the new ship. All later re-signed at Southampton for the maiden voyage. Most were of English origin. At least 34 had strong Liverpool backgrounds. These included Chief Steward Andrew Latimer and 30 of his stewards, Storekeeper Herbert Henry Thompson, Chef Charles Proctor and Chief Baker Charles Joughin.

On the same day, Monday 1 April, Captain Edward John Smith, RNR, having travelled independently to Belfast, took over the command of the ship from Captain Haddock.[22] Sixty-two-year-old Smith was the most senior master mariner or captain of the White Star Line. Since the *Baltic* entered service in 1904 he had commanded all of the company's new liners on their maiden voyages. Born in Hanley, Staffordshire, Smith was the son of a potter. He travelled to Liverpool at the age of 13 to begin his seafaring career as an apprentice on a sailing ship, and then spent almost forty years sailing from the port before moving, like many White Star employees, to Southampton in 1907. From the late 1880s he had made his home in the pleasant north Liverpool suburb of Waterloo. His wife's family was from Winwick, Cheshire, not far from Liverpool.[23] Between 1898 and his departure for Southampton he had lived with his wife and Liverpool-born daughter at 17 Marine Crescent, Waterloo.[24]

Titanic's sea trials and departure from Belfast were originally scheduled for Monday 1 April, but had to be postponed until the following day because of strong winds. This delay probably prevented the ship from making a one-day visit to Liverpool during her delivery voyage to Southampton, as *Olympic* had done the previous year, to acknowledge her official home port.[25] At about 6 am on Tuesday 2 April the tugs steamed up the River Lagan ready to assist the largest ship in the world on the first stage of her trials. Already on board were officers, engineers, deck and engine crew, stewards, cooks and storekeepers, as well as two Marconi wireless operators, namely Jack Phillips and Harold Bride.[26] Phillips, at 24 years of age, was the senior of the two and would soon achieve lasting fame as the man who remained at his post sending distress messages until the very last minutes before *Titanic* sank. Born and educated in Surrey, he had trained as a marine radio operator in 1906 at the Marconi School at Seaforth Sands, near Liverpool. Over the next two years he had then worked on a number of passenger liners sailing from Liverpool, including White Star's *Teutonic*, Allan Line's *Corsican* and *Virginian*, and Cunard's *Lusitania* and *Mauretania*. In late March 1912 he transferred from *Oceanic* to take up his post on *Titanic*.[27] Harold Bride, Phillips' 22-year-old assistant, was born in Hull and later lived at the family home in Kent. Like his senior colleague, he had attended the Marconi School near Liverpool, where he obtained his certificate in Wireless Telegraphy in June 1911.[28] Like Phillips, prior to his appointment to *Titanic* he had worked on several Liverpool-based passenger liners, including *Haverford*, *Lusitania*, *Lanfranc* and *Anselm*.[29]

Apart from officers and crew, also on board during the sea trials were Harold Sanderson for White Star, Thomas Andrews and Edward Wilding for Harland and Wolff, together with support staff and yard workers, and Francis Carruthers, Board of Trade surveyor. The trials lasted all day, and proved wholly satisfactory. At about 7 pm, as the great ship approached Belfast, Carruthers signed the Board of Trade passenger certificate, thereby licensing her for one year. Yard workers and Harland and Wolff staff not travelling to Southampton were taken ashore, and some last-minute kitchen equipment, furniture and food supplies were brought aboard. Andrews and Sanderson signed the papers to formally acknowledge the handing over of the ship from builder to owner and shortly after 8 pm the vessel finally set off for Southampton.[30] The 570-mile voyage took just under thirty hours, and *Titanic* docked safely in the Hampshire port shortly after midnight on the morning of 4 April. Throughout the journey the ship had been in regular wireless communication with White Star's Liverpool offices, and with other ships. In all, 401 officers and crew, plus the two Marconi operators, made this brief

passage. There also appear to have been some Liverpool-related men among the unlisted 'passengers' on the trials and delivery voyage, including Chief Engineer Joseph Bell's son, Frank, who was a young apprentice with Harland and Wolff in Belfast, and three Liverpool-based employees of Weir's Pumps Limited, who were checking on the ship's installation of pumps and pipes. One of these men was John Stone of Walton, Liverpool, but the names of his two colleagues are not known. All three had been hired the previous year as consultants for the same work on *Olympic*. While Frank Bell and John Stone are believed to have left *Titanic* at Southampton, Stone's two Liverpool colleagues left her at Queenstown, and then boarded a train from Cork to Belfast.[31]

Among the 14 passengers listed on the voyage from Belfast was Harold Sanderson, who, as White Star's general manager in Liverpool, was named as *Titanic*'s 'Registered Managing Owner' on the crew lists for this voyage and also for her subsequent, disastrous, maiden voyage. He disembarked at Southampton and did not sail on her maiden voyage. However, about half of the officers and crew who shared the delivery voyage with him, including at least fifty with strong connections with the Liverpool area, were not so fortunate. A few weeks later, on 28 April 1912, Sanderson would meet crew survivors of the *Titanic* sinking on their arrival at Plymouth to ensure that their witness statements were recorded for the Board of Trade prior to their exposure to the press and public. Among those who took down this evidence were clerks of Hill, Dickinson and Company, Liverpool, solicitors for the White Star Line.[32]

Titanic leaves Belfast, with Liverpool tugs in attendance. (© Museums and Galleries Northern Ireland, Ulster Folk and Transport Museum)

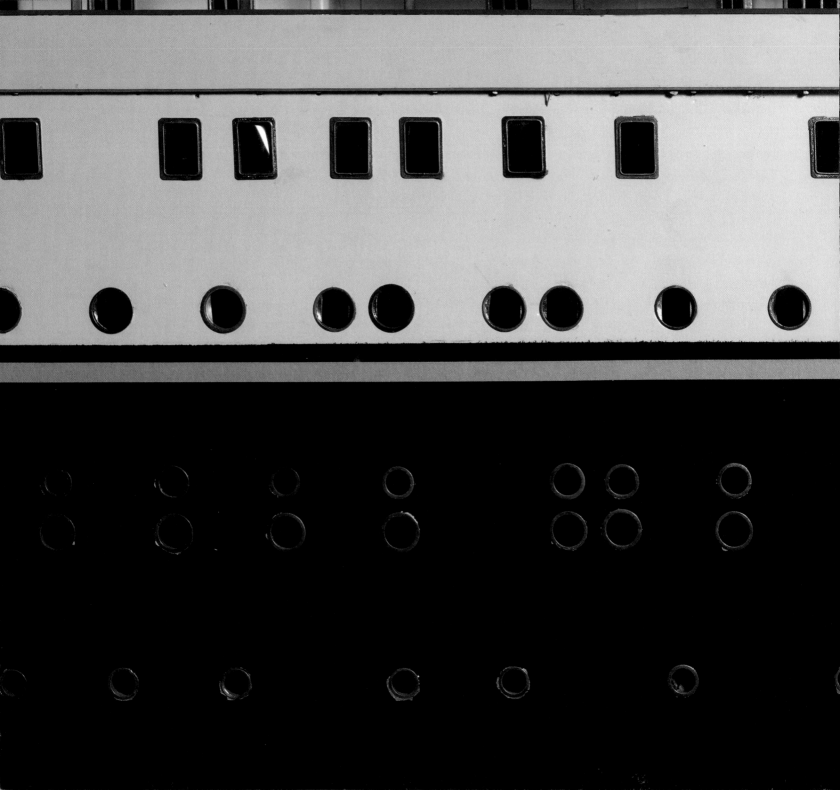

CHAPTER 5

OFFICERS AND CREW

Having fitted out this magnificent vessel, the *Titanic*,
we proceeded to man her with all that was best in
the White Star organisation …

Harold Sanderson
22 April 1912[1]

White Star Line's preparations for *Titanic*'s tragic maiden voyage were directed from Liverpool by Captain Charles Bartlett, the company's marine superintendent in the port, supported by colleagues in Liverpool and Southampton. As we have seen, these arrangements began well before the ship left Belfast with the selection of key officers and crew, involving many transfers of personnel from other White Star ships, and the provision of a wide range of supplies and equipment.

London-born Bartlett had joined the White Star Line in 1894 as Fourth Officer on the *Germanic*. Since 1900 he and his family had settled in Crosby, north Liverpool, a district in which he would reside for most of his later life. Given his first command in 1903, he soon became master of several White Star passenger liners on the North Atlantic, including *Germanic*, *Gothic*, *Republic*, *Cymric* and *Cedric*. Bartlett was a well-respected seaman, with an excellent safety record. In particular, he was known for his apparent ability to 'smell' ice, earning him the nickname 'Iceberg Charlie'. This supposed ability might well have proved invaluable had *Titanic* safely completed her maiden voyage and, as might well have happened, Bartlett succeeded Captain Smith as her master. Sadly, this was not to be. In January 1912 he was appointed to the shore-based position of Marine Superintendent of the

White Star Line in Liverpool. As such he played a major role in organising her maiden voyage, but was unable to prevent her catastrophic fate.[2]

On *Titanic*'s arrival in Southampton, the passengers who travelled from Belfast disembarked, the crew was discharged and the preparations for her maiden voyage intensified. Although the national coal strike ended on 6 April, there was no time for newly mined coal to be shipped to Southampton and loaded on to the ship. Coal from the five other IMM ships in port and surplus coal from *Olympic*, which had left for New York shortly before her sister's arrival, was therefore commandeered for *Titanic*'s vast bunkers. On board, furnishings and fittings were still being added to staterooms and public rooms, while huge quantities of tableware, food supplies and general cargo were delivered, listed and stored. Indeed, such was the lack of time during the ship's one-week stay at Southampton that White Star reluctantly decided not to allow general visitors on board. Instead, on Good Friday, 5 April, the vessel was 'dressed overall' in flags as a salute to the port and its people.[3] In the meantime, the recruitment of crew for the maiden voyage had already begun.

DECK DEPARTMENT

Sixty-six men signed on in Southampton as deck crew for *Titanic*'s maiden voyage, and all sailed.[4] Of these, 42 mostly Able Seamen from southern England, were completely new to the ship. However, two of the newcomers were Liverpool residents, namely Chief Officer Henry Wilde and Able Seaman Thomas Jones. Thirty-nine-year-old Henry Tingle Wilde lived at 24 Grey Road, Walton, Liverpool. A widower with four young children, he was born in Liverpool and had grown up in the Walton district of the city. He first went to sea as an apprentice on the sailing ships of James Chambers and Company, Liverpool. Having obtained his master's certificate while sailing to South America with the Maranhan Steamship Company, he joined White Star as a junior officer in 1905. He then served on a number of White Star ships, mainly on the Australian and New York routes, before joining *Olympic* as Chief Officer under Captain Edward Smith in 1911. According to Charles

Lightoller, Wilde's late appointment as *Titanic*'s Chief Officer was intended by 'the ruling lights of the White Star Line' to be for one voyage only, and was thought desirable due to his previous experience in that role on *Olympic*, the new vessel's sister ship.[5] However, this decision meant that both William Murdoch and Charles Lightoller, despite having conducted themselves well on *Titanic*'s voyage from Belfast, were demoted, to First and Second Officer respectively, for her maiden voyage. David Blair, Second Officer on *Titanic*'s delivery voyage, was not reappointed for the maiden voyage, but assigned to another ship. By mistake, Blair took with him the keys to the locker or drawer on *Titanic* containing the lookouts' binoculars. This explains why the binoculars, which were issued to the lookouts on the ship's crow's nest during her delivery voyage from Belfast to Southampton, were not made available to them on her maiden voyage. It is possible that this error may have contributed to the late sighting of the iceberg by the lookouts on the fateful night of Sunday 14 April 1912.[6]

The other deck officers for the maiden voyage remained the same as for the trip from Belfast. Although working on the ship on Good Friday, 5 April, Wilde only signed on for *Titanic* on Tuesday 9 April 1912, the day before she sailed, and reported for duty at 6 am the following day. On Sunday 7th he wrote a letter from the ship to two of his nieces in Liverpool in which he said that he still did not know whether or not he would be sailing on her the following Wednesday. He had tried to get to Liverpool the day before, but could not manage it. He revealed that *Titanic* was 'very far behind to sail on Wednesday', but that he and the crew were 'working at her night and day'. In his words: 'she is an improvement on Olympic in many respects and is a wonderful ship, the latest thing in shipbuilding'.[7]

One of his tasks shortly before sailing on 10 April was to write to W. Jones & Son, Flagmakers, in Liverpool, to clarify the details of the flags sent by the firm to Southampton for use on the maiden voyage.[8] Wilde was to play an important part in the events leading to *Titanic*'s sinking, which he did not survive. His body, if recovered, was never identified.[9]

Thirty-two-year-old Able Seaman Thomas William Jones was born at Cemaes Bay, Anglesey, Wales. He went to sea at 17, having moved to Liverpool to work for the White Star Line. In April 1912 his home address was 68 Nesfield Street, Walton, Liverpool. Jones apparently joined *Titanic* by chance. He had been an Able Seaman on the *Oceanic*, then out of service due to the coal strike, when he went to look around *Titanic* as she lay at her berth in Southampton prior to the maiden voyage. While he was aboard the ship one of her officers, an old friend, persuaded him to join her.[10] He signed on for the maiden voyage on 6 April. Jones survived the sinking, being put in charge of lifeboat 8, and later testified at the US Senate Inquiry. He continued working for White Star for a further two years, and lived in Liverpool until his death in 1967.[11]

Of the 66 deck crew who sailed on *Titanic*'s maiden voyage, just eight appear to have had strong Liverpool connections. They were as follows:

OFFICERS

Edward J. Smith, 62, Master, born Staffordshire

Henry T. Wilde, 39, Chief Officer, born Walton, Liverpool

William M. Murdoch, 39, First Officer, born Dalbeattie, Scotland

Charles Lightoller, 38, Second Officer, born Chorley, Lancashire

SEAMEN

Frederick Fleet, 24, Lookout, born Liverpool

Thomas William Jones, 32, Able Seaman, born Anglesey, Wales

John Maxwell, 29, Ship's Carpenter, born Liverpool

Walter Wynn, 49, Quartermaster, born Chester, Cheshire

As can be seen, the above group of eight men includes the ship's four most senior deck officers, who controlled the navigation of the ship, and four seamen, each of whom would play a significant part in the dramatic events of the night of 14–15

April. Of the eight individuals listed, only four would survive the sinking, namely Second Officer Charles Lightoller, Lookout Fred Fleet, Able Seaman Thomas Jones and Quartermaster Walter Wynn.

ENGINE DEPARTMENT

Officers and Support Staff

The 36 engineer officers and their support staff for the delivery voyage all re-signed in Southampton for the maiden voyage, and were joined by a further nine colleagues who were not on the delivery voyage.[12] Almost all of these men were English, including Chief Engineer Joseph Bell and the seven other senior engineering and associated staff with strong Liverpool backgrounds who were mentioned in the previous chapter.[13] None of the senior engineers or their support staff would survive the sinking.

Leading fireman Tom Ford. (*Daily Sketch*, 22/4/1912)

Crew

Most of the delivery voyage engine crew of firemen, greasers and trimmers did not re-sign for the maiden voyage, so an almost completely new 'Black Gang' of 280 men signed on at Southampton. Despite some last-minute personnel changes, the same number sailed on the maiden voyage. Of these, the crew list indicates that at least 32 were born, lived in or had strong connections with Liverpool and its surrounding areas. They included eight leading firemen (of 13), fifteen firemen (of 162),[14] six greasers (of 33) and three trimmers (of 72). They were as follows:[15]

Leading Firemen

Frederick Barrett, 28

Thomas Davies, 33

W. Ferris, 38, born Warrington, Cheshire

Thomas Ford, 30

James Keegan, 38, born Liverpool (or Wexford?)[16]
James Mason, 39
William Small, 40
Thomas Threlfall, 44

Firemen
E. Benville, 42
Alexander Black, 28
William Clark(e), 39, born County Louth, Ireland, lived Liverpool
B. Cunningham, 30
Thomas (or James?) Hart, 49, born Manchester[17]
John Jacobson (Jackson?), 29
Thomas Kerr, 26
L. Kinsella, 30
Thomas McAndrew, 36
William McAndrews, born Wigan, Lancashire
Edward Joseph McGarvey (McGoveney?), 34
John Noon, 35, born Wigan, Lancashire
Charles Rice, 32
Thomas Shea, 32
John William Thompson, 35, of 2 Primrose Hill, Vauxhall, Liverpool

Greasers
John Bannon, 32
Joseph Henry Couch, 45
Thomas McInerney, 37
J. Kirkham, 39
Thomas Joseph Fay, 30, of 31 Stamford Street, Kensington, Liverpool 7
Thomas Palles, 42, of 25 Upper Parliament Street, Liverpool

Trimmers

T. Casey, 28

Thomas Patrick Dillon, 24

James McGann (McCann), 26, of 18 St George's Place, Liverpool 1

The high proportion of leading firemen (eight out of 13) from the Liverpool area again reflects White Star's policy of selecting experienced and trusted staff for key positions on the maiden voyages of its most high-profile ships. The job of the leading firemen or 'pushers' involved watching the steam pressure and signalling the next firing or stoking of the boiler by rattling on the stokehold floor with a shovel. This basic but key task required experience of exactly how to keep the glowing mass of coal in such a condition as to produce the maximum heat.[18] According to George Garrett, a Liverpool fireman on the Cunarder *Mauretania* in 1918, these men were 'steam proud': 'they rousted slackers and lent reserve stamina to struggling firemen with boilers below par. Their additional weight on a long slice-bar cracked up clinker beyond a single man's strength.'[19]

In British shipping circles Liverpool firemen had for many years been considered to be 'the best on the western ocean', able to survive and thrive in the harshest stokehold conditions, even though they could also be challenging to manage. Referring specifically to the older Liverpool men, for example, Charles Lightoller, *Titanic*'s Second Officer, later wrote: 'A tougher bunch than the firemen on a Western Ocean Mail boat it would be impossible to find. Bootle seemed to specialise in the Liverpool Irishman, who was accounted to be the toughest of the tough.'[20] Lightoller also commented that there was no call for the tough element in the more modern mail steamers like *Oceanic*: 'in fact it did not exist in Southampton, where the mail boats were now running from'.[21]

Of these 32 men, just seven were originally recorded as having survived the sinking, namely Leading Firemen Barrett and Threlfall, Firemen Clark(e), Rice and

Thompson, and Trimmers Dillon and McGann. As will be seen below, however, there remain some uncertainties regarding the identities and fates of Fireman Thomas (or James?) Hart, Leading Fireman James Keegan, and Trimmer T. Casey. [22]

To summarise, of the total complement of 325 men employed in the engine department during *Titanic*'s maiden voyage, at least 40 had strong Liverpool connections. They included eight of the most senior engineers, and up to eight of the leading firemen. At the time of writing only seven of these 40 men are known to have survived the sinking.

VICTUALLING DEPARTMENT

All 120 victualling or catering crew on *Titanic*'s delivery voyage signed on again for her maiden voyage. However, more than 300 extra victualling staff were also recruited by White Star at Southampton. Eventually, after some last-minute changes, a total of 431 sailed in the victualling department on the maiden voyage. [23] This, by far the largest section of *Titanic*'s crew, was divided into three classes to cater for the three passenger classes on board. In all, 231 individuals, including the two Marconi operators, were categorised as First Class victualling crew, 76 as Second Class and 121 as Third Class and Galley. For convenience, the five postal clerks were usually added to the victualling staff list, even though, like the two Marconi operators, they were not directly employed by White Star. [24] Similarly, the 68 *à la carte* restaurant staff were broadly grouped with the victualling crew, even though they were not members of the White Star crew, but directly employed by the London-based Italian restaurateur Signor Gatti. [25] This brought the full complement of victualling and associated staff who sailed on the maiden voyage to 501.

Victualling, First Class
Among the 231 First Class victualling crew who sailed on the maiden voyage were at least 52 people with strong Liverpool area connections. Their details are given in Table 1.

Table 1. First Class victualling crew with connections to Liverpool and surrounding areas

Surname	Forenames/initials	Sex	Age	Rank/position	Place of birth	Address	Survived?
Allan	Robert Spencer	M	36	Steward	Liverpool	Southampton	No
Ashcroft	Austin Aloysius	M	26	Clerk	Liverpool	Cheshire 28 Canterbury Road Seacombe	No
Boston	William John	M	30	Deck Steward	Liverpool	Southampton	No
Boyes	John Henry (Harry)	M	36	Saloon Steward	Liverpool	Southampton	No
Brown	Walter James	M	28	Saloon Steward	Ormskirk, Lancs	Southampton	No
Bunnell	Wilfred	M	20	Plate Steward	Birkenhead	Southampton	No
Burke	Richard Edward	M	30	Lounge Steward	Liverpool	Southampton	No
Carney	William	M	31	Lift Steward	Bristol	Liverpool 11 Cairo Street West Derby Road	No
Crafter	Frederick	M	27	Saloon Steward	Liverpool	Southampton	Yes
Cullen	Charles	M	45	Bedroom Steward	Liverpool	Southampton	Yes
Davies (Davis)	Gordon Raleigh	M	33	Bedroom Steward	Liverpool	Southampton	No
Dodd	George Charles	M	44	Steward	London	Southampton	No
Donoghue	Frank (? Thomas)	M	35	Bedroom Steward	Liverpool	Southampton	No
Evans	George Richard	M	27 (32)	Saloon Steward	Liverpool	Southampton	No
Faulkner	William Stephen	M	37	Bedroom Steward	Birkenhead	Southampton	Yes
Fellowes	Alfred J.	M	29	Assistant Boots Steward	Liverpool	Southampton	No
Freeman	Ernest Edward Samuel	M	43	Deck Steward	London	Southampton	No
Gregson	Mary (Miss)	F	44	Stewardess	Liverpool	Southampton	Yes
Hamilton	Ernest	M	25	Assistant Smoke Room Steward	Liverpool	Southampton	No
Hewitt (Hewett)	Thomas	M	37	Bedroom Steward	Liverpool	Liverpool 98 Devonfield Road Aintree	No
Hogg	Charles William	M	37	Bedroom Steward	York	Liverpool 24 Pulver Street	No
Holland	Thomas	M	28	Reception Steward	Liverpool	Liverpool 38 Walton Village	No
Hughes	William Thomas	M	33	Steward	Liverpool	Southampton	No

Surname	Forenames/initials	Sex	Age	Rank/position	Place of birth	Address	Survived?
Latimer	Andrew L.	M	55	Chief Steward	Lancaster	Liverpool 4 Glenwyllin Road Waterloo	No
Leather (née Edwards) Elizabeth May (Mrs)		F	41	Stewardess	Liverpool	Cheshire 24 Park Road Port Sunlight	Yes
Lydiatt	Charles	M	28	Steward	Liverpool	Southampton	No
McCarthy	Frederick J.	M	36	Steward	Liverpool	Southampton	No
McElroy	Hugh Walter	M	37	Purser	Liverpool	Southampton	No
McLaren (née Allsop) Harriet (Mrs)		F	40	Stewardess	Liverpool	Southampton	Yes
McMicken	Benjamin Tucker	M	21	Second Pantry Steward	Liverpool	Southampton	No
McMicken	Arthur	M	23 (26)	Saloon Steward	Liverpool	Southampton	Yes
McMurray	William Ernest	M	43	Bedroom Steward	Birkenhead	Liverpool (Southampton on crew list?)	No
Mishellamy	Abraham	M	52	Printer Steward	Lebanon	Southampton, but lived Liverpool	No
Morgan (Bird)	Charles Frederick	M	42	Assistant Storekeeper		Birkenhead 46 Bessborough Road	No
O'Connor	Thomas Peter	M	39	Bedroom Steward	Liverpool	Southampton	No
Revell	William	M	30	Saloon Steward	Liverpool	Southampton	No
Rice	John Reginald	M	25	Assistant Purser	Hull	Liverpool 'Leafield' 311 Kimberley Drive Great Crosby	No
Rimmer	Gilbert	M	27	Saloon Steward	Liverpool	Southampton	No
Roberts	Hugh H.	M	40	Bedroom Steward	Holyhead, Anglesey, Wales	Liverpool 39 Mildmay Road Bootle	No
Roberts (née Humphreys) Mary Keziah (Mrs)		F	30	Stewardess	Liverpool	Nottingham	Yes
Stap	Sarah Agnes (Miss)	F	47	Stewardess	At sea	Birkenhead 41 Bidston Avenue Claughton	Yes
Strugnell	John H.	M	34	Saloon Steward	Liverpool	Southampton	No
Thomas	Albert Charles	M	23	Steward	Liverpool	Southampton? 11 Brunswick Place	Yes
Thompson	Herbert Henry	M	25	Second Assistant Storekeeper	Liverpool	Hampshire	No

Surname	Forenames/initials	Sex	Age	Rank/position	Place of birth	Address	Survived?
Turner	L.	M	28	Saloon Steward	Liverpool or Shropshire	Hampshire	No
Walpole	James	M	48	Chief Pantryman Steward	Southport, Lancs	Southampton	No
Wareham	Robert Arthur	M	36	Bedroom Steward	Liverpool	Southampton	No
Weatherstone	Thomas Herbert	M	24	Saloon Steward	Liverpool	Southampton	No
Webb	Brooke Holding	M	50	Smoke Room Steward	Liverpool	Southampton	No
Wheat	Joseph Thomas	M	29	Assistant Second Steward	Rock Ferry, Cheshire	Southampton	Yes
Wheelton	Edneser Ernest Edward	M	29	Saloon Steward	Liverpool	Hampshire	Yes
Williams	Arthur J.	M	38	Assistant Storekeeper	Liverpool	Liverpool 52 Peter Road Walton	No

The most senior members of this group, and indeed of the entire victualling department, were Purser Hugh McElroy and Chief Steward Andrew Latimer. Thirty-seven-year-old McElroy was born in 1874 at 3 Percy Street, Toxteth, Liverpool. His parents had moved to Liverpool from County Wexford, Ireland. At sixteen he became a student priest, but after two years he decided to follow his father by becoming a merchant seaman. Before joining *Titanic*, McElroy worked for the White Star Line for some thirteen years, during which he spent three years on board the troopship *Britannic* during the Boer War, and served on the *Majestic* and *Adriatic* under the command of Captain E.J. Smith. With Chief Steward Latimer and Ship's Surgeon Dr. William O'Loughlin, he was subsequently transferred to *Olympic*, then *Titanic*. He signed on for *Titanic* on 9 April 1912 as Chief Purser with wages of £20 per month. By this time he was married, and lived with his Wexford-born wife in Southampton.[26] According to Dr. J.C.H. Beaumont, who succeeded O'Loughlin as surgeon on the *Olympic*, McElroy had been woken on several occasions on the *Olympic* by suffocating nightmares, 'which gave way to him having some premonitions about sailing on the *Titanic*. He would have nightmares of being in a dark tunnel, with no means of escape.'[27] McElroy did not survive the sinking of *Titanic*. His body was

Purser Hugh McElroy (© Museums and Galleries Northern Ireland, Ulster Folk and Transport Museum)

First-class steward George Dodd. (*Daily Sketch*, 18/04/1912)

Deck steward Ernest Freeman. (*Daily Sketch*, 18/4/1912)

recovered by the *Mackay-Bennett*, and he was buried at sea on 24 April 1912. He is remembered on the family gravestone at Anfield Cemetery in Liverpool.[28]

Fifty-five-year-old Chief Steward Andrew Latimer was born in Lancaster but sailed from Liverpool for many years on the Dominion Line's Canadian service. He then obtained employment with the White Star Line following the creation of the IMM combine. He joined *Titanic* having been Chief Steward on White Star's *Teutonic*, *Cedric*, *Adriatic* and *Olympic*. In 1912 he lived with his second wife and their four children at 4 Glenwyllin Road, Waterloo, Liverpool. He signed on for *Titanic*'s delivery voyage at Belfast on Monday 1 April, then again for her maiden voyage at Southampton on 6 April. Like McElroy, his pay was £20 per month. Latimer died in the sinking and his body, if recovered, was never identified.[29]

Working closely with Hugh McElroy on *Titanic* was another Liverpool resident, Assistant Purser or Purser's Clerk, John Reginald Rice. Twenty-five-year-old Rice, a single man, was born in Hull but when he signed on for *Titanic* on 9 April 1912 he lived with his parents at 311 Kimberley Drive, Great Crosby, Liverpool. This address was within walking distance of the homes of Chief Engineer Joseph Bell and Chief Steward Andrew Latimer.[30] Rice died in the sinking and his body was recovered by the *Mackay-Bennett*. He was buried in Fairview Lawn Cemetery, Halifax, Nova Scotia, on 8 May 1912. John Rice's father never recovered from the death of his son, and he himself died at the beginning of 1913.[31]

Among the 41 First Class stewards working under Andrew Latimer was Ernest Freeman. Forty-three-year-old Freeman was born in London and gave his address as Southampton on the crew list. His rank or position on *Titanic* was recorded as 'Deck Steward' or 'Chief Deck Steward', and his previous ship had been *Olympic*. Freeman is often described as having been, unofficially, not so much a crew member as a secretary or 'private secretary' to Bruce Ismay while he was on *Titanic*. However, since William Henry Harrison, Ismay's 'official' secretary, was travelling with his employer as a First Class passenger on the voyage it seems more likely that Freeman was, in fact, a former secretary of Ismay who had opted for a career at sea. He did not survive the sinking and is buried in Fairview Lawn Cemetery in Halifax, Nova Scotia. His gravestone bears the inscription 'Erected by Mr. J. Bruce Ismay. To commemorate a long and faithful service'. Ismay also arranged for a personal pension to be paid to Freeman's dependants. Ernest Freeman is further commemorated on a family gravestone in Walton Park Cemetery, Rice Lane, Walton, Liverpool.[32] This suggests that he had lived with his family in the Liverpool area at least since the 1890s.

Another First Class steward with close links to Bruce Ismay was George Dodd. Forty-four-year-old Dodd was born in London, but had formerly served as Bruce Ismay's butler in Liverpool. Having long expressed the desire to go to sea, he was helped by Bruce Ismay to fulfil this ambition. Dodd moved to Southampton in order to work on White Star's largest liners.[33] Like Ernest Freeman, another former 'personal servant' of Ismay in Liverpool, he transferred from *Olympic* to sign on for *Titanic*'s delivery voyage in Belfast, then for her maiden voyage in Southampton. He died in the sinking and his body was not recovered. However, Dodd is remembered on his family's gravestone in Rake Lane Cemetery, Wallasey, Wirral.[34]

Also among the First Class stewards were the Liverpool-born brothers Arthur and Benjamin Tucker McMicken. Both were single men and signed on for *Titanic*'s delivery voyage from Belfast on 1 April 1912, and then, only three days later, for her maiden voyage from Southampton. Both had worked on *Olympic* immediately

Bedroom steward Thomas Hewitt, of Devonfield Road, Orrell Park, Liverpool, with his wife, Ada.

The gold watches exchanged as gifts on their wedding day in 1902 by Ada and Thomas Hewitt. Ada's fob watch is on the left, Thomas's pocket watch on the right. (MMM. 1999.82)

beforehand and were living with their mother, sister and brothers at 43 Suffolk Avenue, Southampton. At 23, Arthur was two years older than his brother and was employed as a saloon steward. Benjamin, who signed on at Belfast and Southampton as 'Benjamin Tucker', presumably to conceal his close family relationship with Arthur,[35] was employed as a second pantry steward. On *Titanic* he worked under chief pantryman James Walpole, who was born in Southport, Lancashire, some twenty miles from Liverpool. Although Arthur survived the sinking, being rescued in lifeboat 11, Benjamin did not, and his body was never recovered.

Bedroom Steward Thomas Hewitt, 37, was born in Liverpool and lived in the city with his wife and two children at 96 Devonfield Road, Aintree. He was on *Titanic*'s delivery trip from Belfast and her maiden voyage from Southampton. Merseyside Maritime Museum has a pair of gold watches which Thomas and his wife, Ada, exchanged as gifts on their wedding day in 1902. As *Titanic* was sinking Thomas is said to have passed his watch to a stewardess, who later returned it to Ada. Thomas died in the disaster and his body was buried at sea on 24 April 1912. Ada remained a widow until her death in 1966.[36]

Of the 19 First Class stewardesses who sailed on *Titanic*'s maiden voyage, four had been born in Liverpool, namely Miss Mary Gregson, Mrs. Elizabeth May Leather (née Edwards), Mrs. Harriet McLaren (née Allsop), and Mrs. Mary Keziah Roberts (née Humphreys). Like most other stewardesses on board, each of these women was about forty years of age. Of the four, in 1912 only Elizabeth Leather was still living in the Liverpool area. She gave her home address as 28 Park Road, Port Sunlight, Liverpool, although Port Sunlight was not part of the city of Liverpool, but nearby, on the Cheshire side of the River Mersey. Like Mary Gregson and Mary Roberts, Elizabeth Leather survived the sinking of *Titanic* in lifeboat 16. Harriet McLaren was the younger sister of First Class Saloon Steward Frank Allsop. Although Harriet was born in Liverpool and lived in Southampton, Frank was born and lived in Devon. While she survived the sinking in lifeboat 5, her brother died. If recovered, his body was never identified.[37]

Assistant 2nd steward Joseph Wheat. (*Daily Sketch*, 18/4/1912)

Chief pantryman steward James Walpole. (*Daily Sketch*, 18/4/1912)

Another First Class stewardess with strong Liverpool connections was Miss Agnes Sarah Stap. She was born at sea around 1865, the daughter of master mariner Henry Stap, who may at one time have sailed out of Liverpool with the White Star Line. In April 1912 she lived near Liverpool at 41 Bidston Avenue, Claughton, Birkenhead. When she signed on for *Titanic*'s maiden voyage on Tuesday 9 April, she gave her age as 31 years, but her actual age was probably about 46. As such, she was the oldest stewardess on board. Like Mary Gregson and Elizabeth Leather, her previous ship had been the *Olympic*. According to her great-nephew, Gordon Stap, she was effectively the ship's matron, rather than a stewardess. Even so, on *Titanic* her monthly wages, like those of most of the other stewardesses, were £3 10s per month. Sarah survived the sinking in lifeboat 11. She later claimed that she owed her survival to 'a young cabin boy' who ignored her protests and lifted her into the lifeboat. She died in Birkenhead on Saturday 27 March 1937, at the age of 72.[38]

Victualling, Second Class

Only three of the 76 Second Class victualling crew who sailed on *Titanic*'s maiden voyage were originally from the Liverpool area, namely the young stewards Charles Andrews and Albert Jones, and the Smoke Room Steward James Witter.

Nineteen-year-old Assistant Saloon Steward Andrews was born in Liverpool in early 1893. When he signed on to *Titanic* on 4 April 1912 he gave his address as 145 Millbrook Road, Southampton. His last ship had been *Oceanic*. Andrews survived the disaster, having helped to row lifeboat 16, and soon afterwards testified at the US Senate Inquiry into the sinking. In later years he served as a steward on the Cunard liner *Aquitania* and as a masseur and swimming pool attendant on the *Queen Mary*. He retired in 1959 and died in Southampton on 2 January 1961, aged 67.[39]

At 17 years of age, Liverpool-born Saloon Steward Albert Jones was one of the youngest stewards on board, apart from the bell-boy stewards.[40] When he signed on to *Titanic* on 4 April 1912 he gave his address as Woodfield, Charlton Road, Southampton. His previous ship had been the *Majestic*. Jones died in the sinking. His body, if recovered, was never identified.[41]

Thirty-one-year-old James William Cheetham Witter was born in Aughton, Lancashire, about ten miles from Liverpool. However, he gave his address as 56 Porchester Road, Woolston, Hampshire when he signed on for *Titanic* in Southampton. Witter survived the sinking in lifeboat 11, having fallen into the boat while trying to stop a hysterical woman from falling overboard. He soon returned to sea with White Star after the disaster, and served on many White Star and Cunard White Star liners in the 1920s and 1930s. He died in Southampton in 1961, aged 80.[42]

One of the Second Class victualling crew who signed on for the maiden voyage but failed to join the ship was Liverpool-born R. Fisher, a 'Second Class Plate Steward'. Fisher was 24 years old and gave his home address as 28 Duncan Street, Portsmouth.[43]

Chef Charles Proctor. (*Daily Sketch*, 18/4/1912)

Chief baker Charles Joughin. (*Daily Mirror*, 22/4/1912)

Walter Ennis, Turkish Bath attendant. (*Daily Sketch*, 18/4/1912)

Victualling, Third Class and Galley

Just four of the 52 Third Class victualling crew who sailed on the maiden voyage were born in Liverpool. These were Chief Third Class Steward James Kieran, and stewards H.P. Hill, William Crispin and William Wright. Steward Henry (or Harry) Ashe is believed to have been born in County Kerry, Ireland, but lived at 15 Wyresdale Road, Walton, Liverpool. Of these men, only 'Glory Hole Steward' William Wright would survive the sinking. Forty-year-old Wright signed on to *Titanic* on 4 April 1912, having previously worked on her sister ship *Olympic*. He gave his address as 9 Emsworth Road, Southampton. As a 'Glory Hole' steward he was responsible for catering for fellow crew members, and not for passengers.[44] Wright survived because he was ordered into lifeboat 13 so as 'to take an oar and assist in sailing the seventy persons the boat contained'. On 16 May 1912 he attended the funeral in West Derby Cemetery, Liverpool, of his fellow steward and former *Olympic* shipmate Arthur Lawrence, one of only two victims of the *Titanic* disaster to be buried in Liverpool.[45]

Of the 69 galley crew who sailed on the maiden voyage, just five appear to have had Liverpool backgrounds. These were, in order of seniority (as indicated via their monthly wages):

Charles Proctor, 40, Chef, born Liverpool, £20 per month
Charles Joughin, 33, Chief Baker, born Birkenhead, Cheshire, £12 per month
John Giles, 30, Second Baker, born Liverpool, £7 per month
James Hutchinson, 29, Vegetable Cook, born Liverpool, £6 10s per month
Henry ('Harry') Shaw, 39, Kitchen Porter, born Liverpool, £3 10s per month

Of these men, only Proctor and Joughin had also sailed on the delivery voyage from Belfast. All had transferred directly from the *Olympic*, except Henry (or Harry) Shaw, whose last ship had been the Pacific Steam Navigation Company's *Orissa*, sailing between Liverpool and South America. When signing on for *Titanic* in Southampton, Shaw gave his home address as 47 Towcester Street, which was in the Litherland district of Liverpool.[46] Although all of the others gave Southampton addresses, James Hutchinson's home address was at 91 Woodcroft Road, Wavertree, Liverpool, while Charles Joughin is also believed to have lived with his family in Liverpool in 1912, possibly in Grasmere Street, Everton.[47] The only one of these five men to survive the *Titanic* disaster was Chief Baker Charles Joughin. His celebrated survival story will be told in a later chapter.[48]

Also included with the galley staff on the crew list were the three Turkish bath attendants, one of whom, Walter Ennis, gave his address as 141 Bedford Road, Birkdale, Southport, Lancashire. Thirty-five-year-old Ennis was born in Northumberland and was married, with two children. *Titanic* was his first ship, and he had previously worked in a similar job at Smedley Hydro in Birkdale. He died in the sinking and his body, if recovered, was never identified.[49]

A la carte Restaurant Staff

Most of the 68 *à la carte* restaurant staff who sailed on *Titanic* from Southampton were from Italy, France or Switzerland. However, the First Cashier was 27-year-old Englishwoman Miss Ruth Bowker. She was born in Wade, Hertfordshire, but in

April 1912 her home was near Liverpool at The Cottage, Little Sutton, Wirral, Cheshire. Like many of her colleagues, she had previously worked on *Olympic*. Ruth Bowker survived the sinking, and escaped in lifeboat 6.

CREW SUMMARY

To summarise, available evidence suggests that the total number of crew and associated staff who sailed on *Titanic*'s maiden voyage from Southampton on Wednesday 10 April 1912 was 892. Of this total, at least 114 were people with Liverpool backgrounds or strong associations with Liverpool and its surrounding area. They included eight deck crew (of 66), 40 engine crew (of 325) and 66 victualling crew and associated staff (of 501). Many had transferred directly to *Titanic* from *Olympic*.

Although this means that only about one in eight of *Titanic*'s maiden voyage crew had strong Liverpool connections, it is clear that many of these individuals were key officers and crew on the ship. This was, no doubt, the natural result of White Star's long association with Liverpool, and of the company's policy of choosing their most trusted and experienced staff for the maiden voyages of their most important ships. The Liverpool connection linked Captain Edward Smith, Chief Officer Henry Wilde, First Officer William Murdoch, Second Officer Charles Lightoller, Chief Engineer Joseph Bell and several of his most senior engineer officers, Chief Steward Andrew Latimer, Purser Hugh McElroy, Chief Electrician Peter Sloan, Chef Charles Proctor, Chief Baker Charles Joughin, right through to stewardesses, stewards, firemen, greasers and trimmers.

The 'Liverpool connection' explains why the long, wide working alleyway which ran the length of *Titanic* on the port side of 'E' deck, providing access to crew quarters, the boiler rooms and to other parts of the ship, was known by the crew as 'Scotland Road'. As Harland and Wolff naval architect Edward Wilding stated in his deposition to the Limited Liability Hearings relating to the *Titanic* disaster held in New York State in May 1915, 'The men called it Scotland Road;

that is the name of a broad, wide road in Liverpool'.[50] The term was also used by Wilding, chef Charles Joughin and chief bathroom steward Samuel Rule during their respective testimonies at the Board of Trade Enquiry in 1912.[51] Each of these men had strong Liverpool connections. Although this nickname continues to bemuse some *Titanic* researchers,[52] Scotland Road was then a notorious Liverpool thoroughfare, not far from the Liverpool waterfront, in and around which generations of seafarers and their families had lived in tightly packed streets and houses. Over many years this gritty, working-class, largely Irish Catholic area, which supplied many of the 'Black Gang' and other crew for Liverpool-based Atlantic liners and other ships trading worldwide, had become the distinctive and turbulent heart of Liverpool's North Docks community. It had also acquired an unenviable reputation as 'an affront to late-Victorian standards of decency and order' due to its squalid living conditions and the habitually unruly behaviour of some of its residents and visitors.[53] As John Belchem has shown, among neighbouring Protestant communities, the expression 'Scotland Road' appears sometimes to have been used almost as a euphemism for hell, as in the insult 'Get to hell or Scotland Road!'[54] Even so, as Derek Whale wrote in his book *The Liners of Liverpool*, 'many a grand vessel would never have sailed without the fire in her belly being stoked by the lads from Scotland Road. From the dismal, gas and candle-lit homes in the warrens of "Scottie" Road's rank terraces and courts, came so many of the tough and hardy "black gangs" of firemen, trimmers and greasers of the age of steam.'[55] It seems likely that the term 'Scotland Road' was used as a nickname for such working alleyways on Liverpool-connected ships long before *Titanic* and continued to be so used for many years after her.[56]

Towards the end of the First World War, Liverpool-Irish fireman George Garrett was working in the stokehold on Cunard's *Mauretania*. He later wrote a short story, clearly derived from his first-hand experiences, in which he described how the firemen arranged their sleeping area:

The widest floor space crossed from the alleyway door to the ship's side. Off this, bunks branched into irregular sized 'cracks' where men grouped according to shore locality. Athol Street, Marsh Lane and Gerard Street were aptly named. A wag altered Gerard Street to Gerard Avenue.[57]

Like Scotland Road, the three localities to which he referred were all situated near Liverpool's North Docks. Indeed, both Athol Street and Gerard Street were just off Scotland Road. Interestingly, in the same short story Garrett also revealed that, 'due to prejudice, religious or geographical', Liverpool firemen on the *Mauretania* who lived south of the Liverpool Landing Stage were regarded as interlopers. He continued: 'The few "Southenders" joining the "Maurie" [*Mauretania*] named their "crack" Park Laney Street'.[58] The Park Lane district was in the area of Liverpool's South Docks, near Canning Place, and 'formed the centre of what was traditionally known as the seamen's ghetto'.[59] It is intriguing that the same working alleyway on *Titanic* known by the crew as 'Scotland Road' was known to at least one of her officers as 'Park Lane'.[60] This was probably just an ironic reference to one of London's most wealthy and select neighbourhoods. However, Garrett's evidence could suggest that the reference was a *double* (or even a treble) *entendre*. Without necessarily attributing this to the subtleties of the legendary Liverpool humour, we have already seen that a number of *Titanic*'s officers had strong Liverpool backgrounds.

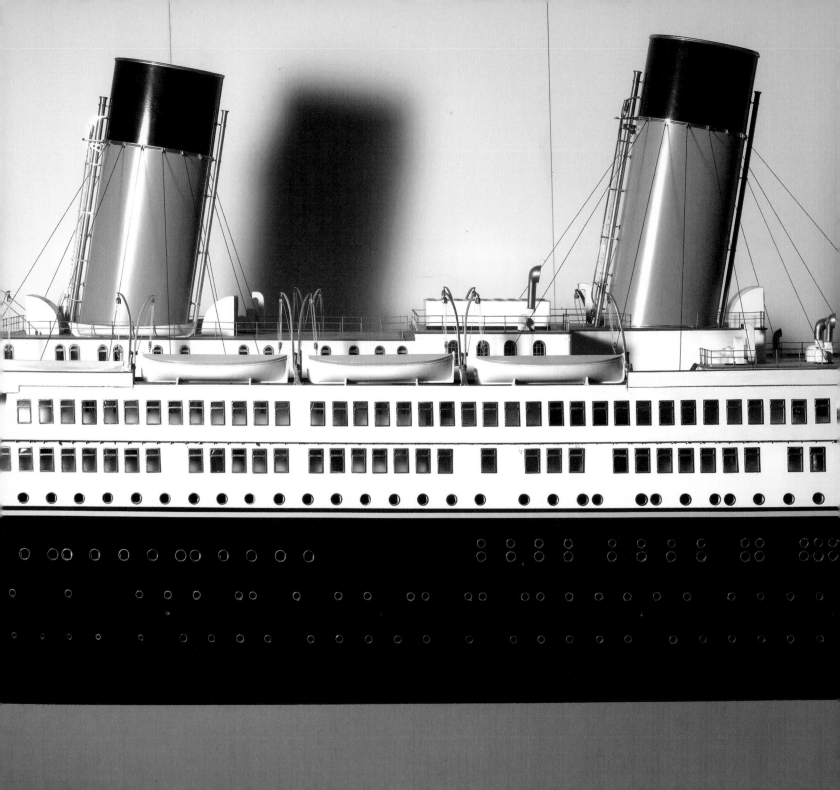

CHAPTER 6

PASSENGERS

Thus, with the largest and most magnificent ship in the world, manned by the finest possible crew, we announced ourselves as ready to send her on her maiden voyage to New York, and booked a large list of passengers.

Harold Sanderson
22 April 1912[1]

It would be surprising if many residents of the Liverpool area, or indeed the northern regions of England generally, had been among the passengers for *Titanic*'s maiden voyage. After all, in 1912 Liverpool was still Britain's largest Atlantic port in terms of overall passenger numbers cleared, and would continue to be so until after the First World War. This was due mainly to the numbers of Second and Third Class passengers emigrating to the United States and Canada.[2] Many such passengers were non-British emigrants who had travelled to Liverpool from Scandinavia and other parts of Europe in order to cross the Atlantic. Liverpool was the home port and only English base of the Cunard Line's celebrated 'ocean greyhounds', *Lusitania* and *Mauretania*, which were still, after over four years' service on the New York run, 'the fastest ships in the world'. The port could also offer the traditional, very popular, weekly New York service provided by three of White Star's '*Celtic* class' liners, each of which could carry over 400 passengers in First and Second Class, and 2000 in Third Class.

Passengers from the northern and Midland counties of England would therefore only choose to cross the Atlantic via Southampton, rather than

Liverpool, if they had a particular reason to do so. After all, for these people Southampton was much further away than Liverpool, requiring a day-long train journey. When departing from Southampton on 10 April 1912, *Titanic* would indeed be the largest and most luxurious ship in the world. However, this alone would not have persuaded many passengers from the North and Midlands of England to book tickets for her maiden voyage.

There was, however, one exceptional circumstance which might have diverted some passengers from Liverpool to Southampton, and perhaps vice versa, in early April 1912. This was the national coal strike, which severely restricted coal supplies in Britain generally and caused some sailings of White Star and other Atlantic liners to be cancelled.[3]

MISSED THE BOAT

In this context, it is interesting that, just five days after the *Titanic* disaster, the *New York Times* reported that there were a number of passengers on the *Mauretania*, which had arrived in New York the previous day, who had booked 'by the *Titanic*', but who, 'for one reason or another, cancelled the booking at the last moment, and waited for the *Mauretania*'. The *Mauretania*, of course, was based in Liverpool, not Southampton. Among the passengers who had done this were 'the venerable T. J. Madden, Archdeacon of Liverpool' and Mr. Charles Lancaster of the Liverpool Chamber of Commerce.[4]

The Very Reverend T. J. Madden, Archdeacon of Liverpool, had cancelled his passage on *Titanic* and instead booked to travel on *Mauretania* from Liverpool to New York to speak at the six-day Christian Conservation Conference which was due to begin at the Carnegie Hall on 20 April. This was the evangelical peace conference in New York which the British journalist and author William Thomas Stead had also been invited to address. Unlike Madden, Stead, who lived and worked in London, did not cancel his passage on *Titanic*, and died in the sinking. The same Carnegie Hall conference was that at which the Reverend J. Stuart Holden, vicar of St Paul's Church, Portman Square, London was due to speak when his plans were interrupted

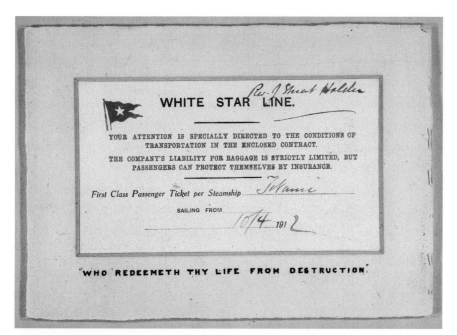

The Reverend J. Stuart Holden's First Class boarding card for *Titanic*'s maiden voyage. He did not sail. (MMM ref. DX/1063/R)

Titanic leaves Southampton, 10 April 1912. (NML ref S2006-00448)

by his wife's sudden illness. On 9 April, a day before *Titanic* sailed, he too had cancelled his voyage on the ship so that he could remain at his wife's side. The Reverend Holden is believed to have returned his First Class contract ticket, but kept his boarding pass, which he later framed, to remind him of God's mercy in saving him from almost certain death. This First Class boarding pass, believed to be the only surviving example for *Titanic*, has for many years been in the collection of the Merseyside Maritime Museum in Liverpool.[5] As John Eaton comments, clergymen appear to have done especially well in 'missing the boat'. Madden and Holden were among four clergymen who cancelled passages previously booked on *Titanic* and were thus spared 'to carry on God's work in greener pastures'.[6]

Charles Lancaster, the other prominent Liverpool man who cancelled his passage on *Titanic* to sail instead on *Mauretania*, was Chairman of the Council of the Liverpool Chamber of Commerce. According to a report published on 2 April 1909 in the *Ledger-Dispatch* of Norfolk, Virginia, Lancaster was 'one of England's greatest capitalists' when he came down from New York to attend the celebration of the opening of the Virginia Railway. The report revealed that he was one of a party of guests, including Dr. Samuel L. Clemens (alias the novelist Mark Twain), who were travelling with Henry H. Rogers, owner of the Virginia Railway. Lancaster was then, evidently, an important and enthusiastic investor in that company.[7] This is an interesting example of how 'Liverpool capital' was being invested in the United States in the immediate pre-*Titanic* years. The precise reasons for Charles Lancaster's last-minute decision to switch from *Titanic* to *Mauretania* in April 1912 are not known. As in the case of the Very Reverend T.J. Madden, however, this decision may well have saved his life.

THE LIVERPOOL LIST
Among the 954 passengers recorded as having embarked at Southampton on 10 April there appear to have been just 16 people with Liverpool area backgrounds or connections. Five were travelling First Class, eight Second Class, and three Third

Class. None of these passengers was among the 24 who left the ship at Cherbourg that evening, after the English Channel crossing.[8] None was among the seven passengers who left at Queenstown in Ireland the following day.[9] However, there was at least one more Liverpool-related person among the 394 additional passengers who boarded the ship during her brief calls at these two ports.[10] This was First Class passenger Victor Giglio, valet or manservant to the American millionaire Benjamin Guggenheim. Liverpool-born Giglio and his employer both embarked on *Titanic* at Cherbourg. In all, therefore, there appear to have been just 17 Liverpool-related passengers among the final total of 1317 who left Queenstown on 11 April, bound for New York. The backgrounds of these 17 people, only four of whom would survive the ensuing disaster, will now be briefly considered.

First Class Passengers

Miss Elizabeth Bonnell, 60
Mr. John Richard Fry, 39, servant (valet) to J.B. Ismay
Mr. Victor Gaetan Giglio, 24, servant (valet) to B. Guggenheim
Mr. William Henry Harrison, 40, secretary to J.B. Ismay
Mr. Joseph Bruce Ismay, 49, shipowner
Mr. Alfred G. Rowe, 59, landowner

J. Bruce Ismay was 49 years old when he boarded *Titanic* at Southampton on the morning of 10 April 1912 accompanied by his wife and three children, his valet John Richard Fry and his secretary William Henry Harrison. He had travelled with his family by car from his London home the previous day, and had then stayed the night with them at the South Western Hotel in Southampton.
Mrs. Ismay and the children were not sailing with him, but would watch *Titanic* depart before setting off for a motoring holiday in Devon and Wales. Ismay was in high spirits, having seen his eldest daughter married just a fortnight previously, and was looking forward to the maiden voyage of his latest, most magnificent

ship.[11] Two months earlier he had made plans for his old friend Harold Sanderson to succeed him as President of the IMM company on 30 June 1913. Everything seemed to be set fair for him to retire smoothly from the shipping business, as his father had done, at the peak of his career.[12] Even so, in a letter to Charles Steele, secretary of Morgan and Company, New York, on 26 February he had struck a cautionary note: 'Of course, the 30th June, 1913, is a "FAR CRY" and much may happen between now and then'.[13]

At noon, in fine April sunshine, *Titanic* left the Ocean Dock with relatively little ceremony or publicity, in contrast to the maiden voyage of *Olympic* the previous year. However, as she passed the American Line ship *New York* which was berthed alongside the quay, the enormous suction of her propellers caused the *New York* to break her moorings and almost resulted in a collision between the two ships. This was narrowly avoided, and the huge new liner proceeded on her way.

During the voyage, Ismay, who was very reserved by nature, played little part in the social activities on board. Indeed, apart from an occasional stroll on the boat deck he appears to have spent most of his time in his suite of staterooms, B52-6 on the starboard side of 'B' deck. On Thursday afternoon, while *Titanic* was at anchor in Queenstown harbour, he was visited in his suite by Chief Engineer Joseph Bell, to discuss the coal to be consumed by the ship and the speed required of her during the voyage.[14] During the voyage Ismay often talked to American passenger Mr. Charles M. Hays, president of the Grand Trunk Railway.[15] Otherwise, his only regular contact on board, except with stewards and other victualling staff, is likely to have been with his valet, Fry, and his secretary, Harrison.[16] One evening he dined with *Titanic*'s designer Thomas Andrews, who revealed his proposal to add a stateroom to the forward end of the ship's Writing and Reading Room. On Saturday he dined with Captain Edward Smith, and on Sunday with Ship's Surgeon Dr. William O'Loughlin.[17]

Surprisingly, throughout his entire business career, Ismay had travelled on the maiden voyages of only two previous White Star liners, namely *Adriatic* in May

1907 and *Olympic* in June 1911.[18] Shortly after the *Titanic* disaster, for which he was immediately scapegoated by sections of the American press, he testified at the US Senate Inquiry that his main aim in travelling on the ship on this particular occasion was 'to inspect the ship and see if there were any defects in her, with the idea of not repeating them in the other ship [i.e. *Britannic*] which we are now building at Belfast'. When questioned further on this matter, he replied that his focus on such occasions was not on technical details but rather on 'passenger conveniences'.[19] As shall be seen, however, his motives for travelling on *Titanic*'s fateful maiden voyage, and his actions before, during and after the voyage, have been subject to enormous scrutiny and controversy ever since.[20]

Thirty-nine-year-old John Richard Fry had been J. Bruce Ismay's valet or butler for ten years. On *Titanic* he occupied First Class cabin B-102. Little is known about his time on board the ship, but he would have been in close attendance whenever required by his employer. Fry lived with his wife and two children at 24 Rose Lane, Mossley Vale, near Ismay's home at 'Sandheys' in Mossley Hill, Liverpool. He died in the sinking and his body, if recovered, was never identified. Ismay never saw him again after the ship collided with the iceberg.[21]

Forty-year-old William Henry Harrison was Ismay's personal secretary when he boarded *Titanic* in Southampton with his employer and John Richard Fry. His home address was near Liverpool at 'Sudbury', Grove Road, Wallasey, Cheshire. Harrison, a pipe-smoker, occupied First Class cabin B-94 on the ship. He was present at the meeting between Ismay and Chief Engineer Bell in the former's stateroom while the ship was anchored at Queenstown.[22] Otherwise, his activities on board have not been recorded. Like his colleague and travelling companion John Richard Fry, Harrison died in the sinking. His body was recovered by the *Mackay-Bennett* and he was later buried at Fairview Lawn Cemetery in Halifax, Nova Scotia. He left a widow, Anne Elizabeth.[23]

Yorkshire-born Miss Elizabeth (Lily) Bonnell, of 17 Welbeck Road, Birkdale, near Southport, Lancashire, was 61 years old when she boarded *Titanic* on 10 April

John Richard Fry, Bruce Ismay's valet or butler (courtesy of the Titanic Historical Society, Inc.)

1912.[24] Lily, one of six children of a master saddler from Bradford, Yorkshire, was a woman of independent means, and 'a prominent worker in connection with the Southport Day Nursery'.[25] She was travelling to the United States to visit her brother, Mr. John Meek Bonnell, and other relatives in the bustling iron and steel manufacturing city of Youngstown, Ohio. She was accompanied by her niece, 26-year-old Miss Caroline Bonnell, of Youngstown, and Caroline's Youngstown relatives Colonel George D. Wick, his wife Mary (Mollie), and their daughter Miss Natalie Wick. The Youngstown party was returning home from a tour of Europe, and may well have arranged to meet up with Lily at the Carlton Hotel in London before travelling together to Southampton. Lily was allocated stateroom C-103 on *Titanic*, near to the staterooms occupied by her companions.[26] At Queenstown she sent a letter home to her two sisters, Jane and Mary, in Birkdale in which she wrote: 'It is simply glorious this morning. The sun is shining. It was most interesting seeing the people come on board at Cherbourg. I changed for dinner last night and was nearly frozen. Shall wear a jacket tonight.'[27]

On the night of Sunday 14 April, Caroline Bonnell and her cousin Natalie Wick were awoken by the collision with the iceberg. The Wick family made their way to 'A' deck, while Caroline went to find her aunt. Both the Bonnells and the Wicks then moved up to the boat deck, where the four ladies were placed in lifeboat 8. According to an Illinois newspaper report dated 17 April 1912:

> Miss Natalia [sic] and the Misses Bonnell were on deck. The four women entered the second life-boat let down. Mrs. Wick said the boat was not launched for an hour after the collision. Mr. Wick stood at the rail as his wife and daughter were helped into the boat and waved his hand as the party left the Titanic. The last seen of him was standing on the deck waving a farewell. Mrs. Wick said the party drifted about in the intense cold for five hours before they were picked up.[28]

Lily Bonnell survived the sinking, and eventually returned to England. On 24 July 1913 she disembarked from the Cunard liner *Caronia* in Liverpool[29] and made her way home to Birkdale, where she is believed to have lived for the rest of her life. She died on Thursday 20 February 1936, aged 85.[30]

Victor Gaetan A. Giglio was the 24-year-old valet of the American mining and smelting millionaire Benjamin Guggenheim. The Guggenheim family believed that Giglio was Egyptian.[31] *Titanic* steward Henry Samuel Etches, who attended to Guggenheim and Giglio on board the ship, believed that he was Armenian.[32] In reality, Giglio was born in Liverpool and as a small child had lived in the city at 22 Linnet Lane, Toxteth Park. The UK Census records for 1891 appear to show that Victor, then just two years old, was the youngest of four sons of D.J. Giglio, the female head of the household. Victor was the only family member recorded in this census as having been born in Liverpool, all the others having been born in Egypt.[33] Ten years later he was a schoolboy boarder at Ampleforth Abbey and College in Yorkshire.[34] In January 1912 Giglio accompanied Guggenheim, who had offices in London and Paris, on a business trip to Europe. Both men arrived on the Cunard liner *Lusitania* at Fishguard in South Wales on 16 January, and eventually made their way to Paris.[35] On 11 April they boarded *Titanic* at Cherbourg for the return journey to New York. Giglio occupied First Class stateroom B-84, one of the suite of rooms booked for his employer. Also embarking at Cherbourg were Guggenheim's mistress, the French singer Mme Leontine Pauline ('Ninette') Aubart, her Swiss maid Emma Sägesser, and Guggenheim's chauffeur, René Pernod. Of these five people, only Mme Aubart and her maid would survive the sinking. Shortly before *Titanic* sank, both Guggenheim and Giglio went to their rooms and changed into their best evening wear. Guggenheim was heard to remark: 'We've dressed up in our best and are prepared to go down like gentlemen.' They then waited calmly to die. Both Guggenheim and Giglio died in the sinking and their bodies were never recovered.[36]

The final First Class passenger with a strong Liverpool background was

59-year-old businessman and landowner Mr. Alfred G. Rowe. Rowe was born in Peru in 1853, the fourth of seven children of John James and Agnes Rowe of 'Dinglefield', Liverpool. His father was partner in the Liverpool ship-owning firm of Graham, Rowe and Company. Alfred was educated at Cheltenham College and then on the Continent before working for the family business for two years. After studying at the Royal Agricultural College in Cirencester, Gloucestershire, he decided to seek his fortune in America, where in 1879 he became a pioneer in cattle farming with his brothers Vincent and Bernard at Glenwood Creek, Donley County, Texas. Just over ten years later the RO ranch which he had established had grown to about 200,000 acres of land. The town of Rowe was named after Alfred, before its flourishing community moved, in 1907, to a new site now known as Hedley.

In 1910 Alfred moved back to England, where he set up home in London with his wife and three children, but he returned to his American ranch at least twice a year. It was for one such trip that he booked a First Class passage on the *Titanic*'s maiden voyage. His home address at the time was 6 Petersham Terrace (now Gloucester Road), London, SW. His wife, Constance, and two young sons went to see him off. During the voyage, he wrote a letter to his wife in which, referring to the near-collision with the *New York* in Southampton, he described his misgivings about the ship:

> My Dearest Girl,
> She is too big, you can't find your way about, and it takes you too long to get anywhere; she has no excessive speed to compensate for all this and is a positive danger to all other shipping in port. The Mauretania and Lusitania are quite good enough and big enough for me. We had the narrowest possible escape of having a hole knocked in us.
> Au Revoir Bientot,
> Your Loving Husband,
> Alfred Rowe

On a lighter note, he remarked in his postscript that he had 'a large and comfortable stateroom' all to himself.[37] Alfred Rowe died in the sinking. His body was recovered and forwarded to Liverpool, where it arrived on the Canadian Pacific liner *Empress of Britain* on 4 May 1912. He was buried ten days later in the family vault at Toxteth Park Cemetery, Smithdown Road, Liverpool.[38]

Second Class Passengers

Mr. William Theodore Ronald Brailey, 24, musician (ship's orchestra)

Mr. John Frederick Preston Clarke, 29, musician (ship's orchestra)

Mrs. Elizabeth Faunthorpe (Wilkinson), 29

Mr. Harry Bartram Faunthorpe, 40, salesman

Mr. Joseph J. Fynney, 35, rubber merchant

Mr. Alfred Gaskell, 16, apprentice barrel-maker

Mr. Wallace Henry Hartley, 33, musician (leader of ship's orchestra)

Mr. Charles Frederick Waddington Sedgwick, 25, electrical engineer

Three of the eight Second Class passengers with known Liverpool area connections, namely William Brailey, Fred Clarke and Wallace Hartley, were members of the ship's orchestra. As such, they were not members of the crew, since the eight musicians comprising *Titanic*'s orchestra were not directly employed by White Star, but by the Liverpool music agents and self-styled 'Music Directors' for the Line, Messrs C.W. and F.N. Black. This firm, managed by two brothers, had an office at 14 Castle Street, Liverpool, on the third floor. At the beginning of 1912 Black's had convinced shipping lines such as Cunard and White Star that they, and not the shipping companies themselves, should supply and employ the musicians for their ships' orchestras, thereby giving the companies 'a better deal'. As Yvonne Carroll observes, this unscrupulous scheme, aimed at creating a virtual monopoly for Messrs Black, would have 'devastating results for sea-going musicians'. The better deal for the shipping companies entailed drastic wage cuts for the men. Having previously been paid £6 10s per month plus a monthly uniform allowance of 10 shillings, they would, in future, receive just £4 per month and no uniform allowance. As before, they were allowed to keep a share of any money given on board as gratuities or tips. Black's also reserved the right to dismiss any musician without notice at the end of a voyage.[39]

Thirty-three-year-old violinist Wallace Hartley was the leader of *Titanic*'s eight-man orchestra, which usually played as two separate units, a quintet and a trio, at different times and in different places on the ship. Hartley was born and raised in Colne, Lancashire, but in 1912 was living at his parents' home in Dewsbury, West Yorkshire. Having led orchestras in Harrogate and Wetherby in Yorkshire, he had been working on Cunard liners on the Liverpool to New York run since at least 1909, when he joined the *Lucania*, followed by *Lusitania* and *Mauretania*. When his ship docked in Liverpool, his soon-to-be fiancée Maria Robinson, from Boston Spa, West Yorkshire, would sometimes be there to meet him.[40] Merseyside Maritime Museum has a programme for a musical concert held in aid of seamen's charities at Liverpool and New York in the First Class Lounge of the *Lusitania*, homeward bound from New York on the evening of Saturday 10 September 1910. The programme lists Wallace Hartley as Second Violin.[41]

In almost three years with Cunard, Hartley had made about eighty transatlantic crossings.[42] At the beginning of 1912, like other members of the Amalgamated Musicians' Union, he had little choice but to accept the inferior terms offered by Messrs Black of Liverpool if he wished to continue to enjoy the glamorous lifestyle offered on the big Atlantic liners.[43]

On the evening of Monday 8 April, Hartley arrived back in Liverpool on the *Mauretania* after yet another fast Atlantic crossing. The next morning he left the ship and called in to the office of Messrs Black in Castle Street, where both he and fellow musician Ellwand Moody were asked if they would transfer to *Titanic*, which was due to begin her maiden voyage from Southampton the following day.

Although reluctant to leave the *Mauretania*, where the musicians were 'a very happy and contented family', Hartley agreed. However, Moody declined the invitation, having completed his twelve-month contract with Cunard that day, and returned to his home in Leeds.

Since this would be his first job for White Star, and *Titanic* was due to sail at noon the following day, Hartley had quickly to find a suitable outfitters in Liverpool where he could buy a White Star uniform, complete with company buttons and lapel badge. This he probably did at the premises of J.J. Rayner and Sons, 'Naval Contractors, Merchant Tailors, Drapers and General Outfitters' at 4 Lord Street. As usual when he was in the city, he made his way to Brooks Alley, a narrow street between Hanover Street and School Lane, near the Bluecoat building, to call at George Byrom's violin shop at number 14. This was clearly a regular visit, since one of his friends, 'Bill', of 62 Lea Road, Egremont, near Liverpool, waited for him at the end of the alley and arrived at Byrom's just after Hartley had left. Instead, Bill wrote to him at '*R.M.S. Titanic, Southampton*' to wish him 'Bon voyage and Bon sante'.[44] After a hectic few hours in Liverpool, during which he also sent a parcel of washing home to his mother, Hartley finally boarded a train at Lime Street station, bound for Southampton and *Titanic*. Hartley died in the sinking, as did all of his seven musician colleagues. His body was recovered on 4 May and arrived at Liverpool on 12 May on SS *Arabic*. It was then taken by hearse to his home town in Colne, Lancashire for burial. Over thirty thousand people are believed to have lined the route to his funeral.[45]

The only one of *Titanic*'s musicians whose home address was in Liverpool was 29-year-old bass violist Fred Clarke. Clarke was born in 1883 in Manchester, his birth being registered in the Chorlton district.[46] At the age of seven he was living with his grandparents in Croydon, Surrey,[47] but by 1912 his home was at 22 Tunstall Street, off Smithdown Road, Wavertree, Liverpool. Clarke was an enthusiastic and accomplished musician who had played in the Liverpool Philharmonic Orchestra. He also enjoyed lighter musical work, for a time

The Musicians' Union tribute to *Titanic*'s musicians. (courtesy of the Musicians' Union)

performing at the Kardomah café in Church Street, Liverpool, and the Argyle Theatre of Varieties in Birkenhead. According to the *Birkenhead News* of 20 April 1912: 'He was in Birkenhead early last week, and said good-bye to friends preparatory to leaving for Southampton to join the *Titanic*. Mr. Clarke is very well known in musical circles. Only two Saturdays ago he was in Birkenhead and was very well. He attended the performance at the Argyle Theatre and met a number of friends there.' The writer added that Clarke 'appeared rather morose and, he said, had hopes of receiving great benefit from his voyage on *Titanic*'. Clarke hoped to embark on a musical season again after completing his services with the White Star Company.[48] He died in the sinking. His body was recovered and buried at Mount Olivet Cemetery, Halifax, Nova Scotia on 8 May 1912.

Pianist William T.R. Brailey was the third member of *Titanic*'s orchestra who had definite links with the Liverpool area. Twenty-four-year-old Brailey, of 71 Lancaster Road, Ladbroke Grove, London, had previously served on the Cunard liner *Carpathia* with cellist Roger Bricoux, his French colleague on *Titanic*. According to the *Liverpool Echo* of 25 April 1912, Brailey was 'at one time associated with Mr. Compton Paterson at the Freshfield aerodrome, and Mr. J. Gaunt at the Southport hangar'. Both aircraft facilities were within the wider Liverpool area, to the north of the city. Whether this means that Brailey was an amateur pilot, an aircraft enthusiast, or neither, is not clear. Brailey was also said to be a member of the Southport Pier Pavilion Band, and was engaged to 'a well-known Southport young lady'.[49] He died in the sinking and his body, if recovered, was never identified.

As regards the remaining five Second Class *Titanic* passengers within the 'Liverpool area' category, the passenger list records that they consisted of one married couple, Mr. and Mrs. Harry Faunthorpe, two male travelling companions, Joseph Fynney and Alfred Gaskell, and one male passenger, Charles Sedgwick, who was travelling alone.

In reality, Mr. Harry Bartram Faunthorpe and his 'wife' Elizabeth ('Lizzie') were not married. Forty-one-year-old Harry was born in 1880 to a farming family in Scotter, Lincolnshire, but in 1912 was a carrot and potato salesman residing in either Liverpool or Manchester.[50] His 29-year-old companion, Elizabeth Ann Wilkinson, or Fox Wilkinson, from Manchester, is said by one researcher to have abandoned her husband of five years to run off to America with Harry.[51] She was certainly not his lawful wife. On board *Titanic*, however, they told fellow English passenger Miss Edwina ('Winnie') Troutt that they had been married in January and were on their way to California for their honeymoon.[52] Although Elizabeth Wilkinson survived the sinking, Harry Faunthorpe did not. His body was recovered and returned to Elizabeth for burial in Philadelphia.[53]

As regards the two male travelling companions, Joseph Fynney and Alfred Gaskell, Fynney was a 35-year-old Liverpool rubber merchant of 13 Park Way,

Fred Clarke of Liverpool, *Titanic* bandsman. (bass violist)

MR. JOSEPH FYNNEY.
Liverpool rubber merchant.

Second Class passenger Joseph Fynney
(*Liverpool Daily Post and Mercury*,
4/5/1912; Liverpool Record Office)

Toxteth. Shortly after *Titanic* sank the *Liverpool Echo* reported that Fynney always took great interest in the welfare of the young men of his local parish church, St James, Toxteth. It appears that his neighbours often complained about the late-night visits of young boys to his house. Fynney made frequent trips to North America to visit his widowed mother and his sister, who lived in Montreal, Canada. A handsome bachelor, he always made these journeys in the company of a different young man. On this particular trip it was with 16-year-old apprentice barrel-maker Alfred Gaskell, who also lived within the Liverpool parish of St James, Toxteth.[54] Both Gaskell and Fynney died in the sinking. Gaskell's body was not recovered, but Fynney was buried in Mount Royal Cemetery in Montreal, Canada. He is remembered on his family gravestone at Anfield Cemetery in Liverpool.[55]

The Second Class passenger with a Liverpool connection who was travelling alone was 28-year-old Mr. Charles Frederick Waddington Sedgwick. Sedgwick was born in Blackpool, Lancashire, in 1884, and a few years later lived with his family in Eckington in Derbyshire.[56] In 1912 he was an electrical engineer who had previously been employed by St Helens Electricity Works, St Helens, Lancashire. At that time his home had been at 68 Ampthill Road, Aigburth, Liverpool. However, when he married his wife, just a week before departing from Southampton on *Titanic*, he was living in London. Sedgwick was travelling on *Titanic* en route to Minatitlan, Veracruz, south-east Mexico, where he had an appointment, presumably in relation to a business or employment opportunity in that area. His wife was due to follow him later. He died in the sinking and his body was never found.[57]

Third Class Passengers
Mr. Thomas Henry Davison, 32, blacksmith
Mrs. Mary E. Davison (née Finck), 34, wife
Mr. Thomas Storey, 51, seaman

Thirty-two-year-old Thomas Henry Davison was born in Chippenham, Wiltshire, in February 1880. In 1901, at the age of 21, he was still living in the family home in Hardenhuish, Wiltshire, where he was employed as an 'Iron Smith' or blacksmith.[58] By 1912 he was living in Liverpool with his American wife, Mary. They boarded *Titanic* in Southampton and were travelling Third Class. Mary was the daughter of Mr. and Mrs. John Finck, Sr, of Cleveland, Ohio. Two days after the *Titanic* disaster the Fincks received a letter from their daughter informing them that she and her husband had booked a passage on the ship. The Davisons had visited Mary's parents four years previously and had decided to return to the United States to settle in Bedford, Ohio. They delayed their journey to travel on *Titanic*, looking forward to enjoying the novelty of the maiden voyage. Thomas died in the sinking and his body was never recovered. Mary survived in lifeboat 16. Having been cared for on arrival in New York by the Junior League, she is believed to have returned to her family home in Ohio. She died in 1939.[59]

Fifty-one-year-old seaman Thomas Storey, who was originally from Liverpool, was an employee of the American Line, like White Star a subsidiary of the IMM company. He boarded *Titanic* at Southampton as a Third Class passenger, together with five other American Line employees, namely Alfred Johnson, William Henry Turnquist, William Cahoon Johnson Jr, Lionel Leonard and Alfred Carver. Storey's exact background is unclear, but he was probably born in Liverpool or its surrounding area in about 1861.[60] Since American Line ships such as the *New York* had been temporarily taken out of service in Southampton due to the coal strike, it seems likely that Storey and his colleagues were travelling to New York, by courtesy of their employers, so as to join one of the Line's ships for the return voyage to Southampton. Storey died in the sinking and his body was buried at Fairview Lawn Cemetery in Halifax, Nova Scotia.

Second Class passenger Charles Sedgwick. (*Liverpool Daily Post and Mercury*, 20/4/1912; Liverpool Record Office)

CHAPTER 7

PLAIN SAILING

The weather during this time was absolutely fine, with the exception, I think, of about ten minutes' fog one evening.

J. Bruce Ismay
19 April 1912[1]

After her two-hour stay in Queenstown harbour, *Titanic* weighed anchor at about 1.30 pm on Thursday 11 April. Within a few hours she had cleared the south-west coast of Ireland and begun to head out into the North Atlantic. The weather remained fine but cold. Both passengers and crew settled into the routine of shipboard life, at the same time familiarising themselves with the lay-out of the huge vessel. In his autobiography, published in 1935, Second Officer Charles Lightoller wrote:

> It is difficult to convey any idea of the size of a ship like the Titanic, when you could actually walk miles along decks and passages, covering different ground all the time. I was thoroughly familiar with every type of ship afloat, from a battleship and a barge, but it took me fourteen days before I could with confidence find my way from one part of that ship to another by the shortest route.[2]

Titanic was more like a floating palace than a ship. Passengers commented that her immense size and remarkable steadiness in the calm weather conditions sometimes made them forget that they were travelling at sea at all. The 2208 people on board mirrored the 'upstairs, downstairs' class divisions of Western society at the time.

Titanic at Queenstown, 11 April 1912. This is one of the last photographs taken of the ship. (© The Father Browne S.J. Photographic Collection, Dublin)

Everyone knew their place. On the bridge, the senior deck officers and their subordinates attended to the navigation of the ship. On the luxurious and spacious upper decks, millionaires and their entourages took in their magnificent surroundings, which included '[oak] panelled corridors leading to smoke room and lounge; revolving doors to keep out the ocean's chill; mirrors, cut glass lighting fixtures, thick carpeting, draperies and furniture in a profusion of colours and textures [...] Suites of cabins in period décor. Broad decks open to the fresh ocean air; decks enclosed from spray and cold. Elevators...'[3]

As they dined in either the great 532-seat dining saloon or the 137-seat *à la carte* restaurant, First Class passengers were entertained by music played by one of the ensembles from the ship's band. They could stroll on the boat deck with their fellow passengers, sample the Turkish and electric baths, the gymnasium or the squash court, or enjoy a good book in the library. The white-jacketed stewards and waiters worked quietly and efficiently, hopeful of eliciting gratuities from passengers, which usually comprised a major part of their income. The presence on board of the White Star chairman and IMM President, Mr. J. Bruce Ismay, no doubt made officers and crew extra keen to impress. In the meantime, several decks below, poor emigrants and ordinary crew members made do with the more basic, but nevertheless comfortable facilities provided for them. Still further below, in the infernal heat and dust of the stokeholds, the 'Black Gang' of firemen, greasers and trimmers toiled away in exhausting four-hour shifts to drive the ship forward. Deprived of the financial perks available to the 'white coats', they would have found ways of procuring food scraps unsuitable for passengers to make the watery 'oodle', 'scouse' or stew which would help to sustain them in their hard physical labour.[4]

As we have seen, more than half of the 891 crew sailing from Queenstown[5] were in the victualling department, busily working in shifts to provide 24-hour catering and welfare services to passengers. In terms of their distribution on the ship, including those of the 67 *à la carte* restaurant staff, one victualling crew member was provided for every one of the 324 First Class passengers, every four of the 285 Second Class passengers, and every 59 of the 708 Third Class passengers.

The second largest section of *Titanic*'s crew was in the engine department, consisting, as we have seen, of 45 officers and support staff and 280 men. However, the actual navigation of the ship was almost entirely in the hands of Captain Smith and his seven deck officers, namely Chief Officer Wilde, First Officer Murdoch and Second Officer Lightoller, assisted by Pitman, Boxhall, Lowe, and Moody. Apart from Captain Smith, who was in overall command of the ship and so 'always on duty', these officers worked on a rota according to the standard system of ship's watches, normally four hours 'on deck' and four hours 'below', except for the two 'dog watches' of two hours each, from 4 to 6 pm and 6 to 8 pm each day.[6] The officers of the watch in charge of the bridge were the Chief Officer and the First and Second Officers. There were always two junior officers on duty as well.[7]

On each day at 10.30 am, except Sunday, in accordance with White Star Line regulations, Captain Smith made a full inspection of the ship, deck by deck, both public and working areas, with Chief Engineer Joseph Bell, Purser Hugh McElroy and Assistant Purser Reginald Barker, Surgeon William O'Loughlin and Chief Steward Andrew Latimer. He had already heard the daily reports of each of his department heads. In the engine room, shortly after noon, Chief Engineer Bell would hand a report to Smith showing 'the estimated quantity of coal consumed since noon the previous day, the quantity of coal remaining, and the nautical miles run by revolutions of the engine since noon the previous day'.[8] Afterwards, the group would return to Smith's quarters on the bridge to discuss any issues arising and to receive the captain's orders before returning to their usual duties. Smith would then meet his deck officers to discuss the inspection and the navigational details for the day.[9]

Favoured by calm seas and clear weather, the voyage progressed from early Thursday afternoon to midday on Sunday in a largely smooth and uneventful manner. *Titanic* maintained a good speed throughout, gradually increasing over every 24-hour period without ever reaching her estimated maximum speed of between 22 and 23 knots. By noon on Friday she had covered 484 miles since leaving Queenstown, by noon on Saturday a further 519 miles, and by noon on Sunday another 546 miles.[10]

In reality, however, it had not all been plain sailing. Apart from routine messages of congratulation and good wishes for the maiden voyage, the ship's wireless operators had received a number of ice warnings from eastbound and westbound ships on the busy North Atlantic sea lanes. These indicated an extensive area of ice near the Grand Banks of Newfoundland, just over half way through *Titanic*'s intended route to New York, at approximate latitude 41°50′ North. One such message was sent to *Titanic* on Friday morning by the Canadian Pacific liner *Empress of Britain*, eastbound from Halifax to Liverpool. In the afternoon a similar message was received from the French Line ship *La Touraine*. Indeed, even before *Titanic* left Southampton, some ships had reported encountering major ice problems in the same area. On 26 March 1912, for example, the Liverpool ship *Lord Cromer* had been badly damaged by ice near where, just a few weeks later, *Titanic* would founder, and had had to proceed to New York for repairs. A few days later another Liverpool ship in the same vicinity, the oil tanker *Lucigen*, had to alter her course to avoid heavy pack ice and icebergs before arriving safely at New York.[11] However, such warnings and incidents were not unusual during a North Atlantic crossing at that time of year and would have caused no particular alarm to Captain Smith and his navigating officers. After all, *Titanic* was following the southern, 'long track' route used by westbound White Star Line steamers in the North Atlantic from 15 January to 23 August to avoid encountering ice in the vicinity of the Grand Banks.[12] Also, Captain Smith, the genial 'Millionaires' Captain', was vastly experienced in North Atlantic voyaging in all conditions, and his impressive record and bearing instilled great confidence among crew and passengers alike.

Of more immediate concern was the fact that, at about 11 pm on Friday, *Titanic*'s wireless equipment suddenly failed. The Marconi operators Phillips and Bride had to work on for several anxious hours, until early Saturday morning, before the problem was eventually found and repaired. There was some more good news a few hours later when Chief Engineer Bell informed Captain Smith that the fire which had burned constantly in boiler room 6 since *Titanic*'s sea trials nearly two weeks earlier had at last been extinguished. Again, this was a fairly common problem with coal-burning ships, and was not considered to be of major concern at the time.[13]

At 9 am on Sunday 14 April, a message was received in *Titanic*'s radio room from the Cunard liner *Caronia*, eastbound from New York to Liverpool via Queenstown. It read: 'Captain, *Titanic* – West-bound steamers report bergs, growlers and field ice in 42°N, from 49° to 51° W, April 12. Compliments, Barr.' This message was delivered to Captain Smith, who posted it in the chart room on the bridge for his officers to read and note. At 1.42 pm a message was sent to Captain Smith by the White Star liner *Baltic*, also eastbound from New York to Liverpool via Queenstown. It read: 'Greek steamer *Athenai* reports passing icebergs and large quantities of field ice today in latitude 41°51′ N, longitude 49°52′ W [...] Wish you and *Titanic* all success. Commander.' Shortly afterwards, Smith handed this message to J. Bruce Ismay, who was on deck at the time. Having 'glanced at it very casually', Ismay put it in his own pocket. Later, Ismay read this message to two female passengers.[14] It was not until 7.15 pm, when Smith asked Ismay for its return, that the message was posted in the chart room. In the meantime, at 1.45 pm a message from the German liner *Amerika* to the United States Hydrographic Office in Washington DC was received and forwarded to Cape Race in Newfoundland by *Titanic*'s wireless operator. It read: '*Amerika* passed two large icebergs in 41°27′ N, 50°8′ W on April 14'. As this message related to navigation, it should also have been sent, as a matter of priority, to the bridge by her Marconi operators for the attention of the deck officers. Unfortunately, even though the message specified a position close to the 'southern track' route which *Titanic* was following, this does not appear to have been done.[15]

By 5.30 pm many passengers walking on deck noticed a rapid drop in the air temperature and moved indoors to get warm. Twenty minutes later the ship's course was altered from S62°W to S85°W, following Captain Smith's written instructions in the night order book. This adjustment would normally have been made about thirty minutes earlier. The resulting delay placed *Titanic* on a course slightly to the south and west of what would have been her standard course. This was considered by the bridge officers to be a precaution by the captain to avoid the ice hazards about which he had been forewarned. However, in his final report at the British Wreck Commissioner's Inquiry, Lord Mersey later commented that the change of course was so insignificant that 'in my opinion it cannot have been made in consequence of information as to ice'.[16]

At 6 pm Second Officer Lightoller took over from Chief Officer Wilde on the bridge. During his four-hour watch two further ice warnings were received by *Titanic*'s wireless operators, only one of which appears to have been delivered to the bridge.[17] This was probably because Harold Bride had gone off duty to take a brief nap, and senior Marconi operator Jack Phillips was preoccupied with sending a large backlog of passengers' messages to the Cape Race shore station. At 8.55 pm Captain Smith excused himself from a dinner party in the *à la carte* restaurant and joined Lightoller on the bridge. According to Lightoller's testimony at the US Senate Inquiry, they discussed the weather:

> He said, 'There is not much wind.' I said, 'No, it is a flat calm.' I said that it was a pity that the wind had not kept up with us whilst we were going through the ice region. Of course he knew I meant the water ripples breaking on the base of the berg …

Lightoller added that, just before retiring to the chart room at about 9.20 pm, Smith said to him: 'If it becomes at all doubtful let me know at once. I shall be just inside.'

Later, at the British Wreck Commissioner's Inquiry, Lightoller stated that the night order book for that night had a footnote about keeping a sharp lookout for ice, and this had been 'initialled by every officer'.[18] Shortly after his conversation with Captain Smith, Lightoller sent a message to the crow's nest, asking lookouts Symonds and Jewell to keep a sharp lookout for ice, 'particularly small ice and growlers'. This message was passed on by them to their colleagues Fleet and Lee, who replaced them at 10 pm. At the same time First Officer Murdoch took over from Lightoller as officer of the watch on the bridge.

As we have seen, *Titanic*'s speed was gradually increased each day during her maiden voyage. This was standard White Star Line policy with new ships to check that all machinery was working properly and thus allow the engines to 'get into their stride'.[19] This procedure had been followed the previous year, for example, during the maiden voyage of *Olympic*.[20] As Bruce Ismay later testified at the US Senate Inquiry: 'The *Titanic* being a new ship, we were gradually working her up. When you bring out a new ship you naturally do not start her running at full speed until you get everything working smoothly and satisfactorily down below.'[21]

This seems thoroughly reasonable and understandable. Rather less understandable, however, in the light of the ensuing disaster, is that, despite having received several ice warnings from other ships, her speed was not reduced as she approached the reported area of danger on the evening of Sunday 14 April. Instead, it was increased. At 7 pm that evening the two or three additional boilers which had been lit twelve hours earlier finally 'came on stream' to drive the engines. This meant that nineteen of *Titanic*'s 24 boilers were then available for use.

From 7 pm until the collision at 11.40 pm, the ship's average speed is believed to have risen to about 22.5 knots, her fastest yet recorded. A number of passengers noticed the increase in the vibration frequency of the engines late that night.[22]

CHAPTER 8

SINKING

I cannot conceive of any vital disaster happening to this vessel.
Modern shipbuilding has gone beyond that.

Captain E.J. Smith
after the maiden voyage of RMS *Adriatic*, May 1907[1]

There was no moon, the stars were out,
and there was not a cloud in the sky.

British Inquiry, Report
30 July 1912[2]

At 11.40 pm Liverpool-born Fred Fleet, one of the lookouts in the crow's nest on
the foremast, noticed a dark shape or 'black mass' in the distance, about five
hundred yards directly ahead of the ship. He immediately rang the warning bell
three times, then telephoned Sixth Officer Moody on the bridge to confirm that
he had seen an 'iceberg right ahead'. Although the instinctive reactions of officer
of the watch Murdoch prevented a head-on collision, the warning had come too
late. By the time the iceberg brushed along *Titanic*'s starboard side, less than half a
minute later, with 'just a slight grinding noise', as Fleet later recalled, it appeared
to him to be about fifty or sixty feet above the water. He breathed a sigh of relief,
thinking that the ship had had 'a narrow shave'.[3] He was wrong.

As we now know, in 'scraping and bumping' along her starboard side, the
iceberg, within about ten seconds, had fatally damaged *Titanic* below the

Fred Fleet, the lookout who first spotted the iceberg. (*Daily Sketch*, 25/4/1912)

waterline. This had the effect of 'opening to the sea's inrush the forepeak, number one hold, number two hold, number three hold, number six hold, number six boiler room, and poking about six feet beyond the bulkhead of number five boiler room'.[4] As Harland and Wolff naval architect Edward Wilding later explained at the British Wreck Commissioner's Inquiry, the ship could have survived with up to four of her forward compartments flooded, but not those four and the forward boiler room also flooded.[5] The Commissioner's report concluded that 'water came into the five forward compartments to a height of about 14 feet above the keel in the first ten minutes. This was a rate of inflow with which the ship's pumps could not possibly have coped, so that the damage done to these five compartments alone inevitably sealed the doom of the ship.'[6]

According to Sir Rufus Isaacs, the Attorney-General, speaking at the same inquiry, the full seriousness of the situation was realised within twenty minutes 'by the Captain and by the Chief Engineer, by Mr. Andrews, who represented the builders, by those, of course, who spoke to Mr. Andrews who were only taking his view, and by Mr. Ismay himself'.[7]

Someone else who already knew that there was a major problem was leading fireman or stoker Fred Barrett, who in over ten years at sea had sailed on White Star liners out of Liverpool, his place of birth.[8] At the time of the collision, Barrett was in charge of eight firemen and four coal trimmers in boiler room 6, which was nine decks below the ship's first or fore funnel. Standing at the aft end of the boiler room on the starboard side, he was talking to the engineer on duty, John Henry (Harry) Hesketh, another Liverpool man. As Barrett later recalled: 'The bell rang, the red light showed. We sang out, "Shut the doors!" [ash doors or dampers, to stop air reaching the furnaces] and there was a crash just as we sung out. The water came through the ship's side.'[9] The water began to pour in from damage caused about two feet above the stokehold floor, and Barrett and Hesketh scarcely had time to jump through the connecting door between boiler rooms 6 and 5 before the watertight door shut down behind them. Barrett quickly found that water was also pouring through 'a hole two feet abaft the bulkhead between sections 5 and 6'[10] into an empty coal bunker in boiler room 5. When Hesketh then ordered all hands to stand by their stations, Barrett and engineer Jonathan Shepherd tried to climb an emergency ladder back into boiler room 6, but found it already flooded to a depth of eight feet.[11]

Most of the other people on board, however, whether crew members or passengers, were either asleep or preparing for bed at the time of the collision. Even after they had been made aware that something untoward had occurred, requiring lifejackets to be worn, many still did not realise until much later that night that the ship could not be saved. This was partly because those originally 'in the know' among the ship's company had been advised to keep the horrific news to themselves, for fear of causing widespread panic.[12]

Amid the growing tension and confusion, Captain Smith and his deck officers began the unenviable task of organising the uncovering, manning, loading and lowering of lifeboats. This they achieved with mixed results. Initial evidence presented at both the American and British Inquiries suggested that the first lifeboat did not leave *Titanic* until 12.45 am, just over an hour after the collision. However, the crew began to prepare the lifeboats for launching shortly after midnight, and recent research by Senan Molony suggests that the first boat, number 7, may have been lowered as soon as fifteen to twenty minutes later.[13] The knowledge that there was lifeboat accommodation for only just over half of those on board must have weighed very heavily indeed on the minds of Captain Smith, Bruce Ismay and Thomas Andrews, in particular. Each, in his own way, had inadvertently played a major part in bringing the ship to this tragic and defining moment in her history.

Thomas Andrews, Managing Director and chief naval architect of Harland and Wolff Limited, had been deeply involved in overseeing the construction of both *Olympic* and *Titanic*. He was leading his company's Guarantee Group on *Titanic*'s maiden voyage, and after an initial inspection of the damage below with

John Henry Hesketh from Kirkdale, Liverpool, Junior 2nd Engineer on *Titanic*. (NML, ref. S2006.00841)

Captain Smith and Purser McElroy, thought that the ship would sink in about thirty minutes. After further investigation, however, he revised this estimate to between one hour and one hour thirty minutes.[14] In the event, the ship sank two hours and forty minutes after the collision. Andrews went down with the ship, having apparently made no attempt to save himself. During *Titanic*'s final hours he wandered the decks, urging passengers to wear their lifebelts and to make their way to the boats. He is thought to have been last seen staring into space by the painting in the First Class smoking room, having apparently discarded his own lifebelt.[15]

At about 12.15 am, having received Fourth Officer Boxhall's hastily scribbled estimate of the ship's position, Captain Smith went to the wireless room and ordered Marconi operator Jack Phillips to begin sending the distress signal 'CQD' 'to all steamers within reach'. This was heard by the shore station at Cape Race, by the London-based steamer *Mount Temple*, en route to St. John, New Brunswick, and by several other steamships. By 12.25 am Boxhall had corrected his estimate of the ship's position and another message was sent: 'Come at once, we have struck a berg'. This message, which caused the Cunard liner *Carpathia*, 58 miles away, to turn round and rush to *Titanic*'s assistance, was followed a minute later by the stark statement: 'Sinking; cannot hear for noise of steam'.

Meanwhile, Boxhall had seen the lights of a vessel in the distance, just off the port bow, and Captain Smith had given him permission for rockets to be sent up as signals of distress. The Fourth Officer ordered Quartermaster George Rowe to fire the rockets from a socket on the boat deck. These signal rockets were designed to explode in the air and throw off white stars. About eight were fired at five- or six-minute intervals until Boxhall left the ship about an hour later. Between firing rockets, both Boxhall and Rowe also used a Morse lamp from the bridge in an attempt to contact the unknown vessel, which Boxhall thought was about five or six miles away. They received no reply. Gradually the light or lights from the vessel diminished and finally disappeared.[16]

One of the first passengers to lend a hand with the lifeboats was Bruce Ismay, who had been awoken by the collision and, having put an overcoat over his pyjamas, immediately rushed to the bridge to find out what had happened. He was informed by Captain Smith that the ship had struck ice, and that the situation was serious. Ismay then returned to his room and put on a suit of clothes before returning to the boat deck to help with the clearing of lifeboats.[17] At about 12.20 am, while assisting Third Officer Pitman to remove the cover from boat 5, on the ship's starboard side, he remarked: 'There is no time to lose'.[18] According to Pitman, who did not recognise Ismay at the time,

> Then this man in the dressing gown [sic] said we had better get her loaded with women and children. So I said, 'I await the Commander's orders,' to which he replied, 'Very well,' or something like that. It then dawned on me that it might be Mr. Ismay […] so I went along to the bridge and saw Captain Smith, and I told him […] So he said, 'Go ahead; carry on.'[19]

Fourth Officer Lowe, who also did not recognise Ismay, then objected to him urging the men to 'lower away', and tetchily ordered him to 'Get the hell out of that'. He later admitted, however, that Ismay was simply 'trying all in his power to help the work'.[20]

Despite these incidents, Ismay continued, for well over an hour, to assist with the loading of lifeboats on the starboard side of the boat deck. Finally, at about 1.40 am, by which time *Titanic* was well down by the head and listing six degrees to port, he helped to load collapsible boat C with women and children, most of whom were Third Class or steerage passengers. With no response to his repeated calls for more women and children to come forward, Chief Officer Wilde gave the order to lower away. It was the ninth and last boat to be lowered from the starboard side, and still had room for a few more people. As the boat began its

Saloon steward Ernest Wheelton, May 1912. (courtesy of the Titanic Historical Society Inc.)

descent, two male First Class passengers quietly stepped in to the after end. One was William Ernest Carter, from Philadelphia, the other was J. Bruce Ismay.[21]

Another Liverpool-born man who was woken up when the ship hit the iceberg was 28-year-old First Class Steward Ernest Edward ('Teddy') Wheelton. At first he thought that the ship had dropped a propeller 'or something like that', and was about to go back to sleep when someone shouted, 'Watertight doors!' As he left his room, off 'Scotland Road' on 'E' deck, he heard the order, 'Get your lifebelts. Get up to boat stations.' He put on trousers and an overcoat over his pyjamas and, still wearing slippers, made his way to the boat deck, where he helped to get lifeboat 5 away. This was the boat to which he had been assigned when he first joined the ship. Soon after, on 'B' deck, having been ordered to go down to the storeroom for provisions, he saw Thomas Andrews, 'who was opening the rooms and looking in to see if there was anyone in, and closing the doors again'.

Wheelton later assisted with boats 7 and 9. At one stage, while working with the lifeboats, he witnessed Fourth Officer Lowe's brief confrontation with Bruce Ismay. He also saw Ismay helping women and children into boat 9 and telling the men, who were standing in a circle around the boat, to 'make way', or 'to make a gap so that a lady could come through'. Eventually, First Officer Murdoch sent Wheelton and another steward down to 'A' deck to load and man boat 11. Once the boat had been loaded, mainly with women and children, it was lowered some seventy feet down to the water. Among the nine crew were two other Liverpool men, stewards Arthur McMicken and Joseph Wheat. As Wheelton later recalled, 'We rowed around and tried to get to the other boats, to get close to them. We pulled toward a light, but we did not seem to get any closer to it, until daybreak. A lady back of me complained of the cold, and I took my coat off and gave it to her.'[22]

Among other Liverpool-connected crew members who were involved in loading or manning the lifeboats were Leading Fireman Fred Barrett, Assistant Steward Charles Andrews and Able Seaman Thomas Jones. Like Wheelton, each of these men survived and gave evidence at either the American or the British Inquiry.

After his traumatic experiences in the stokehold immediately after the collision, Fred Barrett eventually made his way up to 'A' deck, the saloon deck immediately below the boat deck, where he was one of the last people to climb into lifeboat 13, the seventh boat to leave on the starboard side. While being lowered down the side of the ship, the boat, which was virtually full to capacity, was almost swamped by a large stream of water being discharged from the ship's side by the condenser pumps, then narrowly escaped from underneath boat 15. In Barrett's words:

> It [boat 15] was getting lowered about 30 seconds after us. It was coming on top of us. […] When we found the discharge was coming out we stopped lowering and all the hose was tied up in the boat. I had a knife and I cut the hose adrift and shoved two oars over the forward end to shove the lifeboat off the ship's side. We got into the water and there was a bit of a current and it drifted us under No. 15 boat, and I sung out 'Let go the after fall.' Nobody seemed to realise what I was doing. I walked across the women to cut the fall [rope], and the other fall touched my shoulder.

Since no-one else came forward, Barrett placed the rudder in position and took charge of the boat until after *Titanic* sank.[23]

Twenty-year-old steward Charles Andrews, who had sailed with White Star for four years, had been allotted to lifeboat 16 on the Sunday morning before the collision. He came off watch at about 10.45 pm and went down and turned in to his bunk. Soon afterwards he and several fellow stewards were awoken by 'a movement of the ship', thinking that 'something might have gone wrong with the engines'. All hands having been ordered on deck, he went up to the boat deck and stood by boat 16, the farthest lifeboat aft on the port side:

There were lots of people around, and I saw stores brought to the boat, and bread. I did not see the stores put in the boat. I assisted in helping the ladies and children into the boat. After the boat was full the officer called out for able seamen, or any individuals then, to man the boat.[24]

Andrews was one of four male crew in the boat, which also carried three stewardesses and about fifty passengers. Among the female passengers were Mrs. Elizabeth Faunthorpe (in fact Wilkinson) and Mrs. Mary Davison (née Fincke), both of whom, as we have seen, were travelling with Liverpool men.[25] Three Liverpool-born stewardesses, namely Mary Gregson, Mrs. Elizabeth Leather (née Edwards) and Mrs. Mary Roberts (née Humphreys) are also believed to left the ship in this boat.[26] Andrews assisted in putting the rowlocks in, and later helped to row the boat. Eventually, from a distance, he witnessed the sinking: 'When we got away in the boat at the last everything seemed to go to a black mist. All the lights seemed to go out and everything went black.'[27]

Thirty-two-year-old Welshman Thomas (Tom) Jones, originally from Anglesey, was living in Liverpool when he signed on as an Able Seaman for *Titanic*'s maiden voyage. Having previously been a lookout on the *Oceanic*, he had also sailed for six years on the North Atlantic on the White Star liner *Majestic* 'without missing a trip'. During that time he had seen only one iceberg. Tom was 'sitting in the forecastle', presumably in the seamen's quarters on 'E' deck, when the collision occurred. In his words:

I heard something, just the same as a ship going through a lot of loose ice; and everybody ran on deck right away. When we got on deck we could see some ice on the deck. Then I went forward, and I could see a lot of firemen coming up out of the forecastle; and I looked down below, and I heard a rush of water. I went down below, in No. 1 (hatch), and I could see the tarpaulin of the hatch lifting up the same as if there was air coming up there ...[28]

When he went on deck, he saw 'all the firemen coming up from there'. He later observed at the United States Senate Inquiry that they were all carrying their 'bundles' of clothing and belongings, 'not because they thought the boat was going to sink, but because they wanted to take them out of the water, as the water was coming in'.

Having been sent up to the boat deck to help prepare the lifeboats, Tom assisted in getting a collapsible boat ready on the port side, before working on his own allotted boat, number 8. An officer sent him for a lamp, and when he returned the boat was already 'swung out', with 'about thirty five ladies in it'. He jumped into the boat, and Captain Smith asked if the plug was in the bottom, which it was, before making a final request for any more ladies to come forward. As Jones remembered:

> There was one lady came there and left her husband. She wanted her husband to go with her, but he backed away, and the captain shouted again – in fact, twice again – 'Any more ladies?' There were no more there, and he lowered away.

Captain Smith told Jones to row towards the light of what appeared to be a nearby ship, land the passengers and return to *Titanic* to pick up more passengers. According to Jones,

> I pulled for the light, and found that I could not get near the light, and I stood by for a little while. I wanted to return to the ship, but the ladies were frightened, and I had to carry out the captain's orders and pull for that light; so I did so. I pulled for about two hours, and then it started to get daybreak, and we lost the light; and all of a sudden we saw the *Carpathia* coming, and we turned right back and made for the *Carpathia*.

Thomas Jones, able seaman. (courtesy of Henry Aldridge and Son)

At the United States Inquiry Jones revealed that he did not initially believe that *Titanic* would sink and thought that the boats were only being sent away for an hour or so until they could 'square' or steady her by pumping the water out. He confirmed that he, like most of the crew, thought that she was 'unsinkable'. Apart from himself, boat 8 contained only one other 'sailor', two stewards and thirty-five ladies. He believed that it was only half full because when it was being loaded nobody else, woman or man, was ready to leave the ship. When asked if he could name any of the passengers in the boat, he replied, 'One lady. She had a lot to say, and I put her to steering the boat.' When pressed further for her name, he said: 'Lady Rothe. She was a countess or something.'[29]

Jones was the only experienced seaman in the boat. Under his direction, the other men did their best, but their lack of skill as oarsmen was bitterly criticised by some of the women passengers. According to Noelle, Countess of Rothes, 'the little seaman [Jones] had to assume the responsibility. He did it nobly, alternately cheering us with words of encouragement, then rowing doggedly.'[30] Jones was similarly impressed by the Countess, who, with her cousin Miss Gladys Cherry, took the tiller of the boat and encouraged other women to help with the rowing. Although Tom Jones, the Countess and a few other women wanted to go back and try to pick up more survivors, they were overruled by the others in the boat, including the three crewmen. A few weeks later Miss Cherry wrote the following letter to Jones to thank him for his efforts:

> Tom Jones,
> I feel I must write and tell you how splendidly you took charge of our boat on that fateful night. There were only four English people in it – my cousin, Lady Rothes, her maid, you and myself and I think you were wonderful. The dreadful regret I shall always have, and I know you share with me, is, that we ought to have gone back to see whom we could pick

up, but, if you remember, there were only an American lady, my cousin, self and you that wanted to return. I could not hear the discussion very clearly, as I was at the tiller, but everyone forward and the three men refused – but I shall always remember your words – 'Ladies, if any of us are saved, remember, I wanted to go back. I would rather drown with them than leave them.' You did all you could, and being my own countryman, I wanted to tell you this.
Yours very truly,
Gladys Cherry.[31]

The Countess of Rothes. (*Daily Mirror*, 22/4/1912; MMM ref. DX/2130)

A few weeks after receiving this letter, Jones received an inscribed silver watch from the Countess of Rothes, who continued to correspond with him until her death in 1956. This must have been difficult since, as an example of Thomas Jones' handwriting held at Merseyside Maritime Museum shows, his ability to write English was very limited.[32] Perhaps this was because Welsh was his first language when he was a child in Anglesey. It might equally have been because, like many of *Titanic*'s crew, he was from a humble background and so had had little, if any, formal education. At all events, it would appear that both Jones and Miss Cherry were mistaken in thinking that there were only four 'English' people in boat 8. There was at least one other, namely First Class passenger Miss Lily Bonnell, from Birkdale, near Liverpool, who, as previously mentioned, had left the ship with her three female travelling companions from Ohio.[33]

At least five Liverpool-connected crew members who survived the *Titanic* sinking were still on board the ship after the last lifeboat had been lowered. They were Second Officer Charles Lightoller, Chief Baker Charles Joughin, Fireman John Thompson, and Trimmers Thomas Patrick (Paddy) Dillon and James McGann. Apart from Dillon, all initially survived via collapsible boats A and B, which both served as makeshift rafts after floating off the boat deck as *Titanic* sank.

Thirty-five-year-old fireman John Thompson, of 2 Primrose Hill, Vauxhall,

127

Liverpool, originally climbed on to the swamped collapsible A before transferring, with all its other survivors, to boat 14 later in the morning. He somehow broke his arm in his struggle to survive in the water, but did not notice this until he had to climb up the rope ladder on to the *Carpathia*.[34] Collapsible A, with three dead bodies still on board, was discovered by the White Star liner *Oceanic* a month later, some two hundred miles from the scene of the disaster.[35]

When interviewed by the New York *Tribune* on 20 April, Trimmer James McGann said that he was one of about thirty crew, mainly firemen, who clung to collapsible B as it left the ship. As regards the appalling conditions suffered by those on the boat that night, he added: 'All our legs were frostbitten and we were all in the hospital for a day at least.'[36]

Lightoller's harrowing survival story is well known, not least because of his memorable portrayal by Kenneth More in the 1958 British feature film *A Night to Remember*. Having played an admirable part in loading and lowering lifeboats on the port side, he eventually dived into the sea and was sucked under as *Titanic* made her final plunge. Fortunately, he was blown back to the surface when the ship's boilers exploded and found himself clinging to a rope attached to the capsized collapsible lifeboat B. He was then narrowly missed by *Titanic*'s massive forward funnel as it broke loose and toppled into the sea. Lightoller was one of thirty exhausted men who scrambled or were dragged onto the overturned collapsible B. They included three First Class passengers, the Marconi operators Phillips and Bride, and a number of crew, mostly firemen. With great difficulty, they gradually managed to paddle away from the hundreds of other people struggling in the water. Lightoller later transferred, with several others, to boat 12 before the occupants of both boats were rescued by SS *Carpathia*.

Thirty-two-year-old Chief Baker Charles Joughin's dramatic story is also well known because of his colourful testimony at the British Inquiry and its later portrayal in books and feature films. Awoken by the shock of the collision, he soon became involved in organising the supply of bread and other provisions for the lifeboats. Since he had already been assigned to take charge of lifeboat 10, on the port side, he then went up to the boat deck to assist in loading it with women and children. Soon afterwards, as Joughin was waiting for orders from the officer to jump in, the officer (probably Lightoller or Moody) ordered two sailors and steward William (Billy) Burke to get into the boat. Joughin later told the British Inquiry that, although he was supposed to be in charge of boat 10, he did not then try to get in because 'I would have set a bad example if I had jumped into the boat. None of the men felt inclined to get into the boat.'[37]

At one point a woman tried to step into the boat to join her two children but missed her footing due to the large gap between the boat and the ship's side, caused by *Titanic*'s increasing list to port. Luckily, Steward Burke managed to catch her by the foot and she swung head downwards for a few minutes before being pulled into 'A' deck, immediately below.[38]

After watching boat 10 depart, Joughin went down to his room and drank 'half a tumbler' of spirits before returning to the boat deck. Seeing that all the boats had gone, he then went down to the deck below and began throwing deck chairs overboard in the hope that they might help him to survive in the water. Just before the ship sank, when she took a sudden lurch to port, he found himself clinging to the rail on the starboard side of the poop deck. In his words: ' – Well, I was just wondering what next to do. I had tightened my belt and I had transferred some things out of this pocket into my stern pocket. I was just wondering what next to do when she went.'[39] According to Joughin, *Titanic* did not rise far out of the water before she sank. Nor was there any 'great shock'. Instead, he insisted, 'She simply glided away.'[40]

When he entered the water, he did not think that his head went under at all. He estimated that he was paddling and treading water 'for over two hours' until, as dawn was breaking, he swam towards the upturned collapsible boat B. At first, he tried to climb on it, but was pushed off. Then he moved round to the other side, and assistant cook Isaac Maynard helped him to hang on for 'about half an

Trimmer Thomas Patrick (Paddy) Dillon attends the British Enquiry, 9 May 1912. (*Daily Sketch*, 10/5/1912)

hour'. He then swam across to the tightly packed lifeboat 12 with Lightoller and several others from collapsible B. Joughin later recalled that he felt colder in the lifeboat than he had done in the freezing water.[41] By the time boat 12 reached *Carpathia*, Joughin's feet had swollen so much that he had to crawl up the ladder to board her.[42] However incredible certain aspects of his account now seem, he undoubtedly demonstrated remarkable determination and powers of endurance under the extreme circumstances in which he found himself.

Thirty-four-year-old Trimmer Thomas Patrick (Paddy) Dillon was an important witness not only of events in the engine room and stokehold after the collision, but also of the actual sinking itself. Although living in Belfast in 1912, he was born in Liverpool in 1878, the eldest of six children of an Irish dock worker and a Glaswegian mother.[43] He also retained strong ties with Liverpool in later life.

On the night of 14 April Dillon, although usually employed as a trimmer, was engaged in cleaning duties in the engine room, because his own boilers were not lit at the time. Soon after the collision with the iceberg, he was ordered by Chief Engineer Bell to open several of the watertight doors so that the engineers could go forward to attend to the pumps and valves. He remained in the stokehold until about 1.20 am, then obeyed the orders 'All hands on deck!' and 'Put your life-preservers on!'[44] He reached the starboard side of the well deck, where he and the other men 'chased' two female steerage passengers up a ladder to board the last lifeboat. He then joined other male crew and passengers on the poop deck at the stern. Among them were two of his shipmates from Liverpool, namely Greaser John Bannon and Leading Fireman J. Mason, and Greaser Denny Corcoran, from Tipperary in Ireland.[45] They were there for 'about 50 minutes' before the ship sank. Of this small group, only Dillon would survive.

According to Dillon's testimony on Day 5 of the British Inquiry, the ship eventually 'took one final plunge and righted herself again'. Before he left the ship, the aftermost funnel seemed to 'cant up' towards him. Shortly afterwards, he continued, 'I went down with the ship, and shoved myself away from her into the water.' Dillon went 'about two fathoms' (twelve feet) underwater before seeming to 'get lifted up to the surface'. He thought that he saw 'the afterpart of the ship coming up and going down again – final'. He swam around for about twenty minutes, among 'about a thousand' others in the water, before being picked up, unconscious, by lifeboat 4. When he came to he found two dead men lying on top of him. One was Seaman Lyons and the other a passenger.[46]

Two passengers in lifeboat 4, Mrs. Stephenson and Miss Eustis, later provided a rather different account of this incident to First Class passenger Colonel Archibald Gracie. In 1913 Gracie published it in his book, *The Truth about the Titanic*:

> We implored the men to pull away from the ship, but they refused, and
> we pulled three men into the boat who had dropped off the ship and
> were swimming towards us. One man was drunk and had a bottle of
> brandy in his pocket, which the quartermaster, W. J. Perkis, promptly
> threw overboard and the drunken man was thrown into the bottom of
> the boat and a blanket thrown over him.[47]

Other informal evidence from Dillon himself suggests that he and his colleagues drank alcohol to give them 'Dutch courage' just before the ship sank. In the 1930s he told a friend in Liverpool that he and John Bannon tried to swim towards a light, which they thought was a ship, but his friend became exhausted and drowned. He later concluded that the light had been a star.[48] Another source suggests that at one point Dillon found Bannon afloat 'on a grating', but had to leave him there when he could not climb on himself.[49] Like many of his fellow crew survivors, 'Paddy' Dillon soon resumed his seafaring career after the sinking. A single man, in the 1930s he lived with his sister in Walmsley Street, near Great Howard Street, Liverpool.[50] He died in Liverpool in 1939, aged 59.[51]

Titanic sank at 2.20 am, two hours and forty minutes after the collision, taking with her over 1500 lives. At 12.25 am the Cunard Line steamship

Captain Rostron on *SS Carpathia* with American passengers Mr. and Mrs. Ogden, who took photographs of *Titanic*'s approaching lifeboats.

Captain Stanley Lord, from Liscard, Wallasey, master of *SS Californian*. (MMM ref. D/LO/2/2/5/3)

Carpathia, en route from New York to Trieste and other Mediterranean ports with 700 passengers and crew, had received *Titanic*'s urgent CQD distress call. Although 58 miles from *Titanic*'s reported position, Captain Arthur Rostron, a resident of 52 Victoria Road, Great Crosby, near Liverpool, turned his ship around and rushed at full speed to her assistance. This was an anxious time for Rostron, especially in view of *Titanic*'s 'fateful experience'. As he later wrote, 'Icebergs loomed up and fell astern; we never slackened, though sometimes we altered course suddenly to avoid them'.[52]

Nineteen-year-old Ernest St Clair, from West Derby, Liverpool, was a young waiter on board *Carpathia* at the time. In 1982, at the age of 89, he told a *Liverpool Echo* reporter:

> There was a scramble to volunteer in the rescue and we worked like demons in the biting wind, getting up blankets and swinging out the lifeboats. Then, in the greying dawn, we saw the light of a flare and we soon saw the pitiably few lifeboats with the survivors aboard, guided by the rockets we had sent up.[53]

At about 4.00 am, while still over thirteen miles from *Titanic*'s reported CQD position, Rostron had been surprised to encounter one of her lifeboats. At 4.10 am 24 women from lifeboat 2 began climbing aboard, followed by just one man, Fourth Officer Boxhall, who had been ordered to take charge of the boat.

Over the next few hours, one after another, the rest of the tragic liner's lifeboats appeared as they slowly made their way towards the rescue ship. *Carpathia*'s crew, about one hundred of whom, like Rostron, lived in the Liverpool area,[54] helped to bring all 705 exhausted and distressed survivors on board, as well as thirteen of *Titanic*'s lifeboats. The remaining seven lifeboats, having delivered their precious human cargoes, were cast adrift.[55]

At about 8.30 am, as the last lifeboat was being taken aboard, the Leyland Line steamer *Californian*, commanded by Captain Stanley Lord, a resident of 10 Ormond Street, Liscard, near Liverpool, arrived from beyond a large icefield to the west. Lord had been at sea for over twenty years, and a qualified master since 1901. As a young officer he had attended a navigation school in Liverpool with Henry Wilde, later to become *Titanic*'s Chief Officer. He had also become briefly acquainted with William Murdoch, *Titanic*'s future First Officer.[56] Steaming at speed through the ice, Lord signalled that he wished to communicate with *Carpathia*. However, since there was little else to be done, Rostron accepted Lord's offer that the *Californian* continue searching the area for survivors. He then turned his ship westwards and steamed for New York.

The *Californian* spent the next two hours searching for survivors in an area 'practically surrounded by icebergs'. Captain Lord and his crew only saw several abandoned lifeboats and surprisingly little wreckage, given the scale of the disaster. As Lord later stated at the United States Senate Inquiry: 'It seemed more like an old fishing boat had sunk'.[57] Having finally given up the search, Captain Lord set *Californian*'s course for Boston, where she arrived at 4 am on Friday 19 April.[58]

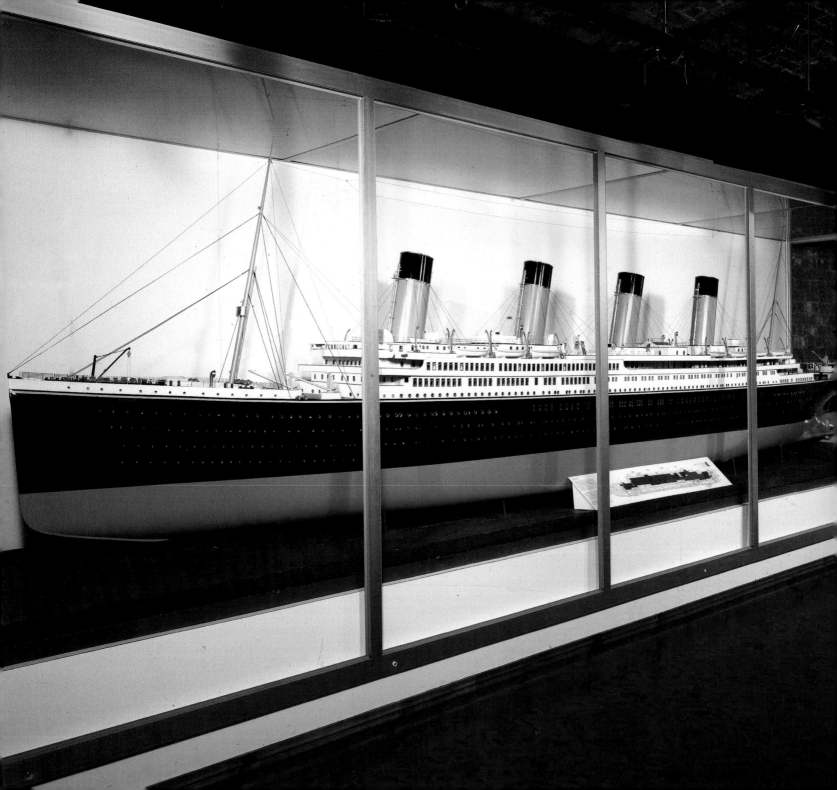

CHAPTER 9

BAD TIDINGS

Such an event is so appalling as to be almost unthinkable.

Liverpool Daily Post and Mercury
16 April 1912

Shortly before 9 pm on Monday 15 April 1912, the same day *Titanic* sank, the entire electricity supply of Liverpool suddenly failed. According to the following morning's *Daily Sketch*: 'The streets were plunged into darkness, electric cars came to a sudden standstill, and all social life was held up. It was fully three-quarters of an hour before normal conditions were restored.'[1] The *Liverpool Daily Post and Mercury* heard that the failure was likely to have originated at the city's main Lister Drive generating station. The problem was thought to have been caused by the sudden return that evening to full power after several weeks of supplying reduced power because of the national coal strike.[2] Even so, in retrospect, the event seems to have been an ominous portent of the appalling news which was yet to come.

Until late on Thursday 18 April, when *Carpathia* arrived in New York with the traumatised survivors of the sinking, many of the news reports circulating on both sides of the Atlantic about *Titanic*'s fate were unclear and contradictory. On Monday 15 April, for example, in reply to an anxious telegram from Sir Walter Howell of the Marine Department of the Board of Trade in London, Messrs Ismay, Imrie & Company (the White Star Line) in Liverpool replied:

Many thanks for your telegram for Mr. Ismay who is on board 'Titanic'
so far our only information is telegram from New York as follows begins

Church Street, Liverpool, 1912.

'Newspaper wireless reports advise Titanic collision iceberg lat 41.46 north long 50.14 west women being put lifeboats steamer Virginian expects reach Titanic ten a.m. today Olympic Baltic proceeding Titanic we have no direct information'.

The postscript to this message contained new details: 'Underwriters have message from New York that "Virginian" is standing by "Titanic" and that there is no danger of loss of life. Latest word from Press agency is "Titanic" proceeding to Cape Race all passengers transferred presumably to "Virginian"'. However, the following morning, Tuesday 16th, the Company sent Howell a brief and devastating update: 'Referring telegram yesterday "Titanic" deeply grieved to say that during night we received word steamer foundered about 675 souls mostly women and children saved'.[3]

Telegram from H. Lee Jones, League of Welldoers, to the White Star Line, dated 16 April 1912. (MMM, ref. SAS 29/22/29)

Also on the morning of 16 April, the *Liverpool Daily Post and Mercury,* while still devoting most of its attention to issues such as Irish Home Rule and the national coal strike, reported that 'A great sensation was caused on both sides of the Atlantic yesterday by the announcement that the White Star liner Titanic, the largest vessel afloat, had met with disaster on her maiden voyage to New York, having collided with an iceberg off the Newfoundland banks late on Sunday night.'[4] The same newspaper commented that the news had come 'like a bolt from the blue' to the people of Liverpool. Although *Titanic* had 'never been seen in this locality' and was 'officially attached to another port', her brief career from shipyard to Atlantic ferry had been viewed 'with friendly solicitude, as affecting the biggest steamer in the world, owned by a company whose headquarters are in Liverpool'. The greatest consternation had prevailed at the White Star office in James Street, where initial scepticism had been replaced by great alarm, particularly as it was common knowledge that 'the head of the

White Star Line acknowledges H. Lee Jones' telegram. (MMM, ref. SAS 29/22/29)

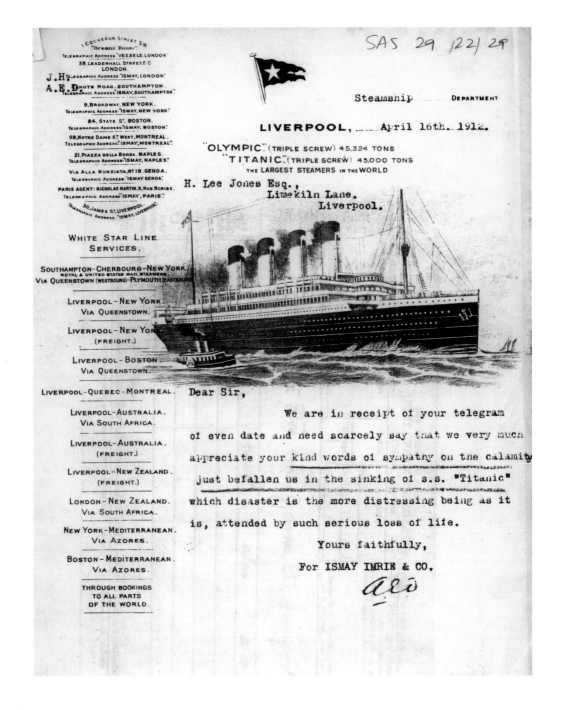

SAS 29 /22/ 29

1 COCKSPUR STREET S.W.
"Oceanic House"
Telegraphic Address "VESSELS, LONDON"
38. LEADENHALL STREET. E.C.
LONDON.
J. H. — Telegraphic Address "ISMAY, LONDON"
A. E. D. — NUTE ROAD, SOUTHAMPTON.
Telegraphic Address "ISMAY, SOUTHAMPTON"
9. BROADWAY, NEW YORK.
Telegraphic Address "ISMAY, NEW YORK"
84. STATE St. BOSTON.
Telegraphic Address "ISMAY, BOSTON"
118. NOTRE DAME St. WEST, MONTREAL.
Telegraphic Address "ISMAY, MONTREAL"
21. PIAZZA DELLA BORSA, NAPLES.
Telegraphic Address "ISMAY, NAPLES"
VIA ALLA NUNZIATA, N°. 18. GENOA.
Telegraphic Address "ISMAY GENOA"
PARIS AGENT: NICHOLAS MARTIN, 5. RUE SCRIBE.
Telegraphic Address "ISMAY, PARIS"
30. JAMES St. LIVERPOOL.
Telegraphic Address "ISMAY, LIVERPOOL"

Steamship   DEPARTMENT

LIVERPOOL, _____ April 16th. 1912.

"OLYMPIC" (TRIPLE SCREW) 45,324 TONS
"TITANIC" (TRIPLE SCREW) 45,000 TONS
THE LARGEST STEAMERS IN THE WORLD

H. Lee Jones Esq.,
      Limekiln Lane.
            Liverpool.

WHITE STAR LINE
SERVICES.

SOUTHAMPTON—CHERBOURG—NEW YORK.
ROYAL & UNITED STATES MAIL STEAMERS
VIA QUEENSTOWN (WESTBOUND)—PLYMOUTH (EASTBOUND)

LIVERPOOL—NEW YORK.
VIA QUEENSTOWN.

LIVERPOOL—NEW YORK
(FREIGHT.)

LIVERPOOL—BOSTON
VIA QUEENSTOWN.

LIVERPOOL—QUEBEC—MONTREAL.

LIVERPOOL—AUSTRALIA.
VIA SOUTH AFRICA.

LIVERPOOL—AUSTRALIA.
(FREIGHT.)

LIVERPOOL—NEW ZEALAND.
(FREIGHT.)

LONDON—NEW ZEALAND.
VIA SOUTH AFRICA.

NEW YORK—MEDITERRANEAN.
VIA AZORES.

BOSTON—MEDITERRANEAN.
VIA AZORES.

THROUGH BOOKINGS
TO ALL PARTS
OF THE WORLD.

Dear Sir,

      We are in receipt of your telegram
of even date and need scarcely say that we very much
appreciate your kind words of sympathy on the calamity
just befallen us in the sinking of s.s. "Titanic"
which disaster is the more distressing being as it
is, attended by such serious loss of life.

      Yours faithfully,

      For ISMAY IMRIE & CO.

White Star Line, Mr. Bruce Ismay, was among the Titanic's passengers'.[5] The newspaper then published a passenger list for the ship, without giving any details of victims or survivors.

That evening the White Star Line in Liverpool received telegrams from both the King and Queen conveying their horror at the 'appalling disaster which has happened to the *Titanic* and the terrible loss of life'. Their Majesties also expressed their deep sympathy 'for the bereaved relatives in their great sorrow'.[6] Over the next few days the company also received similar messages from the Lord Mayor of Liverpool (Lord Derby), the Lord Mayor of London, and a number of foreign dignitaries, including Kaiser Wilhelm IV of Germany.

On Thursday 18 April *The Times* reported that Sir Horace Marshall, treasurer and chairman of the Orphan Working School and Alexandra Orphanage, London, NW, had forwarded copies of a telegram, originally sent to the Lord Mayor of London, to the Lord Mayor of Liverpool and the Mayor of Southampton, offering the care of the institution to twenty children of *Titanic* crew members who had been lost. He suggested that ten children from London and ten from either Southampton or Liverpool would be suitable.[7]

The Lord Mayor of London had already established a Mansion House fund for the relief of those in financial distress due to the *Titanic* disaster. Following his lead, Lord Derby announced on 19 April that he would receive donations from the 'generous people of Liverpool' at the Liverpool Town Hall. These would either 'be added to a local fund, if one is established, or otherwise sent to the Lord Mayor of London's fund'. He felt that, in the first instance, it was not advisable to open a Town Hall fund, but he was prepared to do so later if the circumstances made it necessary for local claims. He hoped that the two Liverpool newspaper offices would agree to the Lord Mayor of London's request to open their columns for any subscriptions which their readers might wish to give. Among the first donations received were the following:

White Star Line	. . . . 1000 guineas
Mr. Harold A. Sanderson (White Star Line)	. . . . . 500 pounds
Mrs. Ismay	. . . . 200 pounds
Miss Lottie Ismay	. . . . 100 pounds[8]

By 26 April more than £14,000 had been collected for Liverpool alone.[9] The Liverpool fund was closed on Monday 13 May, 'the feeling being that sufficient money had been received for the purposes for which it had been intended'. The Lord Mayor expressed the hope 'that a small surplus might be preserved, which would enable them to erect a memorial to the men who had so bravely lost their lives, and left behind them the noblest example that human nature was capable of (applause) …'[10]

On Monday 15 April the *Daily Post and Mercury* had published a White Star Line advertisement which proudly announced the new service provided by 'Olympic and Titanic, the Largest Steamers in the World'. By Wednesday 17th, however, the company's advertisement had reverted to its pre-*Titanic* form: 'Olympic, the Largest Steamer in the World'. On the same day, the newspaper also greatly expanded its *Titanic* disaster coverage, commenting:

> In street and mart, in household and hostelry, on ferryboat and on the river-side, in tramcar and in railway train, man and women talked with bated breath of the tragic tidings to hand.

> The mournful spirit which everywhere prevailed found expression in the flags flying at half mast outside the White Star and other shipping offices, the Town Hall and other municipal buildings.

It also reported that the hymn 'Eternal Father Strong to Save' had been sung in many local schools, observing that 'the awed ring with which the children sang the hymn showed how deep an impression the terrible disaster had made on their young minds'.[11]

Even more poignant is the fact that many children from these schools may already have been kept at home or sent home because their fathers or other close relatives had been, or were thought to have been, on board *Titanic*. This would particularly have applied to schools in the dockland areas of Liverpool. In the late 1960s, for example, Mr. Albert Thompson, a ship's carpenter with Royal Mail Lines, then near retirement age, vividly remembered being in class as a young child in Bootle, near Liverpool's north docks, when he saw a policeman coming into the schoolyard. Soon afterwards the policeman and the headmaster came into the classroom and asked if any of the boys had fathers on the *Titanic*. As Mr. Thompson recalled: 'A good number of hands went up. The headmaster then said for them to go home to their mothers.'[12]

Such heart-rending personal stories seem initially to have escaped the attention of the local press, which was clearly taken by surprise by the extent of the impact of the disaster on the inhabitants of the Liverpool area. For example, the same 17 April edition of the *Liverpool Daily Post* revealed that '[c]ontrary to expectations, a scrutiny of the passenger list and the list of the crew disclosed the names of many people belonging to this city and district'.

While relatives and friends of passengers and crew made anxious enquiries at the White Star office during the morning and afternoon, the officials were unable, in the absence of full details, to give them any definite information. As regards the crew, it appeared that the Southampton crew list was not yet available at the Liverpool offices of the company, and so enquirers were told that, even if their friends or relatives were crew members, it was impossible to tell which of them had been saved. While it was known that some crew had been rescued, it was hinted that 'their names would probably be the last to be given publicity'. As the writer observed: 'The harrowing experiences which the White Star officials were fated to undergo at the Southampton and New York offices did not fall to the lot of the Liverpool staff, but the situation was a sufficiently delicate one, and the inquirers themselves were obviously greatly agitated by the absence of information.'

Evidently grasping at a few straws of information, he continued: 'The majority of the crew reside in Southampton. Several of the officers and the engineering staff hail from Ireland; not a few come from Belfast. A number are well known in Liverpool.' Perhaps more surprisingly, while recording Chief Engineer Joseph Bell's roots in Cumberland and Newcastle, he failed to mention that Bell was also a long-standing Liverpool resident, with a large family to support.[13]

The first substantial list of survivors published by the *Liverpool Daily Post* on 17 April only featured passengers. One enquirer at the White Star Line office was the Reverend Latimer Davies, vicar of St James's, Toxteth, who was anxious as to the fate of three of his parishioners whom he knew were on board *Titanic*. They were Mr. Joseph Fynney and 'a youth named Gaskell', both of whom, as we have seen, were lost in the sinking.[14] It appears that Fynney's sister had received a telegram the previous morning which wrongly stated that all passengers had been saved. Reverend Davies also enquired about a crew member named Pallas, a greaser, presumably Thomas Palles, who had made the delivery trip on *Titanic* before undertaking the first commercial voyage.[15] As we have seen, none of these men survived. Another report in the same newspaper also mentioned 'two ladies from Birkdale', Miss Lily Bonnell, of Welbeck Road, and her niece, Miss Caroline Bonnell. The writer added: 'The crew included about forty persons hailing from Liverpool district, amongst them being several ladies who were serving as stewardesses'.[16]

Another interesting revelation was that Major Archibald W. Butt, of the United States Army, President Taft's aide-de-camp, a First Class passenger victim of the *Titanic* disaster, was the brother of Edward H. Butt, 'who for the last fourteen years has been connected with the Liverpool cotton trade'. E.H. Butt was the eldest of three brothers of an old Southern States family, and was a partner in the Liverpool firm of A.J. Buston and Company, Cotton Brokers, of 48–49 Exchange Building, Edmund Street. At his request, Major Butt, having just visited the Pope and the King of Italy in Rome as part of his official duties, had stayed with him for several days at his home at The Manor, Mickle Trafford, outside Chester, before leaving to join the

Titanic at Southampton.[17] While at his brother's home, according to a report in the same newspaper three days later, he had 'made the acquaintance of a house party of friends from Liverpool and district, who speak enthusiastically of his bright, genial disposition and soldierly qualities'.[18]

To heighten the almost apocalyptic atmosphere developing in the city, between 11 am and 1 pm on Wednesday 17 April Liverpool experienced a partial eclipse of the sun. Local observers reported that during this event, at its peak, 'six sevenths of the sun's disk' were momentarily darkened.[19] This particular solar eclipse, sometimes referred to as the 'Titanic eclipse', was visible in Britain, Western Europe, Russia, the east coast of North America, Guyana and Surinam. As well as in Liverpool, it could be seen in all the other ports most closely associated with *Titanic*, namely Belfast, Southampton, Cherbourg, Queenstown, New York and Halifax, Nova Scotia. It would also have been visible from the position in the North Atlantic at which *Titanic* sank.[20]

By Saturday 20 April the Liverpool newspapers had begun to publish more detailed and accurate information about the disaster. The *Liverpool Daily Post and Mercury* reported:

> After the trying suspense of the last few days the authentic news which reached Liverpool yesterday served to realise the worst fears of the local public as to what had happened in those dreadful early hours of Monday morning after the Titanic struck the devastating iceberg and before she sank to her watery grave.

The report continued:

> During the forenoon the White Star Company issued a list of survivors among the crew, and in this, happily, several local names figured. Later in the day the company sent out a supplementary list of third-class passengers

rescued, but so far as is known it possessed no special local significance, being for the most part representative of Irish and foreign migrants.

The newspaper revealed that many enquiries had been made at the White Star offices by friends and relatives of the missing. Although, in comparison with New York and Southampton, the number of local families affected was small,

the callers at the company's headquarters were sufficiently numerous, and their concern was sufficiently pronounced, to result in some touching displays of joy and thankfulness, or – as, unfortunately, was more frequently the case – of disappointment and despair, when the news of rescue or non-rescue was made known.

Clearly armed with the latest information available from the White Star Line, the writer concluded:

Close upon 100 members of the crew were at one time or other connected with Liverpool, and although only a comparatively small proportion of their families are located in this city and surrounding districts, the extent to which relatives and friends are affected by the disaster is, unhappily, all too great. Information of a reassuring character is still lacking with regard to several of the Titanic's passengers who hailed from these parts.[21]

Later in the same newspaper, under the heading 'Local Members of Titanic's Crew', the photographs of five of the liner's crew and one passenger were published. The crew members were William McMurray, Charles W. Hogg, R.S. Allan and Henry W. Ashe, all of whom were stewards, plus Second Baker John Robert Giles. The passenger whose photograph was included, presumably by

Titanic disaster headlines displayed at the Bridge House Stationers and Tobacconists, 40 Penny Lane, Liverpool, April 1912. (courtesy of Paul Bolger)

Report of 'Local Crew' victims from the *Liverpool Daily Post and Mercury*, 20 April 1912. (Liverpool Record Office)

145

60 Empress Road
Kensington
Liverpool
13.4.12

Dear Father
        It seems ages since
I last seen you. I wish we
where in Southampton with you
it is very lonely without you
Dear Father I have not been
so very well I have had a
a bad throat hoping I will
soon get better for Mana worrie
so much little Ernie as not been

mistake, was Second Class passenger Charles Sedgwick from St Helens, near Liverpool. The text underneath these photographs only gives brief information about four of the men concerned, namely McMurray, Hogg, Ashe and Giles, and adds details of two others not illustrated by photographs, namely the electrician Alfred Middleton and the cook James Hutchinson. Middleton, a native of Ballisadare, County Sligo, Ireland, was the only one featured who did not appear to have a Liverpool background, but he evidently had relatives living in Park Road, Liverpool. The fact that all of these men had been lost in the sinking is strongly implied rather than clearly stated in the article.[22]

Perhaps the most poignant story relating to any of these men involves First Class Bedroom Steward William McMurray. Birkenhead-born McMurray, who was 43 years of age, lived at 60 Empress Road, Kensington, Liverpool, with his wife and three young children. According to the *Liverpool Daily Post*, his wife was 'prostrated with grief' at the sad news of her husband's loss and was being attended to by sympathetic neighbours. The shattering information had reached her on the anniversary of her wedding on 17 April. She stated that the last time she had seen her husband was six weeks earlier, when he had left Liverpool on the Belfast steamer for the *Titanic*, having been transferred from the *Celtic*. Mrs. McMurray, 'even in her great bereavement', had pride in showing a medal which had been presented to her husband for gallantry in connection with the rescue of 1700 souls from the steamship *Republic*, on 24 January 1909, while he was a member of the crew.[23]

As a postscript to this story, one of McMurray's young daughters, May Louise, wrote a letter to him, addressed to '*The Titanic*, Southampton', on 13 April 1912. Since the ship had already left Southampton three days earlier, this letter never reached him, and was returned to the family home after the sinking. It read:

Dear Father,
It seems ages since I last seen you. I wish we where in Southampton with you it is very lonely without you. Dear Father I have not been so very well I have had a bad throat hoping I will soon get better for Nana [Mama?] worries so much little Ernie as not been so well but he as got better now hoping you are keeping well dada so ta love from Ivy and Ernie thank dada for the presents love from all dad hoping to see you soon with love from Ivy and Ma and Ernie xxxxxxxxx kisses for dada x Dada this is my first letter

This letter was donated to Merseyside Maritime Museum in 1989 by May Louise's own daughter, William McMurray's granddaughter.[24]

Letter from young May McMurray to her father, addressed to 'Titanic, Southampton', dated 13 April 1912. Mr. McMurray, a bedroom steward, died in the sinking. The letter was later returned to his daughter. (MMM, ref. DX/1018/R)

Bedroom steward William McMurray. (courtesy of the McMurray family)

At noon on Saturday 20 April a solemn memorial service for those lost in the *Titanic* disaster was held in St Peter's Church in Church Street, Liverpool. The service was attended by the Bishop of Liverpool, the Lord Mayor (the Earl of Derby), and the mayors of Bootle and Birkenhead. Occupying the central aisle with these dignitaries were between three and four hundred White Star Line staff, including office workers, superintendents, ships' captains, officers and sailors. The company's senior managers, namely Harold Sanderson, director and general manager, Henry Concanon, assistant general manager, E.L. Fletcher and A.B. Cauty, joint assistant managers, were joined by their counterparts from other major shipping lines and related organisations based in the port. Mrs. Bruce Ismay, Mrs. Sanderson and Mrs. Fletcher also attended. According to the *Daily Post and Mercury* of 22 April, the service 'brought home very closely to all taking part in it the awful tragedy of the foundering of the *Titanic*'. The congregation was drawn from all classes of the community, and during the service, 'many of the ladies, who formed the greater proportion, were moved to tears by the pathos of the occasion, and the thoughts of all were with the sufferers of the unprecedented calamity of the sea'.[25]

Many other memorial services were held in churches across the city over the next few days and weeks. On Sunday 21 April, for example, at one such service in the Lady Chapel of Liverpool Cathedral, Canon Smethwick described how, '[on] a calm, starlit night the most magnificent steamer that ever breasted the waters of the Atlantic sank like a stone into the depths of the sea'. He continued:

> Many touching incidents have reached us, but none more pathetic than the words of one who was saved on a raft: 'We prayed through the weary night, and there never was a moment when our prayers did not seem to rise above the waves.' Men who seemed long ago to have forgotten how to address their Creator, recalled the prayers of their childhood, and murmured them over and over again.

On Monday 22 April the *Daily Sketch*, under the heading 'A Lady's Dream', told 'a dream story of the *Titanic*' from Ellesmere Port, near Liverpool. Mrs. Shrubsall, the wife of a draughtsman, was said to have dreamt the previous Sunday night (14–15 April) that the *Titanic* was sinking. She woke her husband to tell him about her dream, but he dismissed it as a fancy, saying that she was probably just anxious because she had relatives on board. Mrs. Shrubsall's sister, a member of the crew of the vessel, was 'among the drowned'.[26]

On Sunday 12 May a memorial service to the children who perished on the *Titanic* was held in the Gay Street Mission, Scotland Road, Liverpool. The platform was decorated with the Union Jack, 'emblematic of British heroism'. Mr. Harold Bower gave an address 'commending the act of Captain Smith, who, as the Titanic sank, swam with a child in his arms, placing it safe in the lifeboat'. This somewhat unlikely account of Captain Smith's final actions, which was widely circulated at the time, has never been proven. Finally, the children gave 'a beautiful rendering of that splendid children's hymn, "Safe in the Arms of Jesus"'.[27]

Of the 17 passengers with strong connections to the Liverpool area who sailed on *Titanic*'s maiden voyage, 13 died and only four survived the sinking. The survivors were:

First Class Passengers
Miss Elizabeth Bonnell, 60
Mr. Joseph Bruce Ismay, 49, shipowner

Second Class Passenger
Mrs. Elizabeth Faunthorpe (Wilkinson), 29

Third Class Passenger
Mrs. Mary E. Davison (née Finck), 34, wife

Of the 115 'Liverpool-connected' crew identified as having sailed on *Titanic*'s maiden voyage, 87 died and only 28 survived. The listed survivors are shown in Table 2. The intriguing cases of Leading Fireman James Keegan, Fireman Thomas Hart, and Trimmer T. Casey, who were all listed among the crew who sailed and died, but who may not actually have done so, will be considered in Chapter 10.

Table 2 Survivors among *Titanic*'s crew with Liverpool connections

Surname	Forenames/initials	Age	Department	Rank/position
Andrews	Charles Edward	19	Victualling, Second Class	Steward
Barrett	Frederick William	28 (or 33)	Engine	Leading Fireman
Bowker	Ruth	27	A la carte restaurant	First Cashier
Clark(e)	William	39	Engine	Fireman
Crafter	Frederick	27	Victualling, First Class	Saloon Steward
Cullen	Charles	45	Victualling, First Class	Bedroom Steward
Dillon	Thomas Patrick	34	Engine	Trimmer
Faulkner	William Stephen	37	Victualling, First Class	Bedroom Steward
Fleet	Frederick	24	Deck	Lookout
Gregson	Mary (Miss)	44	Victualling, First Class	Stewardess
Jones	Thomas William	32	Deck	Able Seaman
Joughin	Charles John	32	Victualling, Galley	Chief Baker
Leather (née Edwards)	Elizabeth May (Mrs)	41	Victualling, First Class	Stewardess
Lightoller	Charles Herbert	38	Deck	Second Officer

Surname	Forenames/initials	Age	Department	Rank/position
McGann	James	26	Engine	Trimmer
McLaren (née Allsop)	Harriet (Mrs)	40	Victualling, First Class	Stewardess
McMicken	Arthur	23 (26)	Victualling, First Class	Saloon Steward
Rice	Charles	32	Engine	Fireman
Roberts (née Humphreys)	Mary Keziah (Mrs)	30	Victualling, First Class	Stewardess
Stap	Sarah Agnes (Miss)	47	Victualling, First Class	Stewardess
Thomas	Albert Charles	23	Victualling, First Class	Steward
Thompson	John William	35	Engine	Fireman
Threlfall	Thomas	38 (44)	Engine	Leading Fireman
Wheat	Joseph Thomas	29	Victualling, First Class	Assistant Second Steward
Wheelton	Edneser Ernest Edward	29	Victualling, First Class	Saloon Steward
Witter	James William Cheetham	31	Victualling, Second Class	Smoke Room Steward
Wright	William	40	Victualling, Third Class	Glory Hole Steward
Wynn	Walter	41	Deck	Quartermaster

CHAPTER 10

COMING HOME

But, oh! What a pitiful ending has come to it all.

Harold Sanderson
22 April 1912[1]

While the people of Liverpool were beginning to come to terms with the devastating news, other major scenes of the drama were unfolding in New York. As soon as *Carpathia* reached New York on the evening of Thursday 18 April, the exhausted and distressed survivors had been subjected to a press frenzy, intent on uncovering the full story of the sinking. Since Captain Smith and his two most senior navigating officers were not among the survivors, much of the attention was directed at J. Bruce Ismay, Chairman and Managing Director of the White Star Line and President of the International Mercantile Marine Company.

Unfortunately for Ismay, even before the ship reached New York he was already being widely blamed in the American press as bearing the main responsibility for the disaster. This was largely due to the huge influence of newspaper baron William Randolph Hearst, who had long disliked Ismay, resented his presidency of an American-owned trust and was evidently intent on destroying his reputation. One example of the viciousness of this personal vendetta was revealed by the full-page cartoon in one of Hearst's newspapers depicting Ismay in a lifeboat, watching the sinking of *Titanic* and captioned 'This Is J. Brute Ismay. [...] We respectfully suggest that the emblem of the White Star be changed to a yellow liver.' As Karen Kamuda comments, '[Hearst's] editorials and cartoons portrayed Ismay as a cruel, power-hungry, money-driven businessman. Hearst tried and convicted the man in his newspapers before Ismay arrived in New York on the *Carpathia*.'[2]

Telegram sent from *Carpathia* by Bruce Ismay to the White Star Line, New York, written on 15 April but not sent until 17 April 1912. It reads: 'Deeply regret advise you Titanic sank this morning, fifteenth after collision iceberg resulting serious loss life further particulars later Bruce Ismay.' (MMM, ref. D/TSA)

Like most of his fellow survivors, Ismay had been traumatised by the sinking. Although he himself had not lost a member of his own family, he had lost old friends and close colleagues and was deeply affected by the distress suffered by his fellow survivors. On board *Carpathia*, he was said to have been 'completely shattered' and 'overwhelmed by the tragedy'.[3] Over four days he never left his room, 'lived on soup' and was given opiates by the ship's doctor.[4] As Charles Lightoller testified at the US Senate Inquiry:

I may say that at that time Mr. Ismay did not seem to me to be in a mental condition to finally decide anything. I tried my utmost to rouse Mr. Ismay, for he was obsessed with the idea, and kept repeating, that he ought to have gone down with the ship because he found that women had gone down.[5]

Shortly after coming on board, Ismay was visited by Captain Rostron, who suggested that he should notify White Star's office in New York about the disaster. He wrote a note on a piece of paper and handed it to Rostron. Addressed to 'Islefrank, New York' (Philip Franklin, the American vice-president of the IMM), it read: 'Deeply regret advise you Titanic sank this morning fifteenth after collision iceberg, resulting serious loss of life; further particulars later. Bruce Ismay'.[6]

After consulting *Titanic*'s surviving officers, Ismay sent another message to Franklin, asking him that the White Star liner *Cedric*, then in New York, should be held until *Carpathia*'s arrival. This was apparently so that *Titanic*'s surviving crew could be kept together and returned to England on that ship as soon as possible. This request was declined by Franklin, who feared that such an action would give the impression that the White Star Line had something to hide. In the event, when *Carpathia* arrived in New York Ismay and selected *Titanic* crew members were immediately ordered to remain in the city to await the United States Senate Inquiry into the sinking.

The Senate Inquiry opened in the East Room of New York's Waldorf Astoria Hotel on Friday 19 April, the day after *Carpathia*'s arrival in New York. The hearings, which later moved from New York to Washington, DC, took place over eighteen days, between 19 April and 25 May. Apart from Bruce Ismay, four officers and 34 members of *Titanic*'s crew were detained as possible witnesses. Of these, at least one officer, Charles Lightoller, and five crew, namely Charles Andrews, Thomas Jones, Fred Barrett, Fred Fleet and Ernest Wheelton, had strong connections with the Liverpool area. All of these men testified at the Inquiry.

Meanwhile, on Saturday 20 April the remaining 172 *Titanic* crew members who had not been detained for the Inquiry were allowed to leave for England on the Red Star Line steamer *Lapland*. Upon arriving in Plymouth on Monday 29 April, they were all herded into a Third Class dockside waiting room for the taking of depositions, or sworn witness statements, relating to the disaster. In addition, all had to appear before the Receiver of Wrecks before they could be

Bruce Ismay answering questions at the United States Senate Inquiry. (*Daily Sketch*, 1/5/1912)

released. This required them to stay overnight in the same waiting room, which had duly been equipped with bedding, tables and other basic facilities. The following afternoon they were allowed to leave for their homes.[7] Two of the crew concerned, namely Leading Fireman Thomas Threlfall, and another man, initially thought to have been a passenger, travelled by train from London and arrived at Lime Street Station in Liverpool at 9.30 on the evening of Wednesday 1 May. They may well have been the first local survivors to return to Liverpool. According to the *Liverpool Daily Post and Mercury* on Thursday 2 May, 'For each of the men a small knot of friends and relatives were in waiting, and the passengers were hurried off to escape the local journalists who had been apprised of their coming'. The report stated that the passenger, 'who looked worn and ill', declined to disclose his identity or make any statement of his experiences. The other man, who appeared to be 'in an agitated state, and disinclined to answer questions', was surrounded by 'a number of females, who hurried him away, urging that he had people at home anxiously waiting his arrival'. One of the women said that the man's name was Thomas Threlfall, and that he was a leading fireman on board the

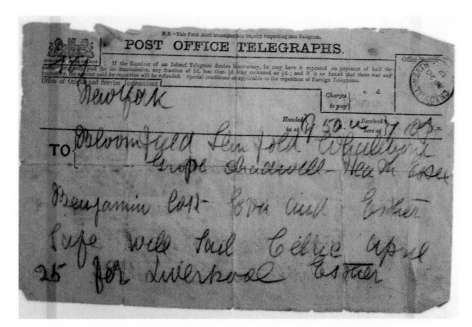

POST OFFICE TELEGRAPHS.

Telegram sent from New York by survivor Esther Hart: 'Benjamin lost, Eva and Esther safe. Will sail Celtic April 25 for Liverpool, Esther.' (MMM, ref. DX/1549R)

ill-fated liner. Threlfall, however, refused to make any statement.[8]

Since Bruce Ismay was the only male passenger survivor from the Liverpool area, it is probable that the 'passenger' mentioned was, in fact, another crew member. A likely candidate is *Titanic* First Class Bedroom Steward William Faulkner, who was reported in the same newspaper the following day (3 May) as having reached his home in Tranmere, near Birkenhead, 'yesterday'.[9] Among the prominent American passengers to whom Faulkner had been assigned on *Titanic* were Colonel John Jacob Astor and his teenage bride, Mr. and Mrs. Isidor Strauss, and Colonel Archibald Gracie. He had also attended to Miss Caroline Bonnell of Ohio, the niece of Miss Lily Bonnell of Birkdale, near Liverpool. Faulkner would later attend the British Wreck Commissioner's Inquiry, although he did not testify, before returning to sea on White Star's *Adriatic* from Liverpool on 13 June 1912.[10]

On 2 May the *Liverpool Daily Post and Mercury* reported that a telegram from Boston, USA, stated that Captain Fenton, of the steamer *Sagamore*, from Liverpool, had sighted two bodies and a considerable quantity of wreckage in latitude 41°21′ North, longitude 49°30′ to 49°36′ West, about five miles north of

Titanic survivors Bertram Dean and Eva Hart at Merseyside Maritime Museum in 1988. (courtesy Mr. T. Miller)

the position where the *Carpathia* rescued the *Titanic*'s survivors.[11] Two days later the same newspaper reported that the body of the Liverpool rubber merchant Mr. Joseph Fynney, a Second Class passenger on *Titanic*, had been recovered by the cable ship *Minia*, the second of four ships chartered by the White Star Line to search for bodies in the aftermath of the sinking. The newspaper added: 'On 'Change [the Exchange in Liverpool] and in commercial circles he will be greatly missed and the deepest sympathy is felt for his relatives'.[12]

On Saturday 4 May, the White Star liner *Celtic* arrived in Liverpool. On board were *Titanic* lookout Reginald Lee and quartermaster Robert Hichens, both of whom had testified at the United States Inquiry. Also on board were Second Class passenger survivors Mrs. Esther Hart and her seven-year-old daughter Eva. Eva and her parents were travelling on *Titanic* as emigrants to Winnipeg, Canada, where Mr. Hart planned to open a drug store. The last time she saw her father was when he placed her and her mother in lifeboat 14, telling her to 'hold Mummy's hand and be a good girl'. Mr. Hart did not survive the sinking and his body, if recovered, was never identified. In 1988 Eva Hart visited Merseyside Maritime Museum in Liverpool with fellow *Titanic* survivor Bertram Dean. She later donated to the Museum the telegram which her mother sent from New York in April 1912 informing relatives in Chadwell Heath, Essex that she and Eva were safe. It reads: 'Benjamin lost Eva and Esther safe will sail Celtic April 25 for Liverpool, Esther'.[13] Eva Hart died on 14 February 1996 at her home in Chadwell Heath at the age of 91.[14]

Another arrival in Liverpool on 4 May was a coffin containing the body of First Class passenger Alfred Rowe, who had died in the *Titanic* disaster. His body was recovered by the cable ship *Mackay-Bennett* and then taken to Halifax, Nova Scotia. At the request of his Liverpool relatives it had then been forwarded to Liverpool on the Canadian Pacific passenger liner *Empress of Britain*. Rowe's body was buried in the family vault at Toxteth Park Cemetery, Smithdown Road, Liverpool, after an impressive funeral on Tuesday 14 May. The service was conducted by the Reverend W.C. Sims of St Anne's Church, Aigburth.[15]

On Thursday 2 May, having being permitted to leave the United States Senate Inquiry, Bruce Ismay, four surviving officers, and over thirty crew members departed from New York for Liverpool, via Queenstown, on the White Star liner *Adriatic*. Ismay was described by *The Syracuse Herald* as being 'in a state of near collapse'. Before leaving, he made a brief statement to newspapermen: 'I am quite satisfied with the way the senatorial investigation was conducted. I am perfectly willing to give every possible bit of information which I possess regarding the Titanic disaster, both here and in England. I expect to be called during the investigation in London.'[16]

It is clear, however, that Ismay had been a reluctant witness at the Senate Inquiry, and was far from satisfied with his treatment at the hands of certain sections of the American press. This explains why, on 23 April, he sent a cable from New York to the *Times* newspaper in London attempting to justify his escape

from *Titanic*, and that of American First Class passenger Mr. Carter, in one of the last lifeboats. The following extract gives a good idea of Ismay's viewpoint:

> I hope I need not say that neither Mr. Carter nor myself would, for one moment, have thought of getting into the boat if there had been any women there to go in it. Nor should I have done so if I had thought that by remaining on the ship I could have been of the slightest further assistance. It is impossible for me to answer every false statement, rumour, or invention that has appeared in the newspapers. [17]

Returning to England at about the same time as *Adriatic* was the Leyland Line steamer *Californian*, which had left Boston on Saturday 27 April and arrived in

Titanic fireman John Thompson (left of centre, in striped suit) arrives in Liverpool, his home city, from RMS Adriatic, 11 May 1912. He is clutching his left arm, which he broke during his struggle to survive after Titanic sank. (© Getty Images Inc./Hulton Archive/ Topical Press Agency/Stringer)

Titanic stewards arrive in Liverpool from RMS Adriatic, 11 May 1912. Bedroom steward Henry Etches is second from the left. (© Getty Images Inc./Hulton Archive/ Topical Press Agency/Stringer)

Liverpool on Friday 10 May. As we have seen, the *Californian* had arrived near *Carpathia* on the morning of 15 April and had searched the surrounding area in vain for survivors of the *Titanic* disaster. Two days before leaving Boston, however, the *Boston American* newspaper had published serious allegations against Captain Stanley Lord regarding his part in the *Titanic* disaster. On the night of the 14–15 April the *Californian* had been stationary, surrounded by ice, in the general vicinity of *Titanic*. According to a sworn affidavit from one of his crew, assistant donkeyman Ernest Gill, Captain Lord had failed to respond to *Titanic*'s distress rockets, which had been reported to him by several of his officers. As a result of Gill's statement, Lord and his wireless operator Cyril Evans had been summoned to appear the following day at the United States Senate Inquiry into the *Titanic* disaster in Washington, DC. Lord was happy to attend, and later felt that he had been treated well at the Inquiry and

Bruce Ismay (centre, with moustache) returns to Liverpool on RMS *Adriatic*, Saturday, 11 May 1912. Behind him on the gangway are his wife, his brother (Bower) and Harold Sanderson. (© Getty Images Inc./Hulton Archive/ Topical Press Agency/Stringer)

able to explain his conduct on the night in question.[18]

Shortly after the *Californian* docked in Liverpool, Captain Lord and his three navigating officers were called to the office of the Leyland Line's chief marine superintendent, Captain Fry. Fry questioned them about what had happened on the night *Titanic* was lost. Lord and Herbert Stone, his Second Officer, confirmed their opinion that the ship which had stopped nearby was not a passenger ship. However, much to Lord's surprise, as Leslie Harrison comments, his Third Officer, Charles Victor Groves, 'not only asserted that she was, but also expressed his opinion that the rockets seen coming from her had been distress signals'.[19] With a few other members of the crew, Lord and his officers then went to the local Board of Trade office to make formal statements about events on the night of the *Titanic* disaster. Since the Board's formal investigation into her loss had opened in London on Thursday 2 May, its officials immediately arranged for nine

Mr. and Mrs. Ismay approaching their motor car at the Liverpool Landing Stage after arriving on the White Star liner *Adriatic*, 11 May 1912.

The crowd cheers Mr. Ismay (in car). (*Daily Sketch*, 13/5/1912)

witnesses from the *Californian* to travel down to London to attend the hearings.[20]

In meantime, Mrs. Ismay, her brother-in-law Mr. Bower Ismay, and Mr. Henry Concanon of the White Star Line had sailed from Liverpool on the *Oceanic* to join Ismay at Queenstown for the return to Liverpool on the *Adriatic*.[21] Another man who boarded *Adriatic* at Queenstown was Mr. Furniss, of Hill, Dickinson and Company, Liverpool, solicitors for the White Star Line. He interviewed *Titanic*'s surviving officers and others during the final leg of the voyage.[22] The ship arrived at the Princes Landing Stage in Liverpool at 7.30 am on Saturday 11 May. Her arrival, as the *Liverpool Daily Post and Mercury* observed, 'had been anxiously anticipated': 'Friends and relatives of the Titanic's survivors had come from various parts of the kingdom to greet their loved ones, and when these landed there were many moving and pathetic scenes.' Yet, the reporter added, there was nothing in the way of 'undue demonstrativeness', and the calm looker-on was afforded

> a striking illustration of the philosophical way in which English men and women bear alike their pleasures and their sorrows. It is doubtful if any homecoming has ever been equalled in the matter of self-restraint. There was no fuss, no hustle – just a hearty handshake and a muffled greeting far more eloquent than high-flown words.[23]

Officer Harold Lowe arrives in Liverpool on RMS *Adriatic*, 11 May 1912. (*Daily Sketch*)

As well as a large staff of officials, present on the stage was 'almost an army of Pressmen and photographers'. Most crew survivors were taken off the *Adriatic* by tender before she reached the landing stage, presumably to avoid contact with the press. However, officers Lightoller, Lowe, Boxhall and Pitman, and lookout Fred Fleet were among the first passengers to descend the gangplank to the landing stage. All 'were disposed to great reticence' except Fourth Officer Lowe. Looking 'neat, dapper, and well groomed', Lowe 'bore no trace of the terrible ordeal which he and others had gone through'. With his 'characteristic breeziness of diction', he said that he had nothing to tell, but paid a warm tribute to the manners of British journalists. As for the American pressmen, however, 'Mr. Lowe, with a suggestive swing of the arm, said he would like to have some of them shot, at sight'. The reporter added that, in this connection, 'a marine official of high standing' had complimented the press of Liverpool for its courteous behaviour towards Mr. Ismay, 'so strikingly at variance with the ungentlemanly and pushful methods of Yankee journalists'.[24]

While members of the press were not permitted to board *Adriatic*, several prominent White Star officials were, including Harold Sanderson, E.L. Fletcher, A.B. Cauty, J. Shelley, A. Fletcher and H.H. Noble. Ismay did not descend the gangway until nearly all the saloon passengers had filed down first, but 'he was in the queue and took no special position to draw attention to himself'. He was accompanied by Mrs. Ismay, who had joined the ship at Queenstown. Both she and her husband were 'attired in deep black'. According to one local journalist: 'As soon as Mr. Ismay reached the Stage welcome cheers rang out. These were mingled with cries of "Welcome Home!" "Welcome back to Mr. Ismay!" and other expressions appropriate to the occasion.' The reporter continued: 'Mr. Ismay seemed very sad, and looked decidedly ill. He bore evident traces of the severe trial through which he had passed, and was obviously touched by the sympathetic attitude of the Pressmen present.'

Officers Herbert Pitman (centre with cap) and Charles Lightoller (in bowler hat) arrive in Liverpool on RMS *Adriatic*, 11 May 1912. (© Getty Images Inc./Hulton Archive/Topical Press Agency/Stringer)

Titanic crew survivors bound for Liverpool on the *Adriatic*. William (Billy) Burke is second from the left on the back row (with hat and moustache). Ernest Wheelton is sitting just behind the lady with the baby. The baby is Millvina Dean. (courtesy of the Titanic Historical Society, Inc.)

Survivors from *Titanic*'s emergency lifeboat No. 1 shown on board Carpathia. Laura Francatelli is standing between Lady Duff-Gordon and Sir Cosmo Duff-Gordon. (*Daily Mirror*)

Just before Ismay came ashore, the journalists of the landing stage had been handed a statement on his behalf, as follows:

> Mr. Ismay asks the gentlemen of the Press to extend their courtesy to him by not pressing for any statement from him. First, because he is still suffering from the very great strain of the Titanic disaster and subsequent events. Again, because he gave before the American Commission a plain and unvarnished statement of facts, which have been fully reported. And also, because his evidence before the British Court of Inquiry should not be anticipated in any way.
>
> He would, however, like to take this opportunity of acknowledging with a full heart the large number of telegraphic messages and letters from public concerns and business and private friends, conveying sympathy for him, which he much appreciates in the greatest trial of his life.[25]

Amid 'unaffected expressions of sympathy', Mr. and Mrs. Ismay entered their motor car, which at once set off for their home in Mossley Hill. As they left, many in the crowd saluted when they caught sight of 'the wan face, on which were graven so many indications of grief and responsibility'.[26] On reaching home, Ismay intended to visit Mrs. Fry, the widow of his valet, John Richard Fry, who had accompanied him on *Titanic* and had died in the sinking. However, at this time she was too shocked and grief-stricken to see anyone. Ismay immediately made arrangements to provide an annuity for her and her children, and she later took the position of cook at 'Sandheys'.[27]

Three other *Titanic* passengers also disembarked in Liverpool from the *Adriatic* on 11 May. They were Mrs. Eva Dean, who had lost her husband in the sinking, and her two small children. In a brief interview, Mrs. Dean said that she was now recovering, though naturally still much distressed. One of her children, Elizabeth Gladys ('Millvina'), nearly six weeks old at the time of the sinking,[28] was the youngest survivor of the disaster. The two children, she said, were none the worse for their extraordinary experience, and much kindness had been shown towards them. A collection had been made on the *Adriatic* for the benefit of Mrs. Dean and her children, realising a sum of £55. Before she died, aged 97, on 31 May 2009, Millvina Dean was the last survivor of the *Titanic* disaster. She had spent her final years in a nursing home near Ashurst, West Sussex. She, her mother and her brother had been placed in lifeboat 10 and were among the first Third Class (or steerage) passengers to escape the sinking liner. As mentioned above, in 1988 her brother Bertram visited Merseyside Maritime Museum in Liverpool with fellow *Titanic* survivor Eva Hart. Bertram died in Southampton on 14 April 1992, aged 81.[29]

On Tuesday 14 May, just three days after *Adriatic*'s arrival, the Cunard liner *Lusitania* arrived in Liverpool, having sailed from New York six days earlier. On board were *Titanic* First Class passenger survivors Sir Cosmo Duff Gordon, his wife Lady Lucie and her secretary Laura Mabel Francatelli. Having disembarked, apparently unnoticed by newspaper reporters,[30] they immediately took the train to

The cotton apron worn by Laura Francatelli on the night of *Titanic*'s sinking. (MMM.2003.221)

London, where they would shortly attend the British Inquiry. All three survived in lifeboat 1, which had a capacity of forty persons, with just two other male First Class passengers and seven crewmen. On board *Carpathia* Sir Cosmo asked Miss Francatelli to write out a £5 cheque to each of the seamen from this lifeboat. Although he insisted, plausibly, that this was to pay for new kit to replace what the men had lost during the sinking, this incident led to accusations of bribery. The British Inquiry later concluded that the Duff Gordons' departure from *Titanic* was 'within the acceptable bounds of civilised behaviour'. Even so, the stigma of this unsubstantiated accusation proved very difficult to live down. Merseyside Maritime Museum has a white cotton apron said to have been worn by Laura Francatelli on the night of the sinking. Some of her other mementoes of the sinking, including the life-jacket she wore that night, signed by fellow survivors from the lifeboat, were sold at auction in London in 2007. Miss Francatelli later married and lived for a time in Switzerland. She died in London in 1967, aged 84.[31]

On Friday 17 May, also virtually unnoticed by the press, the White Star liner

Arabic steamed into Liverpool from Boston, Massachusetts. After all of her passengers had disembarked, however, she was quietly moved to her berth at the west end of South Canada Dock. There, three coffins were unloaded onto hearses waiting on the quayside. The coffins contained the embalmed bodies of *Titanic* victims Arthur Lawrence, Owen Allum and Wallace Hartley. Apart from crew members and dock workers, the only spectators present were some White Star officials, undertakers' staff, relatives of the deceased and a limited number of pressmen.[32]

According to the *Liverpool Echo,* the body of First Class Saloon Steward Arthur Lawrence, 34, had been picked up 'about 200 miles from the scene of the disaster' by the United States cable ship *Mackay-Bennett*. It was taken to Halifax, embalmed, then transhipped to Boston, whence it was brought to Liverpool. Although he had lived in Rochford, Essex, with his wife and young son, Lawrence was buried in West Derby Cemetery in Liverpool. This was evidently on behalf of his widow, who stayed with her brother and his wife at Freshfields, near Liverpool, until the funeral had taken place. By special request of the deceased's relatives the funeral was very quiet. The funeral procession consisted of a hearse and four coaches. Of the many wreaths, the most touching was one bearing the inscription 'A broken-hearted wife'. Among the mourners was *Titanic* crew survivor William Wright, a Liverpool-born 'Glory Hole' steward who had been a shipmate of Lawrence for about five years. Although he had not been a close friend of the deceased, he described him as having been a 'quiet, conscientious worker, one ever ready to do his utmost not only for the comfort of the passengers, but for the welfare of his fellow shipmates'.[33] Steward Arthur Lawrence and First Class passenger Alfred Rowe were the only two victims of the *Titanic* disaster to be buried in Liverpool.

The second body brought to Liverpool on the *Arabic* was that of Third Class passenger Owen George Allum, an eighteen-year-old gardener, who had boarded *Titanic* in Southampton in order to meet his father in New York. He was buried on 22 May at Clewer Parish Churchyard in Windsor.[34]

The third body was that of *Titanic*'s bandmaster Wallace Hartley, who, as we have seen, was no stranger to Liverpool during his lifetime. His elderly father was waiting for him at the quayside. Hartley's body was placed on a horse-drawn hearse before embarking on the sixty-mile journey to his home town, Colne, in Lancashire, for burial in the family grave. In Colne the route to the cemetery was lined by an estimated thirty thousand people.[35]

On 18 May another *Titanic* survivor, junior wireless operator Harold Bride, arrived in Liverpool from New York on board the *Baltic*. He was met by his father. Bride had already made a donation towards the provision of a local memorial for his former colleague Jack Phillips in the latter's home town of Godalming in Surrey. He later testified at the British Wreck Commissioner's Inquiry.[36]
In the meantime, other Liverpool-connected *Titanic* crew survivors who had disembarked from the *Lapland* at Plymouth returned home to their relieved families, whether in Liverpool, Southampton or elsewhere in Britain. So too, it is claimed, did two 'Liverpool men' who were thought to have died in the sinking. The men concerned were Thomas Hart and James Keegan.

On Thursday 9 May Manchester-born marine fireman Thomas Hart, 49, listed among *Titanic*'s crew victims, was reported by the *Cork Examiner* to have arrived at his mother's home. According to this report,

> Messrs Quilliam, Liverpool, solicitors, acting on behalf of relatives of
> Thos. Hart, marine fireman, of Liverpool, supposed to have been lost in
> the *Titanic* disaster, have received a statement from his mother. She says
> that her son has turned up, and informs her that he had his discharge book
> stolen from him. Someone evidently signed on the *Titanic* with Hart's
> name and credentials, and it was he and not Hart who had drowned.[37]

It appears that Hart's mother, who lived with her son in Southampton, had been notified by White Star that he was dead, and had begun to make arrangements for

Harold Bride (centre), *Titanic*'s Assistant Marconi operator, meets his father (left) on arriving in Liverpool on RMS *Baltic*, 18 May 1912. (*Daily Sketch*)

his memorial service. On 8 May, however, he turned up on her doorstep. John Eaton states that Hart had got drunk after signing on for the voyage on 6 April, and someone had stolen his discharge book: 'Following the theft, Hart walked about Southampton in a confused state, too ashamed to return home. Expediency finally overcame fear and shame. It was never determined who stole Hart's book, used it, and was lost.'[38] Thomas Hart's dependants were named under Case Number 131 in the Mansion House *Titanic* Relief Fund booklet of March 1913 as 'Skilton, Maria (sister) and Cornford, Mary Ann (sister)'.[39] However, it has recently been suggested that the man who died may have been James Hart, whose obituary appeared in the *Southampton Echo* in April 1913. According to Peter

James Keegan (Wexford-born) and family, Liverpool, c. 1900. (courtesy of Mr. W. Bowe, Liverpool)

Engberg-Klarstrom, this man was 'remembered by his mother, brother Thomas et al.'[40] This raises the possibility that Thomas Hart's brother had sailed and died in his place. Further investigation is clearly required on this issue, as it is regarding what direct link, if any, there was between the Hart family and Liverpool.

An equally intriguing story involves another 'Liverpool crew member' who was listed as having died on *Titanic*, namely Leading Fireman James Keegan. When Keegan signed on at Southampton on 6 April, like several of his 'Black Gang' colleagues, he used a cross instead of a signature, possibly suggesting that he could not write. He gave his age as 38, and his place of birth as Liverpool, even though his current address was 2 West Place, Southampton.[41] His previous ship had been *Olympic*. Keegan was listed among those who died in the sinking, and his body was never recovered. As Brian Ticehurst has recently shown, Keegan's dependants were recorded under Case Number 156 in the Mansion House *Titanic* Relief Fund booklet of 19 March 1913 as 'Keegan, Alice Maud, widow. Children: Joseph John,

James Keegan's grave, Ford Cemetery, Liverpool (courtesy of Mr. W. Bowe, Liverpool)

Titanic memorial serviette published by the Palatine Printing Company, Wigan, Lancashire, 1912. It gives a very incomplete list of crew members (14) from Liverpool and Birkenhead, including 'James Keegan, fireman'. (MMM, Archives ref. DX/1109)

Lawrence, Sydney Francis, Alice Ellen. Mother: Dunhill (or Keegan), Mrs'.[42] At that time all of these dependants appear to have lived at 2 Crosshouse Road, Chapel, Southampton, except Keegan's widowed mother, Mrs. Dunhill (Durnil or Keegan), who lived in Liverpool. The Relief Fund appears to have continued payments to Keegan's surviving dependants in Southampton until 1925. In the late 1920s one of Keegan's children also agreed to serve an apprenticeship paid for by the Relief Fund.[43]

The problem is that in Liverpool today there are descendants of one James Keegan who claim that although he signed on in Southampton as a leading fireman for *Titanic*'s maiden voyage, he did not sail on her. According to his grandson, having fortunately 'missed the boat' in Southampton, Keegan returned to Liverpool, where he had a wife and two adult children. He told them that he 'went to a party' the night before the ship sailed and lost his discharge book, so that someone else must have 'sailed and died in his place'. He later read reports that he had died in the *Titanic* disaster. Despite this strange experience, Keegan went back to sea until about 1913, when he had an accident which rendered him unfit for the work. He then worked until retirement as a nightwatchman at various warehouses around Liverpool's north docks. He died in Liverpool in May 1932, aged 74 years, and was buried at Ford Cemetery, Kirkdale.

This particular James Keegan was born to a farming family in Wexford, Ireland, in about 1858, and so would have been about 54 years old in April 1912. His early seaman's discharge certificates, the only ones still in his Liverpool family's possession, show that by the early 1880s he had moved to Liverpool and was regularly working as a fireman, greaser or trimmer on the Liverpool–New York routes. Until the early 1890s he worked mainly for the Inman Line, always sailing from Liverpool, except for one trip, in March 1893, from Southampton to New York on the *City of New York*. From 1894 to 1897 he was regularly employed by the White Star Line as a fireman, and occasionally as a greaser, on its Liverpool to New York route, usually on the *Majestic*.[44]

In some respects the story of 'Wexford-born, Liverpool-based' James Keegan is remarkably similar to that of Thomas Hart. Keegan always maintained that someone else had sailed and died on *Titanic*'s maiden voyage using his discharge book and name. His family in Liverpool appear to have had no reason to doubt him. As with Thomas Hart, more research is needed to finally establish the truth in this case.

Even more recently, courtesy of an *Encyclopedia Titanica* website posting by one of his relatives, the name of Liverpool-born trimmer T. Casey has also been added to the list of unusual crew survival stories which require further investigation. Telling a very similar story to those mentioned above, Casey was

Captain Arthur Rostron of SS *Carpathia* is presented with a silver loving cup by Mrs. Margaret (Molly) Brown of Denver on behalf of the Titanic Survivors Committee in New York, 29 May 1912. (Daily Sketch)

Silver loving cup presented to Captain Rostron on behalf of the survivors of the *Titanic* disaster, New York, 29 May 1912. (courtesy of the Rostron family)

Gold medal of the United States Congress presented to Captain Rostron of the *Carpathia* by President Taft, 'in the name of the American people'. The medal shows Rostron's image in profile. (courtesy of the Rostron family)

said by his nephew to have turned up, alive and well, at his family home in 1932, twenty years after the sinking.[45] Casey is listed as Case Number 81 in the *Titanic Relief Fund* booklet of 19 March 1913. His dependants at that time were named as 'Carroll – Annie, sister & 4 nieces'.[46]

In July 1912 a special benefit performance in aid of the mother and sisters of Mr. Fred Clarke, the bass viola player in *Titanic*'s band, was held at the Philharmonic Hall, Myrtle Street, Liverpool. According to *Progress: The Journal of Lever Brothers, Port Sunlight*, Clarke had for many years been 'a familiar and popular ally of our Philharmonic Society at their special concerts'.[47]

On 23 April 1912 a member of the House of Representatives in Washington introduced a resolution calling for Federal recognition and decoration of the captain, officers and crew of the Cunarder *Carpathia* for their gallant service in the rescue of the survivors of the *Titanic*. It provided 'that the President on behalf

The American Cross of Honor presented to Captain Rostron on behalf of the American Cross of Honor Society. (courtesy of the Rostron family)

Gold medal of the Liverpool Shipwreck and Humane Society, presented to Captain Rostron. (courtesy of the Rostron family)

Bronze medal, made by Dieges and Clust of New York, presented to crew members of SS *Carpathia* for their part in rescuing all the survivors of *Titanic*. (MMM ref. 53.114.554)

of the Government, present medals of honor to Captain A.H. Rostron, lieutenant of the Royal Navy [sic], the officers, petty officers, and crew of the Carpathia and proposes an appropriation of $5,000 to pay for striking these medals from dies to be made at the Philadelphia mint'.[48] In New York on 29 May 1912 Captain Arthur Henry Rostron was presented with a silver loving cup and special commemorative medals on behalf of the committee of *Titanic* survivors by Mrs. Margaret (Molly) Brown.[49] The gold, silver and bronze medals, by Dieges and Clust of New York, were later distributed to more than three hundred officers and crew of the *Carpathia* who were on board during the rescue voyage. Shortly afterwards, Rostron was presented with a signed letter of thanks by President Taft at the White House in Washington. A few months later the President also presented him with the Congressional Medal of Honor, the highest award the United States could confer upon him. On the same day Lord Bryce, British Ambassador in Washington, presented him with the American Cross of Honor, on behalf of the American Cross of Honor Society.[50] Several of these items have been displayed at Merseyside Maritime Museum in recent years, by courtesy of the Rostron family.

On 6 June 1912, at the Underwriters' Room, Exchange Flags, Liverpool, Captain Rostron was presented with the gold medal and certificate of the Liverpool Shipwreck and Humane Society. The following December, at Liverpool Town Hall, the Earl of Derby, Lord Mayor of Liverpool, made various presentations to the engineers and electricians of the *Carpathia* who gave service on the night of the *Titanic* disaster. Mr. A. Johnstone, Chief Engineer, received a substantial cheque, a silver tea and coffee service and a punch bowl. The other engineers received gold watches with suitable inscriptions and monograms. A cheque for £48 was also presented to the Sailors' and Firemen's Union to be divided among the 48 greasers, firemen and trimmers, 'if the men could be found', failing which the money would be 'devoted to the Union's sick fund'.[51]

CHAPTER 11

A GREAT CALAMITY

We meet here today under the shadow of a great calamity
which has befallen the Oceanic Steam Navigation Company,
which we have the honour to serve.

Harold Sanderson
White Star Line Special Meeting, 22 April 1912[1]

The *Titanic* disaster was a bitter blow to the port and people of Liverpool. When
she embarked on her one and only voyage, the liner was the largest and most
luxurious in the world. Although she sailed from Southampton, where most of her
crew lived, she was owned and managed by the White Star Line of Liverpool. As
we have seen, the connection between the company and its Liverpool base was
very close and strong.

As in all other ports and communities affected by the tragedy, in Britain and
beyond, the blow fell hardest on the families and friends of the victims. At least
100 people with Liverpool area backgrounds, 13 of whom were passengers and 87
crew, were lost when *Titanic* sank. As we have seen, a further three 'Liverpool
crew', namely Thomas Hart, James Keegan and T. Casey, also appear on the official
list of victims of the disaster, but some doubts remain regarding their actual fates.

In all, including band members, the cases of some 74 'Liverpool' crew
victims are listed in the records of the Mansion House *Titanic* Relief Fund for
March 1913.[2] This fund was raised by public subscription on the invitation of the

Lord Mayor of London 'for the aid and relief of the widows, orphans and dependent relatives of the persons (whether crew or passengers) who lost their lives' due to the sinking of *Titanic*. An initial assessment of these records suggests that around 200 dependants of 'Liverpool area' victims were eligible for help from the fund, of whom about 100 were children. The allowances for children ceased at the age of sixteen for males and eighteen for females. A substantial proportion of these 'Liverpool-related' dependants, especially widows and children, lived in or around Southampton, as indeed did the overwhelming majority of all crew victims of the disaster and their dependants. In a number of cases 'Liverpool' crew victims had dependants in both Liverpool and Southampton.

The administration of cases was divided between 'local' committees in various parts of the UK, most notably for the London, Southampton, Exeter, Belfast and Liverpool areas. Initially the Earl of Derby, Lord Mayor of Liverpool, was chairman not only of the Liverpool Committee, but also of the National Committee for the distribution of the relief. He was said by the *Liverpool Daily Post and Mercury* to have taken the keenest interest in the work, carefully ensuring 'that full justice is meted out to every case according to its needs'.[3]

On 11 May 1912, however, two days before the Liverpool Relief Fund collection was closed, the same newspaper reported that there had already been some criticism by the Liverpool Trades and Labour Council that the money locally subscribed was being 'hoarded' or 'fenced off' from the sufferers. The latter, it was alleged, would 'have to be content with what they obtained under the Workmen's Compensation Scheme'. The Liverpool Committee immediately issued assurances that '[the] Liverpool subscriptions will be utilised solely for the dependants of local victims of the calamity, but an effort will be made to secure a uniformity in the scale of relief provided by various funds administered here, in London, or at Southampton'. In the meantime, considerable preliminary investigations were being undertaken 'by the committee and a number of ladies' into the various cases, to whom they were able to offer temporary relief with the promise of a larger grant to follow, depending on the particular circumstances of the family concerned. The report added: 'So far as the complaint that they should consult their parish clergy is concerned it need only be said that many of the applicants are illiterates, and ministers can well be relied upon sympathetically to advise them in advancing their claims'.[4]

Liverpool-based *Titanic* researcher Geoff Whitfield, who has examined the records of the Liverpool Committee, notes that the appointed 'visitor', who made regular calls on the homes of all Liverpool area recipients, was Mrs. Mary Harrison, of Baden Road, Knotty Ash, Liverpool, the widow of Norman Harrison, *Titanic*'s Junior Second Engineer.[5] She herself was one of the Liverpool area 'A' class dependants eligible for assistance from the fund.[6]

In 1916 the Mansion House Committee was reconstituted, accepting supervision of the *Titanic*, *Empress of Ireland* and *Lusitania* Relief Funds and any other funds which the Lord Mayor might entrust to them. Geoff Whitfield states that in Liverpool, at any rate, this merger took place in 1914–15.[7] In 1958–59 the *Titanic* and *Empress of Ireland* Relief Funds were liquidated and annuities purchased for surviving dependants, while the balance of the General Fund was transferred to the Shipwrecked Fishermen and Mariners' Royal Benevolent Society.[8]

By British law, the crew's employment had been ended with the sinking of the ship. However, very soon after the sinking, White Star agreed to pay all the survivors for the total time they spent away from Britain. Most received their pay for the six days of the voyage, plus an extra thirteen days' pay. Those who stayed in the United States to testify received more. At the United States Inquiry, J. Bruce Ismay undertook to employ any survivor who was willing and some certainly took up the offer. Dependants of the deceased crew received up to £300 under the Workmen's Compensation Act.[9] The amount they received was taken into account when dependants were later assessed for help from the *Titanic* Relief Fund.

On Sunday 12 May, the day after arriving back in Liverpool on the *Adriatic*, although still recovering from the horror of the *Titanic* disaster and the strain of the

United States Senate Inquiry, Bruce Ismay effectively went back to work. From 'Sandheys', his home in Mossley Hill, he wrote a letter to Lord Derby which began:

> The terrible disaster to the *Titanic* has brought prominently to my mind the fact that no permanent fund exists to assist the widows of those whose lives are lost while they are engaged upon active duties upon the mercantile vessels of this country.

He then suggested that a fund, named the 'Mercantile Marine Widows' Fund', should be created to provide pensions for the widows concerned. Ismay himself offered to donate £10,000 to this,[10] and his wife a further £1,000. He also proposed that this fund should be administered by the Liverpool-based Mercantile Marine Service Association, which already had care of the Liverpool Seamen's Pension Fund and the Margaret Ismay Fund, both of which had been established some years earlier by his father. Lord Derby readily agreed to these proposals, and the fund was duly founded.[11] It still exists today as the Mercantile Marine (Widows') Fund.

On Tuesday 14 May Ismay chaired the weekly committee meeting of the Liverpool and London Steamship Protection and Indemnity Association at 10 Water Street, Liverpool.[12] As managing director of White Star, one of its largest customers, he was chairman of this organisation, which had been created by his late father and some of his business friends in 1881 as a private insurance company for shipowners. As regards *Titanic*, the Association 'protected and indemnified' White Star for the claims relating to people or cargoes, including personal possessions, lost or damaged during the sinking.[13]

At the above meeting, chaired by Ismay, the Association authorised the settlement of all claims relating to *Titanic* crew victims under the Workmen's Compensation Act. Understandably, the chairman's signature on the minutes of this particular meeting appears to be much less confident than it had been at previous,

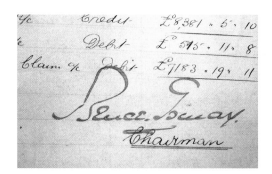
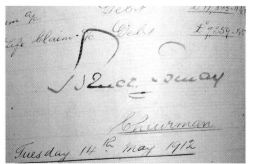

Bruce Ismay's confident signature just before leaving Liverpool for *Titanic*'s maiden voyage. (Minute Book of the Liverpool & London Steamship P & I Association, vol. 12, p.194, 26 March 1912, courtesy of Liverpool & London Steamship P & I Association)

Bruce Ismay's signature shortly after his return to Liverpool, between US and British Inquiries. Less confident, or just written in haste? (Minute Book of the Liverpool & London Steamship P & I Association, vol. 12, p.222, 14 May 1912, courtesy of Liverpool and London Steamship P & I Association)

pre-disaster meetings.[14] For most claims, Liverpool and London made direct payment to survivors or the executors of victims lost in the disaster. This led to the speedy disposal of claims. Within four months 638 claims were made of which 566 were settled, totalling over £112,000. The average amount paid out for each crew-related claim was £218.[15] As Paul Louden-Brown observes, during this very distressing period Ismay must have relived the disaster 'at virtually every meeting'.[16]

By May 1915 White Star and the Liverpool and London Association had also paid almost £87,000 for passenger claims brought in England and, by the following July, £326,960 ($1.6 million) for those brought in the United States. As well as paying its own substantial share of the total US claims and costs, White Star paid a further £21,074 towards the US claims.[17] Today (2009), the equivalent value of all these claims and costs, even after all liabilities had been duly limited by legal compromises, would be many millions of pounds. As J.G. Gregson observes, these costs 'had to be borne by the members from their own resources without the benefit of any reinsurance'.[18] Since most of the member shipping companies concerned were based in Liverpool, the financial effect on the city's shipowning community would have been significant. The Association's *Titanic* files were closed in the 1920s, but Bruce Ismay remained as chairman until 1933.[19]

Another major concern for Ismay, White Star and the IMM was that *Titanic* herself was significantly under-insured. Her hull and machinery had been only partly insured through a policy led by Commercial Union and supported by

Lloyd's Underwriters and other companies.[20] This reflects not only White Star's own financial strength at the time, but also its confidence in the quality and safety of its ships in the pre-*Titanic* era. However, in the case of *Titanic*, as *The Times* commented on 24 April 1912, since there was 'no prospect of salvage',

> the best part of a million sterling is now being found by the British insurance markets, assisted by the Continent and the United States. The owners of the *Titanic* will know what to do with the money, for though, no doubt, some time will elapse before they will want to pay for her successor, it is generally assumed that they were uninsured to the extent of between £500,000 and £750,000.[21]

This situation was confirmed at the United States Senate Inquiry a few days later by Philip Franklin, New York-based Vice-President of the IMM. He said that he did not believe that there was any company crossing the Atlantic that carried such a large proportion of its own insurance as the subsidiary companies of the IMM. As regards *Titanic*, he stated: 'This ship was insured from outside underwriters for $5,000,000, in round figures. It was, in pounds, about a million pounds. The company carried the remainder, up to about $600,000 – between $500,000 and $600,000. That is, our insurance fund carried the remainder.'[22] Bruce Ismay also confirmed these figures at the United States Inquiry, adding that the ship cost $7.5 million (or £1.5 million). He further stated that he himself had very little to do with the insurance arrangements, which were 'dealt with and handled in New York'.[23] At the British Inquiry on 4 June Ismay estimated that the initial loss borne by his company was £200,000 (equivalent to about £16.2 million in 2009).[24]

As Mark Chirnside observes, since *Titanic* cost £1.5 million and was insured for just £1 million, she was therefore only insured for two-thirds of her cost.[25] Although the financial loss caused by her sinking did not break the IMM, or indeed the White Star Line, it was certainly a considerable setback to both of them. In the event, following a temporary upsurge in transatlantic emigration, White Star enjoyed a significant rise in profits in 1913. However, thirteen months after J. Bruce Ismay resigned the First World War began and both companies faced many further problems. In April 1915 the IMM, which had been in serious financial difficulties for some time, was formally declared insolvent.[26]

In the immediate aftermath of the *Titanic* disaster, as Oldham observes, Ismay's treatment by the American press had aroused 'the sympathy and indignation' of many people around the world, and he received hundreds of letters expressing these sentiments. One, from a doctor in Kent, began: 'I am very pleased to see that the people of Liverpool had the decency to give you a hearty welcome after the callous and heartless way you were treated in America'. Another, from a British army officer, advised him that 'so long as you enjoy the confidence and esteem of your fellow townsmen you can afford to disregard vapid utterances of journalists'.[27] On the other hand, as Oldham reveals, Ismay also received 'a good many brutal anonymous letters, from which he had already suffered in America'. At this time, the White Star chairman was 'in a state of complete nervous exhaustion; he was sleeping very badly and had terrible nightmares, often waking the household with his shouts and screams as he relived in his dreams those terrible scenes aboard the sinking ship'. He was particularly distressed on one occasion when he was turned away from the door by an old friend in Liverpool whom he had tried to visit.[28]

On 28 May the United States Senate Inquiry published its findings. It made a number of recommendations for improving safety at sea, notably regarding the capacity and manning of lifeboats, boat drills, the provision of 24-hour wireless communication and the use of rockets at sea for distress signals alone. In his summing up, however, Senator William Alden Smith, the Inquiry's chairman, strongly condemned Captain Stanley Lord, master of the *Californian*, for his apparent negligence in failing to respond to *Titanic*'s distress signals. Perhaps

surprisingly, given his dealings with the White Star chairman before and during
the Inquiry, he was rather less harsh on Bruce Ismay. In his words:

> I think the presence of Mr. Ismay and Mr. Andrews stimulated the ship
> to greater speed than it would have made under ordinary conditions,
> although I cannot fairly ascribe to either of them any instructions to this
> effect. The very presence of the owner and builder unconsciously
> stimulates endeavour, and the restraint of organised society is absolutely
> necessary to safety.[29]

By this time, the British Board of Trade Inquiry into the disaster was well under way in
London. This was held over 36 days between 2 May and 26 July 1912 under the
Wreck Commissioner Lord John Charles Bigham, QC, Baron Mersey of Toxteth
(Lancashire). Bigham was born in Liverpool in 1840, the son of the Liverpool

merchant John Bigham and his wife Helen. A former pupil of the Liverpool Institute grammar school,[30] he later attended London University before completing his studies in Berlin and Paris. After a successful career as a barrister, then a judge, divided by a short period as Liberal Unionist MP for the Liverpool Exchange Division, he retired in 1910 before being raised to the peerage the following year. In May 1912, at the age of 71, he was appointed by Prime Minister Asquith as commissioner to inquire into the loss of the *Titanic*. As Senan Molony observes, Bigham and Bruce Ismay had occasionally attended the same events in Liverpool since the 1880s. Bigham, Ismay and Professor John Harvey Biles, later one of the Board of Trade assessors at the *Titanic* Inquiry, were all long-time members of the Shipwrights' Company, a professional club of which Lord Pirrie was also a member. In June 1909 all four men were guests at one of the Company's dinners in London. The previous year, at the Annual Dinner of the Chamber of Shipping, Bigham had given a toast to the full chamber in which he proposed that all connected with the industry should ensure 'that nothing was done by

Captain Lord at the British Wreck Commission's inquiry. (*Daily Sketch*)

legislation, or in other ways, which would decrease the carrying power of this great country'.[31] In Molony's opinion, Bigham was here advocating 'nothing less than a freemasonry of big shipping, whose members would act in the industry's sole interest at all times'.[32] Certainly, for a government intent on protecting the interests of the Board of Trade and the major British shipping lines, Bigham was an understandable choice as Wreck Commissioner for the *Titanic* Inquiry.

The White Star Line was represented at the Board of Trade Inquiry by a 'formidable battery of counsel' headed by the Right Honourable Sir Robert Finlay, KC, MP, and instructed by Messrs Hill, Dickinson and Company of Liverpool.[33] Among the key witnesses were Bruce Ismay and Harold Sanderson for White Star, and Edward Wilding for Harland and Wolff. Of the 48 former officers and crew of *Titanic* summoned as witnesses, at least eight had strong links with the Liverpool area, namely Charles Lightoller, Fred Barrett, Patrick Dillon, Fred Fleet, Charles Joughin, Elizabeth Leather, Joseph Wheat and Walter Wynn. Among other Liverpool-related witnesses were Captain Stanley Lord of the *Californian*, Captain Arthur Rostron of *Carpathia*, Captain Joseph Ranson of White Star's *Baltic*, and John Pritchard, former master of the Cunard Line's *Mauretania*.[34] Mr. Leonard S. Holmes, senior partner of the Liverpool firm of Miller, Taylor and Holmes, solicitors, was also in attendance. His firm was representing the Imperial Merchant Service Guild, to which five of *Titanic*'s officers belonged.[35]

Accompanied by his wife, Bruce Ismay attended the Inquiry on 4 and 5 June (Days 16 and 17), when he answered over eight hundred questions covering the history of *Titanic* from construction to disaster, including his own controversial survival of the sinking. In some ways the experience was even more gruelling for him than the United States Senate Inquiry, mainly due to the hostility which he felt some of the counsel displayed towards him.[36] Many years later Florence Ismay would privately refer to these hearings as 'that terrible Inquiry'. Afterwards, the Ismays went to Scotland for a short holiday at Bruce's brother's home in Perthshire. Harold Sanderson's letters to Ismay at this time show that he was very concerned about his old friend's 'morbid' state of mind. So, too, was the Reverend Canon George Harford, MA, vicar of Mossley Hill Parish Church, near Ismay's home in south Liverpool. In July he wrote a sympathetic letter to his parishioner which included the following comments:

> Least of all, it seems to me, have you anything to reproach yourself for. [...] That you did not commit suicide by refusing to take an empty place in a boat, which there was no one else to take – so far from being to your discredit – was, to my mind, a mark of courage, whereas the suicide is commonly a coward, and a mean one at that.[37]

The report of the British Inquiry was published on 30 July. It concluded that *Titanic*'s loss was 'due to collision with an iceberg, brought about by the excessive speed at which the ship was being navigated'. In considering what Captain Smith should have done, Lord Mersey observed that for at least a quarter of a century liners using the same track in the vicinity of ice and in clear weather had kept to the course, maintained speed and kept a sharp lookout. This practice had 'been justified by experience, no casualties having resulted from it'. However, *Titanic*'s loss had shown that this practice was 'bad': 'Its root is probably to be found in competition and in the desire of the public for quick passages rather than in the judgement of navigators'. With regard to Smith, the Commissioner concluded: 'He made a mistake, a very grievous mistake, but one in which, in face of the practice of past experience, negligence cannot be said to have had any part'.[38]

Other conclusions followed in a similar vein. The Inquiry found that a proper watch was not kept, that the ship's boats were not properly manned, that the Leyland liner *Californian* might have reached *Titanic* if she had attempted to do so, and that there was no discrimination against Third Class passengers in the saving of life. Lord Mersey also severely censured the Board of Trade for its failure to revise the shipping rules of 1894 regarding lifeboat provision for the largest passenger liners. A number of recommendations were then made to improve regulations and practices relating to safety at sea.[39]

In his revealing memoirs of his seafaring career, published in 1935, Charles Lightoller, *Titanic*'s most senior surviving officer, gave his verdict on the Board of Trade Inquiry. In his view:

> A washing of dirty linen would help no-one. The B.O.T. [Board of Trade]
> had passed that ship as in all respects fit for sea in every sense of the word,
> with sufficient margin of safety for everyone on board. Now the B.O.T. was
> holding an enquiry into the loss of that ship — hence the whitewash brush.
> [...] I think in the end the B.O.T. and the White Star Line won.[40]

As regards Bruce Ismay, the Inquiry effectively exonerated him from an attack which had been 'made in the course of the inquiry' as to his moral conduct during the sinking. Although Lord Mersey considered such matters to be 'no part of the business of the Court', he rejected the suggestion that some moral duty was imposed on Mr. Ismay, as managing director of the steamship company, to wait on board until the vessel foundered. In his words: 'Mr. Ismay, after rendering assistance to many passengers, found "C" collapsible. the last boat on the starboard side, actually being lowered. No other people were there at the time. There was room for him, and he jumped in. Had he not jumped in he would merely have added one more life, namely his own, to the number of those lost.'[41]

Captain Stanley Lord was not so fortunate. He had attended the Inquiry on Tuesday 14 May, and answered over seven hundred questions. Based on the time it took his ship to arrive at *Titanic*'s wreck site in the morning of 15 April, Lord estimated that the *Californian*, when she stopped for the night, must have been between twenty-five and thirty miles away from *Titanic* when the latter struck the iceberg.[42] He also maintained that the steamer which had approached *Californian* at about 11 pm, which he believed had fired rockets later in the evening, was only six or seven miles away, and was much too small to be *Titanic*.[43] As he plausibly argued, 'a ship like the *Titanic* at sea it is an utter impossibility for anyone to mistake'.[44]

Unfortunately, the evidence given by some of his crew contradicted him. Furthermore, Lord Mersey, in his final report, stated that he was convinced by the evidence presented to him 'that the ship seen by the *Californian* was the *Titanic*, and if so, according to Captain Lord, the two vessels were about five miles apart at the time of the disaster. When she first saw the rockets the *Californian* could have pushed through the ice to the open water without any serious risk and so have come to the assistance of the *Titanic*. Had she done so she might have saved many if not all of the lives that were lost.'[45]

Captain Lord's own verdict was that Lord Mersey 'had made up his mind before he started the inquiry, and was disinclined to listen to any further evidence'.[46] He felt that he had, in effect, been convicted without trial, and been made 'a goat' for the disaster. However, his requests for a re-hearing of the evidence were refused. The Board of Trade also decided not to prosecute him for allegedly failing to go to the assistance of a vessel in distress. Lord had been a witness at the Inquiry, not a defendant, but if the Board had attempted to withdraw his master's certificate he would have been able to call his own witnesses and cross-examine others.[47] Despite retaining the full confidence of the Liverpool managers of the Leyland Line, he was soon forced to resign from his position with the company. He was informed that the board of directors in London had decided that public opinion was against him.[48] Within a few months he had accepted a job as master with the Nitrate Producers' Steamship Company of London. He served at sea with the company throughout the First World War, and continued to command its vessels until March 1927, when he was forced to retire due to poor eyesight.[49]

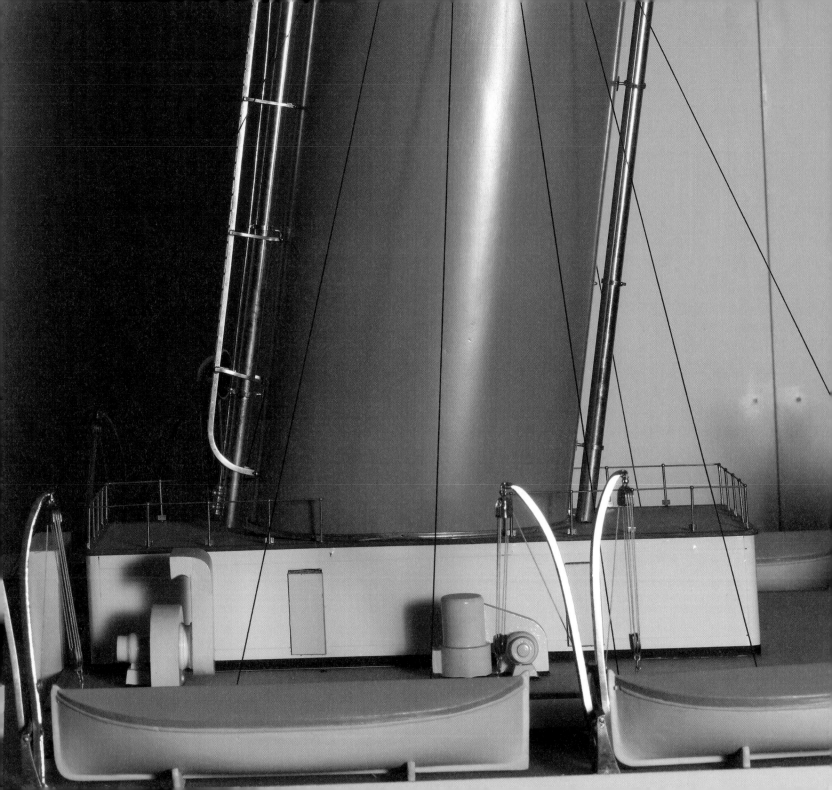

CHAPTER 12

A LONG SHADOW

The *Titanic* disaster almost ruined our lives.

Florence Ismay (wife of J. Bruce Ismay)[1]

Unfortunately for Bruce Ismay, his sympathetic treatment by Lord Mersey regarding his escape from *Titanic* was not the end of the matter. In late February 1912, several weeks before *Titanic* sailed, he and Harold Sanderson had agreed that he would retire as president of the IMM, to be succeeded in this post by his old friend on 30 June 1913. This proposal had been provisionally accepted by Charles Steele, secretary to Morgan and Company, New York. In private, however, Ismay's requests, following the loss of *Titanic*, to remain as either chairman or director of the White Star Line were rejected by the board of the IMM in October 1912, due, no doubt, to the treatment which their president had received in the press. In the event, on 30 June 1913 Ismay retired not only from the presidency of the IMM but also, much more reluctantly, from the chairmanship of White Star, being succeeded in both positions by Harold Sanderson. This marked the end of the long involvement of the Ismay family in the direct management of the White Star Line.[2]

Over the next few years the White Star Line had to defend itself vigorously against claims of negligence brought by *Titanic* passengers and their dependants in court cases in London and New York State. In May 1915 Bruce Ismay made sworn depositions for the New York State hearings in reply to questions about whether or not he influenced the speed of the ship, her intended arrival time in New York, or her design, including her lifeboat provision. As at the United States Senate and British Board of Trade inquiries, he denied suggestions that, while on board, he had played any part in influencing the speed of the ship. He also denied that he had any direct role in determining the number of lifeboats carried. With regard to the ship's speed and her intended arrival time in New York, he stated, referring to his meeting with Chief Engineer Bell while *Titanic* was at Queenstown: 'The whole thing was arranged beforehand. It is a regular rule of the Company that the ships when they are on the long track are not to arrive at New York before Wednesday morning, and it was simply confirming what Mr. Bell already knew. It has been the practice of the Company for fifteen years, I should think.'[3]

With this key issue in mind, on his retirement from White Star and the IMM Ismay had entrusted his Liverpool-based solicitor, Mr. F.M. Radcliffe,[4] with copies of correspondence which he had had, between July and September 1911, with Philip Franklin, his IMM vice-president in New York, regarding *Olympic*'s arrival times in New York. Office copies of these very significant documents were donated to the Merseyside Maritime Museum in 1984.[5] They reveal that, only a few months before *Titanic*'s maiden voyage, Bruce Ismay had resisted strong pressure from Philip Franklin and other American directors of the IMM in favour of *Olympic* arriving in New York on Tuesday evenings, rather than Wednesday mornings, as originally scheduled. As Paul Louden-Brown argues, these documents certainly add considerable weight to Ismay's repeated denials that he ever urged either Chief Engineer Bell or Captain Smith to increase *Titanic*'s speed so that she would arrive in New York on Tuesday evening.[6] Also in this collection is a handwritten letter sent from New York by Chief Engineer Joseph Bell to the 'Chief Engineer' in White Star's steamship department in Liverpool, in which he reports on the performance of *Olympic*'s engines and other machinery immediately after her maiden voyage. A further important document is a draft cable from the White Star Line in Liverpool to its New York office regarding emergency coaling arrangements for *Olympic* and *Titanic* due to the coal strike.[7]

Although he was broadly successful in limiting the financial damage to White Star as a result of the *Titanic* disaster, Bruce Ismay was never able fully to repair the damage done to his own reputation by the unproven allegations and insinuations made against him at the time. However, although perhaps 'never the same again'[8] after *Titanic*, Ismay was not, as is sometimes claimed, a broken man, and he did not become a recluse. After retiring from both the IMM and the White Star Line, he was involved, almost until the day he died, as chairman or director of several important companies in Liverpool and London.[9] Deeply moved by the huge death toll of ordinary sailors during the First World War, in 1919 he donated £25,000 (approximately £1.25 million today) to found the National Mercantile Marine Fund to make provision for the widows and children of merchant sailors, giving preference to dependants of sailors born in Liverpool.

Largely at his wife's insistence, in 1920 Ismay sold 'Sandheys' in Mossley Hill and his house in Hill Street, London became his main residence.[10] Most Sunday evenings he would travel by train to Liverpool to conduct his remaining business and charitable interests in the city, before returning to London on Wednesday. He always stayed at the North Western Hotel on Lime Street, and enjoyed attending concerts in nearby St George's Hall. According to Oldham, he would purchase two tickets, the second one for his hat and coat.[11] Bruce Ismay's health began to fail when he was about seventy years old. Following a circulatory problem his right leg was amputated below the knee. He died of a stroke in 1937, aged 74. In Liverpool, flags on civic buildings were flown at half-mast.[12] J. Bruce Ismay's estate amounted to almost £700,000.

Soon after the disaster a scheme was launched in Liverpool to erect a 'national memorial' in the city to the engine-room staff of the *Titanic*. On 27 April 1912 *The Times* reported that a committee of engineers and members of allied professions had been formed in Liverpool to organise a fund on an extensive scale to erect such a memorial. As the writer observed: 'Out of a trained staff of 32 men, including engineers, electricians, and boilermakers, on board the Titanic not one was saved, and the memorial will indicate public appreciation of this marked devotion to duty'.[13]

Further details of this scheme were revealed by the *Liverpool Daily Post and Mercury* on 4 May. With the approval of the Lord Mayor of Liverpool, Lord Derby, preliminary measures were being taken by the committee, which included 'all the superintendent engineers of the great steamship lines in Liverpool, together with representatives of other branches of the engineering profession and of the University'. A 'very influential general committee' was in course of formation, and Mrs. Asquith, wife of the Prime Minister, had already forwarded the sum of £15 to the fund 'and expressed her high appreciation of such a brave deed'.[14]

The following day *The Observer* reported that the memorial committee, under the chairmanship of Lord Derby, had decided that the memorial would consist of 'an elaborate group of statuary [...] the riverside scheme at present in contemplation will [...] surpass in architectural beauty the Statue of Liberty at New York'.[15] Further progress was made at a meeting six weeks later, with the Earl of Derby again in the chair, seconded by Sir William Lever. Having referred to recent 'labour unrest', and the despondency spread by 'pessimists', Lord Derby said that the deeds of the 'Engine Room Heroes' proved that England's people were 'composed of the same material as those who made England great in the past'.[16]

The sculptor chosen for the project was Sir William Goscombe John, who, between 1912 and 1913, produced a design featuring four seven-foot-high figures in granite to represent the 36 engineers and more than two hundred stokehold crew who did not survive the sinking. At the suggestion of Liverpool city councillor Percy Corkhill, Goscombe John chose local seamen as models for the four figures which dominate the design.[17]

By the end of July a signboard had been placed in position to mark the site of the proposed monument. 'More artistic in design than the majority of such erections', as the *Liverpool Daily Post* commented, this notice had been placed in a 'commanding situation at a point on the Pierhead where it not only overlooks the Landing-stage, but must inevitably attract the attention of all proceeding to or emerging from the Princes Parade'.[18] The writer concluded by praising the 'peculiar appropriateness and effectiveness' of the chosen site.

However, not everyone in the city agreed with this assessment. In a meeting of Liverpool City Council in September 1912, Councillor David Jackson moved that the resolution allocating a site for the memorial on the river front should be withdrawn. Without wishing to deprecate the heroism of the *Titanic*'s engine-room men, he said that they did not want, on the river at all events, 'a whited sepulchre keeping in mind for all time the greatest calamity of the sea. It would be a gravestone reminding all people who come to Liverpool of the terrors of the sea.' Councillor Jackson argued that the Council should regard the matter 'commercially as well as sentimentally'. They were troubled by the cry of 'lifeboats for all', but if before people went on board ship they were taken past such a memorial on the river front they would exclaim 'Look at this! Enough! Good-bye!'[19]

Although Councillor Jackson's rescinding motion was comfortably rejected by the meeting, it still gained considerable support from writers to newspapers and others in the city. The controversy raged for well over a year. In September 1914, for example, Liverpool's satirical journal *Porcupine* stated:

> there are some tragedies so stupendous, so appalling in their nature, that
> it is best to draw the kindly veil of oblivion over them. Such an one was
> the fate of the "Titanic". We do not want it continually thrust upon our
> memory, but, if the Council persists in its pig-headedness, it is likely to be
> so. [...] There are many more appropriate sites in our city, and
> Mr. Jackson's suggestion of a suitable spot in St. John's Garden could
> hardly be improved on. But place it anywhere – except at the Pierhead.[20]

By this time, however, the fundraising campaign for the memorial had been overtaken by that of Southampton, which by late April 1914 had already erected a memorial, specifically to *Titanic*'s 'Engineer Officers', in that city's Andrews

The 'Titanic memorial' near Liverpool's Pier Head, 2007.

Park.[21] The following month the Liverpool campaign was further overshadowed by the sinking, in late May 1914, of the Liverpool-based Canadian Pacific liner *Empress of Ireland*. This horrific incident followed a collision, at night and in thick fog, with the Norwegian collier *Storstadt* in the St. Lawrence River, Canada. Most of the *Empress*'s 1054 passengers and 413 crew were asleep at the time. Largely because she sank in less than fifteen minutes, even more passengers (840) died on the *Empress* than on *Titanic* (817). No less than 172 crew, mostly from the Liverpool area, also died.[22] An even greater setback to the *Titanic* memorial project was the outbreak, a few months later, of the First World War.

By the time the memorial was unveiled on Liverpool's Pier Head in May 1916, thousands of British merchant seamen had been killed and hundreds of British and Empire ships had been sunk, mainly since Germany had unleashed its campaign of unrestricted submarine warfare in February 1915. The largest and most significant victim of this campaign had been the Liverpool-based Cunard liner *Lusitania*, sunk in May that year with the loss of 1201 lives. As with the *Empress of Ireland* disaster just before the war, most of the hundreds of crew members lost were from the Liverpool area.[23] In the meantime, many others had died on less well-known ships. The memorial was therefore dedicated to 'The Heroes of the Marine Engine Room', including the many engineers and support staff who had died due to enemy action during the war. Although originally conceived specifically as a memorial to the engineers of the *Titanic*, and paid for by international subscription, it thereby became, in effect, as Jonathan Black observes, 'one of the first Great War memorials to be erected in the United Kingdom'.[24] Even so, the monument is still identified most strongly with the *Titanic* and arouses great interest because of this. Its real significance in British public sculpture, as Joseph Sharples comments, is that it is 'an exceptionally early monument to the heroic working man'.[25]

Today in Liverpool there are a few other *Titanic*-related memorials which were erected in the aftermath of the sinking. One is a stained glass window

Bronze tablet at the Philharmonic Hall, Liverpool, dedicated to the 'Members of the Band on board the Titanic. They bravely continued playing to soothe the anguish of their fellow passengers until the ship sank in the deep. April 14th 1912. Courage and compassion joined make the hero and the man complete.'

commemorating Captain Smith, which was installed in Liverpool's Anglican Cathedral in 1914. Like the statue of Smith erected in Hanley, Staffordshire, where he was born, this was funded by public subscription and organised by the Smith Memorial Committee, mainly consisting of wealthy Britons and Americans who had sailed with him.[26] Another is a bronze plaque to the memory of *Titanic*'s bandsmen, which can be seen at the city's Philharmonic Hall in Myrtle Street. This may well have resulted from the special benefit performance held at the Hall in May 1912 for the mother and sisters of *Titanic* bandsman Fred Clarke, a former member of the Liverpool Philharmonic Orchestra.[27] There is also a brass and wooden plaque to the bandsmen in the Liverpool City Mission, Jubilee Drive, Edge Hill, Liverpool. Originally in the Beacon Hall, Wavertree Road, Edge Hill, Liverpool, this was funded shortly after the disaster by public subscription.[28] Finally, there is a memorial plaque at St Faith's Church, Waterloo dedicated to *Titanic*'s Chief Engineer Joseph Bell and his staff, all of whom were lost in the sinking.[29]

As we have seen, there are only two graves of *Titanic* victims in Liverpool today, namely those of First Class passenger Alfred Rowe and Saloon Steward Arthur Lawrence.[30] However, at least 16 of the ship's officers and crew victims are remembered on family gravestones in or near the city. They are listed in Table 3. Second Class passenger Joseph Fynney is also remembered on the family gravestone at Anfield Cemetery in Liverpool.

Seven Liverpool crew victims were buried at Fairview Lawn Cemetery, Halifax, Nova Scotia. These were: Henry (Harry) Ashe, William Carney, Alfred Fellowes, Ernest Freeman, James Hutchinson, John Reginald Rice and Robert Arthur Wareham. Bandsman Fred Clarke was buried at Mount Olivet Cemetery in the same port. The bodies of four Liverpool crew were recovered before being buried at sea, namely Thomas Hewitt, Hugh McElroy, Hugh Roberts and L. Turner. At least 66 other Liverpool crew victims were either never found, or never identified.

As we have seen, at least four passengers and 28 crew with close connections to the Liverpool area survived the *Titanic* disaster.[31] Two of the passengers, namely

Table 3 *Titanic* officers and crew remembered on family gravestones in the Liverpool area.

Surname	Forenames/Initials	Rank / position	Family gravestone location
Ashcroft	Austin Aloysius	Clerk	St Peter & St Paul RC Church, Crosby, Liverpool
Ashe	Henry (Harry) Wellesley	Glory Hole Steward	Kirkdale Cemetery, Walton, Liverpool
Davies (Davis)	Gordon Raleigh	Bedroom Steward	Kirkdale Cemetery, Walton, Liverpool
Dodd	George Charles	Steward	Wallasey Cemetery, Rake Lane, Cheshire.
Farquharson	William Edward	Senior Second Engineer	Toxteth Park Cemetery, Smithdown Road, Liverpool
Fay	Thomas Joseph	Greaser	Ford RC Cemetery, Litherland, Liverpool
Freeman	Ernest Edward Samuel	Deck Steward	Walton Park Cemetery, Walton, Liverpool
Harrison	Norman E.	Junior Second Engineer	Knotty Ash Parish Church, Liverpool
Maxwell	John	Carpenter / Joiner	Kirkdale Cemetery, Walton, Liverpool
McElroy	Hugh Walter	Purser	Anfield Cemetery, Liverpool
McInerney	Thomas	Greaser	Ford RC Cemetery, Litherland, Liverpool
Morgan (Bird)	Charles Frederick	Assistant Storekeeper	Flaybrick Hill Cemetery, Tollemache Road, Birkenhead
Sloan	Peter	Chief Electrician	Anfield Cemetery, Liverpool
Wilde	Henry Tingle	Chief Officer / Chief Mate	Kirkdale Cemetery, Walton, Liverpool
Williams	Arthur J.	Assistant Storekeeper	Anfield Cemetery, Liverpool
Wilson	Bertie	Senior Assistant Second Engineer	St Luke's Churchyard, Crosby, Liverpool

Bruce Ismay and Lily Bonnell, soon returned to live in the area. It is not yet known how many of the Liverpool-connected crew did likewise. Most appear to have resumed their seafaring careers as soon as possible after the sinking, either from Southampton or from Liverpool. Among those who are thought to have returned to live in the Liverpool area at about this time were:

William Clark(e), Fireman
Ruth Bowker, First Cashier, *à la carte* restaurant
Patrick Dillon, Trimmer (died Liverpool 1939)
William Faulkner, Bedroom Steward
Charles Joughin, Chief Baker (died Paterson, New Jersey, USA, 1956)
Thomas Jones, Able Seaman
Elizabeth Leather (née Edwards), Stewardess
Arthur McMicken, Saloon Steward
Sarah Stap, Stewardess (died Birkenhead, 1937)
John Thompson, Fireman
Thomas Threlfall, Leading Fireman (died 1934)
William Wright, 'Glory Hole' Steward

Liverpool-Irish fireman William Clark, from Bootle, not only survived *Titanic*, but, two years later, also survived the sinking of the *Empress of Ireland*.[32] Joughin and Thompson emigrated to the United States.[33] Another who eventually settled in Liverpool was Irish-born steward William Burke. As we shall see, he was certainly living in Liverpool in the 1950s. Whether or not he had previous links with the city is not yet known.

Stewardess Annie Robinson, from Bedford, moved to Liverpool soon after the disaster and worked for the Mersey Docks and Harbour Board. When presented to King George V and Queen Mary during their visit to Liverpool in 1913, she said that she preferred not to think about the disaster. Sadly, she died the following year, having thrown herself from the Leyland Line steamer *Devonian* during a heavy fog in the North Atlantic. Mrs. Robinson had been intending to visit friends and relatives in Boston, Massachusetts. Officers of the vessel reported that she had been in a high state of excitement because of the fog and the sounding of the foghorn. This tragic incident may well have been due to what we now call post-traumatic stress disorder. A few years before the *Titanic* disaster, Mrs. Robinson had been on board another ship which had collided with an iceberg in the North Atlantic, namely the Liverpool-based Canadian Pacific steamer *Lake Champlain*. It may also be significant that the *Carpathia*, having rescued all of the *Titanic*'s survivors, including Mrs. Robinson, had sounded her foghorn as she carefully moved away from the rescue site.[34]

Stewardess Annie Robinson talks to *Titanic* steward J. Whitter at Plymouth after the disaster. (© Southampton City Council Arts & Heritage Services)

However, for most of the shipping community in Liverpool, despite the enormous shock caused by the *Titanic* disaster, life and business soon returned to normal. The Liverpool Steam Ship Owners' Association, for example, according to its centenary historian L.H. Powell, considered the public's 'natural alarm' at the catastrophe as 'perhaps, a little hysterical'. It thus held firm to its previous policy that 'the safety of life at sea must, in the main, be dependent on the ship herself, the ship being the highest type the naval architect and the shipbuilder were able to provide'. In its view, the skill and care with which ships had been navigated were indicated by the fact that, 'during the twenty years preceding the loss of the Titanic, upwards of 8,000,000 passengers were carried across the North Atlantic in vessels belonging to the Association with the loss of only twenty-four lives'.[35]

It was soon also 'business as usual' for the White Star Line, which in 1913 achieved a significant rise in profits due to a surge in transatlantic emigration. In April 1915, on the other hand, its parent company, the IMM, was declared bankrupt.[36] Having played a major part in assisting the Allied cause during the First World War, White Star, like all North Atlantic shipping companies, suffered badly from the effects of the Immigration Restriction Act passed in the United States in 1921. As Paul Louden-Brown comments, the complicated and unwieldy

The builder's model of *Olympic/Titanic/Britannic* leaves Liverpool Museum for Pinewood Studios, Surrey, for research prior to the production of the British film *A Night To Remember*. (1958)

Titanic's former 4th Officer Joseph Boxhall examines Liverpool Museums' *Olympic/Titanic/Britannic* model at Pinewood Studios prior to production of the British film *A Night To Remember*. (courtesy of the Titanic Historical Society, Inc.)

quota system introduced by this Act 'spelt financial ruin' for all the shipping companies concerned. In November 1926 the IMM sold White Star to the Royal Mail Steam Packet Company, and the Line became entirely British-owned and British-controlled once more. However, Lord Kylsant's huge Royal Mail Group proved to be unmanageable, and White Star, according to one observer, was 'sucked dry like the proverbial orange' to pay dividends for the other companies.[37] In May 1934, having returned losses for four years and under pressure from the British government, the company's managers signed an agreement with Cunard to form a combined company known as Cunard White Star Limited. In 1949 Cunard took overall control of the company, and the White Star name was removed from its title. The last ship to fly the White Star flag was *Britannic* (III), which was scrapped in December 1960.[38]

Even in its later years the White Star Line still retained some of the quality and prestige which it had displayed in its late Victorian and Edwardian heyday. Nevertheless, the loss of *Titanic* undoubtedly marked the end of a 'golden era' in the company's history. Never again would it quite rise to the lustrous heights it had achieved in those heady years before the disaster.

On Monday 4 August 1958 three *Titanic* crew survivors attended one of the first Merseyside showings of the British film *A Night To Remember* at the Odeon cinema in London Road, Liverpool. They were Tom Jones (age 78), William (Billy) Burke (76) and Arthur McMicken (69). Two members of the crew of the rescue ship *Carpathia*, namely Tom Gould and John Kirkpatrick, also attended.[39] These men had responded to an invitation from Mr. C.H. Dracott, general manager of the cinema, to all survivors of the *Titanic* and anyone who had been aboard *Carpathia* when the survivors were rescued. Tom Jones had previously been invited to attend a showing of the same film at the Odeon cinema in Crewe, Cheshire, followed by an evening reception. The next morning he had been introduced to Kenneth More, one of the stars of the film, who presented him with a copy of Walter Lord's book, on which the film had been based. According to the *Liverpool Echo*, 'When Mr. Jones congratulated him on his performance, Mr. More replied that it was he who was to be complimented. It was an honour, he said, to have met him.'[40]

When interviewed 'over a noggin or two' after the Liverpool showing, John Kirkpatrick, former quartermaster of the *Carpathia*, commented: 'I saw many dreadful things at sea during the wars afterwards, but never anything that horrified me half so much as that loss of the *Titanic*.'[41] Some years later, Mr. Kirkpatrick presented a metal nameplate from one of *Titanic*'s lifeboats, which he had acquired as a souvenir while on *Carpathia*'s rescue voyage, to the Mercantile Marine Service Association in Liverpool. This nameplate is now in the collection of Merseyside Maritime Museum.[42] The Museum also has a pair of thole pins and a survivor's lifejacket, retrieved from another of *Titanic*'s lifeboats, which were donated in 1962 by ex-*Carpathia* waiter Mr. Ernest St Clair, of West Derby, Liverpool.[43]

Someone who did not attend the showing of *A Night To Remember* in Liverpool was 81-year-old Captain Stanley Lord, former master of the Leyland Line steamer *Californian*. Having lost his wife the previous year, and with rapidly failing

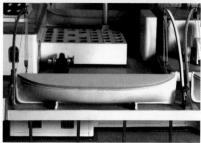

The twenty-foot builder's model of *Olympic/Titanic/Britannic*, on display as *Titanic* at Merseyside Maritime Museum, Liverpool.

Detail from the *Titanic* model at Merseyside Maritime Museum, Liverpool.

Titanic brass lifeboat nameplate, souvenir of *Carpathia* quartermaster J.J. Kirkpatrick. (MMM ref. 1966.15)

A lifejacket worn by a *Titanic* survivor, later donated to Liverpool Museums by Ernest St. Clair, former waiter on SS *Carpathia*. The securing tapes have been cut, probably when the jacket was removed from the survivor. (MMM ref. 1962.342.1)

Thole pins (rowlocks) from a *Titanic* lifeboat, souvenirs of Ernest St. Clair, waiter on SS *Carpathia*. (MMM ref. 1962.342.2)

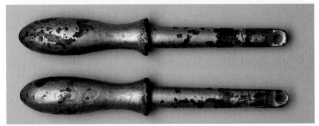

Brass White Star Line burgees or flags from a *Titanic* lifeboat, souvenirs of *Carpathia* able seaman Morgan. The original white and red paint surface has worn away. (Courtesy of Mr. Morgan, Lancaster)

eyesight, he was still living in Wallasey, Cheshire, just across the River Mersey from Liverpool. He had recently read the serialisation, in the *Liverpool Echo*, of the book by Walter Lord on which the new film had been based. He had not been impressed. He then read a review of the film in the *Sunday Express* which stated:

> Only ten miles away the lights of another ship, the *Californian*, winked as she rode at anchor. Her only radio operator was in bed. Her officers watched the *Titanic*'s desperate flares going up and wondered why a big ship was firing rockets so persistently into the middle of the night. They did nothing. As Captain Smith realised that, to all intents and purposes a ship which could save them all was watching and ignoring, he murmured: 'God help them'.[44]

This reignited the deep sense of injustice which had tormented Captain Lord for over half a century. The next morning, he took the ferry across to Liverpool and walked the short distance to the head office of the Mercantile Marine Service Association, in Rumford Place. Lord had been a member of this organisation since 1897, and he asked it to take up his case and finally clear his name. The association agreed, and Leslie Harrison, its General Secretary, became responsible for leading

a long campaign on Lord's behalf.[45] Merseyside Maritime Museum holds Captain Lord's career papers and documents concerning the MMSA's campaign from 1958 onwards to clear his name.[46] The Board of Trade refused to reopen Lord's case, choosing to stand by the findings of Lord Mersey's inquiry of 1912 which had condemned him without right of appeal.

Captain Stanley Lord died, at the age of 84, in 1962, and was buried in Rake Lane Cemetery, Wallasey. His gravestone makes no mention of his long seafaring career.[47] Sadly, he died long before the exact position of *Titanic*'s wreckage was found. This discovery, in 1985, appeared to confirm his estimate, given at both the American and British Inquiries, that his ship had been at least nineteen miles from *Titanic* when she was sinking.[48] Largely because of this, in 1990–92 an official reappraisal of the evidence was carried out by the Marine Accident Investigation Branch of the Department of Transport in Britain. Regrettably, the report's findings

White Star Line 3rd Class hot chocolate cup, salvaged from *Titanic*'s wreck site. (courtesy of Liverpool & London Steamship P & I Association)

United States five dollar bill, salvaged from *Titanic*'s wreck site. (courtesy of Liverpool & London Steamship P & I Association)

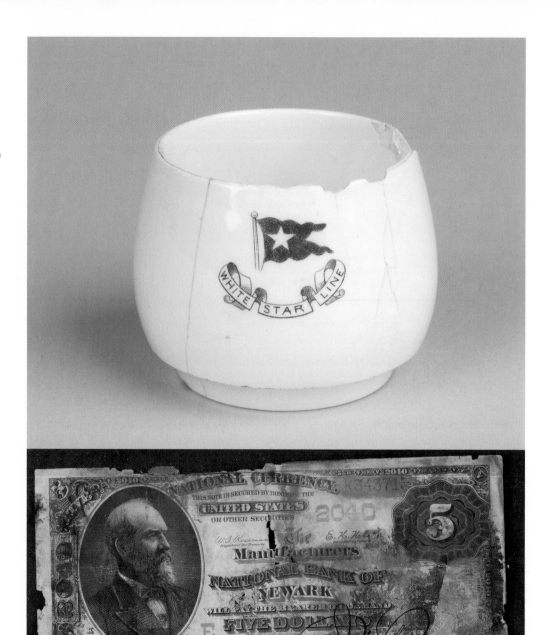

were ambiguous and inconclusive. Although it declared that the *Californian* had probably been 'between seventeen and twenty miles from *Titanic*', the opinions of the inspectors concerned were divided. On the one hand, the investigation found that *Titanic*'s distress signals had been seen on the *Californian* and that no proper action was taken. On the other hand, it stated that any reasonable action by Captain Lord would not have led to a different outcome to the tragedy, since his ship would have arrived on the scene well after *Titanic* had sunk. Today, nearly fifty years after Captain Lord's death, the fierce controversy surrounding his role, and that of his ship, in the *Titanic* story shows no signs of abating.[49]

After the discovery of *Titanic*'s wreck site in 1985, almost six thousand artefacts from the ship and its debris field were recovered by Atlanta-based salvors RMS *Titanic* Inc. When the original *Titanic* salvage case was filed in the US District Court for the Eastern District of Virginia in 1993, the only claimant to appear at the court was a representative of the Liverpool and London Steamship Protection and Indemnity Association.[50] As we have seen, soon after the disaster, this Liverpool-based insurance company, of which Bruce Ismay was chairman, paid compensation to many victims and their families for injuries, loss of life and property. In 1994 the 'salvors-in-possession' presented the company with a small number of artefacts from the wreck site to acknowledge the important role it played in the aftermath of the sinking. A selection of these items has recently been displayed at Merseyside Maritime Museum.

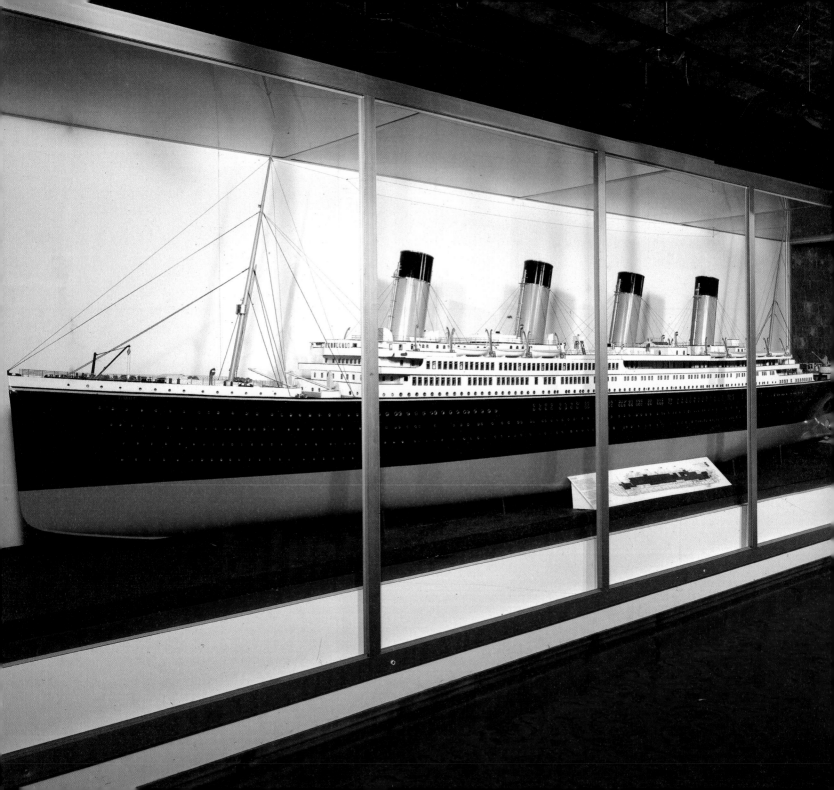

CONCLUSION

In 1912 Liverpool was the world's foremost liner port and 'the supreme example of a commercial port at a time of Britain's greatest global influence'.[1] For any ship to have Liverpool as her port of registration was therefore a matter of great significance, especially if that ship happened to be the largest and most luxurious in the world at the time. In the case of *Titanic* it meant that, even though in her brief career she never visited her 'official home port', she was still very much a Liverpool ship.

Born of the long-standing collaboration between the White Star Line of Liverpool and Harland and Wolff shipbuilders of Belfast, *Titanic* was also a by-product of American financier J.P. Morgan's doomed attempt to secure a monopoly of the lucrative North Atlantic passenger trade. The Morgan Combine's purchase of the White Star Line in 1902 was belatedly seen by the British government as a serious threat to Britain's commercial and naval interests. It therefore intervened by funding the Cunard Line, White Star's main Liverpool-based rival, to build *Lusitania* and *Mauretania*, which on completion in 1907 became 'the largest and fastest ships in the world'. It also insisted that White Star and other British lines acquired by Morgan must only fly the British flag and employ British crews.

In January 1907, as *Lusitania* and *Mauretania* were nearing completion, Bruce Ismay, chairman of White Star and then also president of Morgan's International Mercantile Marine Company, decided to switch White Star's New York mail steamers from Liverpool to Southampton. This was partly to avoid the fierce competition of the two new Cunarders 'on his own doorstep' in Liverpool, and partly to challenge the fast German liners which had been capturing much of the First Class passenger trade from the United Kingdom to New York by calling at Southampton. This explains why both *Olympic* and *Titanic* would later sail from Southampton rather than Liverpool.

A few months after this decision, Ismay and Pirrie, with the enthusiastic endorsement of J.P. Morgan, decided to build the first two 'Olympic' class liners, of which *Titanic* would be the second. Whether this would ever have happened had the Morgan Combine not previously acquired White Star and thus substantially 'changed its terms of reference' is a matter for speculation. In the event, the scene was set for one of the most appalling disasters in maritime history.

Yet if both *Olympic* and *Titanic* were thus, in a sense, pieces in an international chess game, their immediate destinies remained very much in the hands of the White Star Line of Liverpool. Even the considerable cost of financing these ships appears to have been arranged by White Star itself, at its own expense, without direct assistance from J.P. Morgan. After the essential details of design, construction and fit-out had been agreed with Harland and Wolff, most of the major decisions regarding both ships were either made or approved in White Star's head office in Liverpool. These included the scheduling and routing of voyages, the provision of supplies, the insurance of cargoes and passengers and the selection of officers and other senior crew. This also largely explains why so many of the key personnel on *Titanic*'s delivery and maiden voyages had strong Liverpool area backgrounds.

The overwhelming majority (656) of *Titanic*'s crew gave addresses in the Southampton area on the crew list for her ill-fated maiden voyage.[2] In terms of crew casualties, Southampton thus suffered far more than any other British port as a result of the disaster. However, at least 80 of the crew who gave a Southampton address on the crew list also had strong links with the Liverpool area, including, in some cases, homes and families. A further 31 specifically gave home addresses in the Liverpool area. In all, therefore, more than a hundred, or about one in eight, of *Titanic*'s crew on her maiden voyage had strong or long-standing connections with the Liverpool area.

More significant, however, was the fact that on the British side it was mainly Liverpool-based or Liverpool-connected people who played the most prominent roles in her tragic maiden voyage and its aftermath. These included Bruce Ismay, Captain Smith, Henry Wilde, William Murdoch, Charles Lightoller, Fred Fleet, Joseph Bell and most of his senior engineers, Hugh McElroy, Andrew Latimer, Fred Barrett, Tom Jones and Charles Joughin. Then there was Captain Arthur Rostron of the rescue ship *Carpathia*, Captain Stanley Lord of the *Californian*, and Lord Mersey of Toxteth, Wreck Commissioner for the British Board of Trade Inquiry.

Liverpool was one of number of ports and cities on both sides of the Atlantic which played major roles in the *Titanic* story. The others were Belfast, Southampton, Cherbourg, Queenstown, New York and Halifax, Nova Scotia. Until now, however, in terms of due historical coverage, the most notable and surprising 'ghost at the feast' has been Liverpool. It is hoped that this book will help to correct this unfortunate imbalance and finally lay the ghost to rest. It shows clearly that, via the crucial involvement of its people, the port of Liverpool, home of the White Star Line, was central to the *Titanic* story from beginning to end.

In June 1961 a journalist from the *Southern Evening Echo* in Southampton interviewed 74-year-old Fred Fleet, the Liverpool-born lookout who first spotted the iceberg which sank *Titanic*. He wrote: 'At first he was a little shy and I was surprised that the Liverpool accent has lingered on in spite of 54 years living in Southampton.'[3] As a later generation of Liverpool people would say: 'You can take the ship out of Liverpool, but you can't take Liverpool out of the ship.'

Appendix. *Titanic* Officers and Crew with strong Liverpool area links (115 listed)

Surname	Forenames/Initials	Sex	Age	Dept	Rank/position	Place of Birth	Address	Survived?
Allan	Robert Spencer	M	36	Victualling1	Steward	Liverpool	Liverpool 70 Menzies Street, Dingle	No
Allsop	Alfred	M	34	Engine	Assistant Electrician	Manchester	Southampton	No
Andrews	Charles Edward	M	19	Victualling2	Steward	Liverpool	Southampton	Yes
Ashcroft	Austin Aloysius	M	26	Victualling1	Clerk	Liverpool	Wirral, Liverpool 28 Canterbury Road, Seacombe	No
Ashe	Henry (Harry) Wellesley	M	32	Victualling3	Glory Hole Steward	prob Co Kerry	Liverpool 15 Wyresdale Road, Aintree	No
Bannon	John	M	32	Engine	Greaser	Liverpool	Southampton	No
Barrett	Frederick William	M	28 (or 33)	Engine	Leading Fireman	Liverpool	Southampton	Yes
Bell	Joseph	M	51	Engine	Chief Engineer	Maryport, Cumberland	Liverpool 1 Belvidere Road, Crosby	No
Benville	E	M	42	Engine	Fireman	Liverpool	Southampton	No
Black	Alexander	M	28	Engine	Fireman	Liverpool	Southampton	No
Boston	William John	M	30	Victualling1	Deck Steward	Liverpool	Southampton	No
Bowker	Ruth	F	27	A la Carte Restaurant, 1st Cashier		Ware, Hertfordshire	London and The Cottage Little Sutton, Cheshire	Yes
Boyes	John Henry (Harry)	M	36	Victualling1	Saloon Steward	Liverpool	Southampton	No
Brown	Walter James	M	28	Victualling1	Saloon Steward	Ormskirk, Lancs	Southampton	No
Bunnell	Wilfred	M	20	Victualling1	Plate Steward	Birkenhead	Southampton	No
Burke	Richard Edward	M	30	Victualling1	Lounge Steward	Liverpool	Southampton	No
Carney	William	M	31	Victualling1	Lift Steward	Bristol	Liverpool 11 Cairo Street, West Derby Road	No
Casey	T	M	28	Engine	Trimmer	Liverpool	Southampton	No
Clark(e)	William	M	39	Engine	Fireman	County Louth, Ireland	Liverpool (but Southampton on crew list)	Yes
Couch	Joseph Henry	M	45	Engine	Greaser	Liverpool	Southampton	No
Crafter	Frederick	M	27	Victualling1	Saloon Steward	Liverpool	Southampton	Yes
Crispin	William	M	32	Victualling3	Glory Hole Steward	Liverpool	Eastleigh, Hampshire	No
Cullen	Charles	M	45	Victualling1	Bedroom Steward	Liverpool	Southampton	Yes
Cunningham	B	M	30	Engine	Fireman	Liverpool	Southampton	No
Davies	Thomas	M	33	Engine	Leading Fireman	Liverpool	Southampton	No
Davies (Davis)	Gordon Raleigh	M	33	Victualling1	Bedroom Steward	Liverpool	Southampton	No
Dillon	Thomas Patrick	M	34	Engine	Trimmer	Liverpool	Southampton (but home in Belfast ? Liverpool in 1930s	Yes
Dodd	George Charles	M	44	Victualling1	Steward	London	Southampton	No
Donoghue	Frank (?Thomas)	M	35	Victualling1	Bedroom Steward	Liverpool	Southampton	No
Ennis	Walter	M	35	Victualling/Galley	Turkish Bath Attendant	Northumberland	Birkdale, Southport Lancs, 141 Bedford Road	No

Surname	Forenames/Initials	Sex	Age	Dept	Rank/position	Place of Birth	Address	Survived?
Evans	George Richard	M	27 (32)	Victualling1	Saloon Steward	Liverpool	Southampton	No
Farquharson	William Edward	M	39	Engine	Senior 2nd Engineer	Liverpool	Southampton	No
Faulkner	William Stephen	M	37	Victualling1	Bedroom Steward	Birkenhead	Southampton	Yes
Fay	Thomas Joseph	M	30	Engine	Greaser	Liverpool	Southampton	No
Fellowes	Alfred J	M	29	Victualling1	Assistant Boots Steward	Liverpool	Southampton	No
Ferris	W	M	38	Engine	Leading Fireman	Warrington, Cheshire	Southampton	No
Fleet	Frederick	M	24	Deck	Lookout	Liverpool	Southampton	Yes
Ford	Thomas	M	30	Engine	Leading Fireman	? Liverpool	Southampton (but originally from Liverpool)	No
Freeman	Ernest Edward Samuel	M	43	Victualling1	Deck Steward	London	Southampton (but originally Liverpool ?)	No
Giles	John Robert	M	30	Victualling/Galley	2nd Baker	Liverpool	Liverpool 28 Compton Street	No
Gregson	Mary (Miss)	F	44	Victualling1	Stewardess	Liverpool	Southampton	Yes
Hamilton	Ernest	M	25	Victualling1	Asst Smoke Room Steward	Liverpool	Southampton	No
Harrison	Norman E	M	38	Engine	Junior 2nd Engineer	Liverpool	Liverpool 27 Baden Road, Knotty Ash	No
Hart	Thomas	M	49	Engine	Fireman	Manchester	Southampton	N/A
Hesketh	John Henry	M	33	Engine	Junior 2nd Engineer	Liverpool	Liverpool, Kirkdale	No
Hewitt	Thomas	M	37	Victualling1	Bed Room Steward	Liverpool	Liverpool 98 Devonfield Road, Aintree	No
Hill	H P	M	36	Victualling3	Steward	Liverpool	Southampton	No
Hodgkinson	Leonard	M	45	Engine	Senior 4th Engineer	Stoke Staffordshire	Liverpool Thurnham Street, Kensington	No
Hogg	Charles William	M	37	Victualling1	Bed Room Steward	York	Liverpool 24 Bulwer Street, Breck Road, Everton	No
Holland	Thomas	M	28	Victualling1	Reception Steward	Liverpool	Liverpool 38 Walton Village	No
Hughes	William Thomas	M	33	Victualling1	Steward	Liverpool	Southampton	No
Hutchinson (Hutchison)	James	M	28	Victualling/Galley	Vegetable Cook	Liverpool	Liverpool 91 Woodcroft Road	No
Jacobson (Jackson)	John	M	29	Engine	Fireman	Liverpool	Southampton	No
Jones	Albert	M	17	Victualling2	Steward	Liverpool	Southampton	No
Jones	Thomas William	M	32	Deck	Able Seaman	Anglesey, North Wales	Liverpool 68 Nesfield Street Anfield/Walton	Yes
Joughin	Charles John	M	32	Victualling/Galley	Chief Baker	Birkenhead	Liverpool Grasmere Street, Everton	Yes
Keegan	James	M	38	Engine	Leading Fireman	Liverpool	Southampton (& Liverpool ?)	?

Surname	Forenames/Initials	Sex	Age	Dept	Rank/position	Place of Birth	Address	Survived?
Kerr	Thomas	M	26	Engine	Fireman	Liverpool	Southampton	No
Kiernan (or Kieran)	James W	M	32	Victualling3	Chief 3rd Class Steward	Liverpool	Southampton	No
Kinsella	L	M	30	Engine	Fireman	Liverpool	Southampton	No
Kirkham	J	M	39	Engine	Greaser	Liverpool	Southampton	No
Latimer	Andrew L	M	55	Victualling1	Chief Steward	Lancaster	Liverpool 4 Glenwyllin Road, Waterloo	No
Leather (nee Edwards)	Elizabeth May (Mrs)	F	41	Victualling1	Stewardess	Liverpool	Cheshire 24 Park Road, Port Sunlight	Yes
Lightoller	Charles Herbert	M	38	Deck	Second Officer	Chorley, Lancs	Hampshire	Yes
Lydiatt	Charles	M	28	Victualling1	Steward	Liverpool	Southampton	No
Mason	James	M	39	Engine	Leading Fireman	Liverpool	Southampton	No
Maxwell	John	M	31	Deck	Carpenter/Joiner	Liverpool	Southampton	No
McAndrew	Thomas	M	36	Engine	Fireman	Liverpool	Southampton	No
McAndrews	William	M	20	Engine	Fireman	Wigan, Lancs	Wigan 17 New Capley Bridge	No
McCarthy	Frederick J	M	36	Victualling1	Steward	Liverpool	Southampton	No
McElroy	Hugh Walter	M	37	Victualling1	Purser	Liverpool	Southampton	No
McGann	James	M	26	Engine	Trimmer	Liverpool	Southampton	Yes
McGarvey (McGoveney)	Edward Joseph	M	34	Engine	Fireman	Liverpool	Southampton	No
McInerney	Thomas	M	37	Engine	Greaser	Liverpool	Liverpool 58 Elston Street, Everton	No
McLaren (nee Allsop)	Harriet (Mrs)	F	40	Victualling1	Stewardess	Liverpool	Southampton	Yes
McMicken	Arthur	M	23 (26)	Victualling1	Saloon Steward	Liverpool	Southampton	Yes
McMicken	Benjamin Tucker	M	21	Victualling1	2nd Pantry Steward	Liverpool	Southampton	No
McMurray	William Ernest	M	43	Victualling1	Bed Room Steward	Birkenhead	Liverpool (Southampton on crewlist?)	No
Mishellamy	Abraham	M	52	Victualling1	Printer Steward	Lebanon	Liverpool (Southampton on crew list)	No
Morgan (Bird)	Charles Frederick	M	42	Victualling1	Asst Storekeeper		Birkenhead 46 Bessborough Road	No
Murdoch	William McMaster	M		Deck	First Officer	Scotland, Dalbeattie, Dumfries	Southampton	No
Noon	John	M	35	Engine	Fireman	Wigan, Lancs	Southampton, Sailors' Home	No
O'Connor	Thomas Peter	M	39	Victualling1	Bed Room Steward	Liverpool	Southampton	No
Palles	Thomas	M	42	Engine	Greaser	Liverpool	Liverpool 25 Upper Parliament Street, Toxteth	No
Proctor	Charles	M	40	Victualling/Galley	Chef	Liverpool	Southampton	No
Revell	William	M	30	Victualling1	Saloon Steward	Liverpool	Southampton	No
Rice	Charles	M	32	Engine	Fireman	Liverpool	Southampton	Yes

Surname	Forenames/Initials	Sex	Age	Dept	Rank/position	Place of Birth	Address	Survived?
Rice	John Reginald	M	25	Victualling1	Assistant Purser	Hull	Liverpool 'Leafield', 311 Kimberley Drive Great Crosby	No
Rimmer	Gilbert	M	27	Victualling1	Saloon Steward	Liverpool	Southampton	No
Roberts	Hugh H	M	40	Victualling1	Bed Room Steward	Holyhead Anglesey, Wales	Liverpool 39 Mildmay Road, Bootle	No
Roberts (nee Humphreys)	Mary Keziah (Mrs)	F	30	Victualling1	Stewardess	Liverpool	Nottingham	Yes
Shaw	Henry ('Harry')	M	39	Victualling/Galley	Kitchen Porter	Liverpool	Liverpool 47 Towcester Street	No
Shea	Thomas	M	32	Engine	Fireman	Liverpool	Southampton	No
Sloan	Peter	M	31	Engine	Chief Electrician	Liverpool	Liverpool Ferndale Road, Sefton Park	No
Small	William	M	40	Engine	Leading Fireman	Liverpool	Liverpool (Southampton on crew list)	No
Smith	Edward J	M		Deck	Master	Hanley, Staffs	Southampton	No
Stap	Sarah Agnes (Miss)	F	47	Victualling1	Stewardess	At Sea*	Birkenhead 41 Bidston Avenue, Claughton	Yes
Strugnell	John H	M	34	Victualling1	Saloon Steward	Liverpool	Southampton	No
Thomas	Albert Charles	M	23	Victualling1	Steward	Liverpool	Southampton ? 11 Brunswick Place	Yes
Thompson	Herbert Henry	M	25	Victualling1	2nd Assistant Storekeeper	Liverpool	Hampshire	No
Thompson	John William	M	35	Engine	Fireman	Liverpool	Liverpool 2 Primrose Hill, Vauxhall	Yes
Threlfall	Thomas	M	38 (44)	Engine	Leading Fireman	Liverpool	London	Yes
Turner	L	M	28	Victualling1	Saloon Steward	Liverpool or Salop ?	Hampshire	No
Walpole	James	M	48	Victualling1	Chief Pantryman Steward	Southport, Lancs	Southampton	No
Wareham	Robert Arthur	M	36	Victualling1	Bed Room Steward	Liverpool	Southampton	No
Weatherstone	Thomas Herbert	M	24	Victualling1	Saloon Steward	Liverpool	Southampton	No
Webb	Brooke Holding	M	50	Victualling1	Smoke Room Steward	Liverpool	Southampton	No
Wheat	Joseph Thomas	M	29	Victualling1	Assistant 2nd Steward	Rock Ferry, Cheshire	Southampton	Yes
Wheelton	Edneser Ernest Edward	M	29	Victualling1	Saloon Steward	Liverpool	Hampshire	Yes
Wilde	Henry Tingle	M	39	Deck	Chief Officer/Chief Mate	Liverpool	Liverpool 24 Grey Road, Walton	No
Williams	Arthur J	M	38	Victualling1	Asst Storekeeper	Liverpool	Liverpool 52 Peter Road, Walton	No
Wilson	Bertie	M	28	Engine, Senior Assistant to 2nd Engineer		Liverpool	Hampshire	No
Witter	James William Cheetham	M	31	Victualling2	Smoke Room Steward	Aughton, Lancs	Woolston, Hampshire	Yes
Wright	William	M	40	Victualling3	Glory Hole Steward	Liverpool	Southampton	Yes
Wynn	Walter	M	41	Deck	Quartermaster	Chester, Cheshire	Southampton	Yes

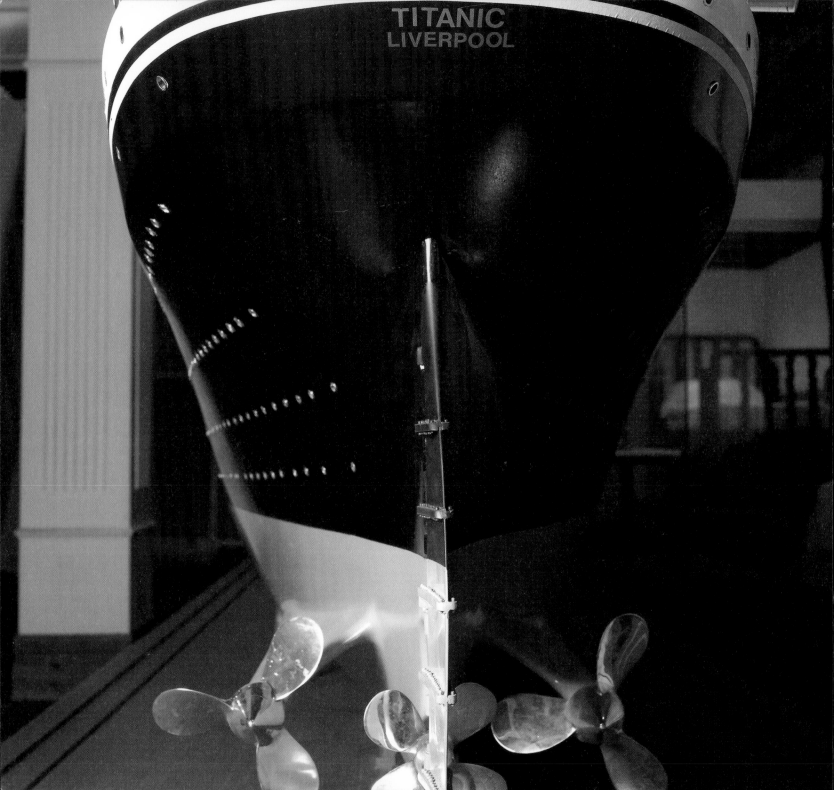

NOTES

PREFACE

1 'White Star Odyssey', *Sunday Business Post Online*

INTRODUCTION

1 S. Barczewski, *Titanic: A Night Remembered* (London and New York: Hambledon & London/Palgrave Macmillan, 2004).

2 Barczewski, *Titanic: A Night Remembered*, p.xviii.

3 Barczewski, *Titanic: A Night Remembered*, p.272.

CHAPTER 1

1 Liverpool Customs Registers, Maritime Archives, MMM, ref. C/EX/L/4/105, fol.123 (item 24/1912).

2 See G.J. Milne, 'Maritime Liverpool', in J. Belchem (ed.), *Liverpool 800: Culture, Character and History* (Liverpool: Liverpool University Press, 2006), pp.257–61.

3 'Liverpool: Port, Docks and City', *Illustrated London News*, 15 May 1886.

4 T. Lane, *Liverpool: City of the Sea* (Liverpool: Liverpool University Press, 2nd rev. edn, 1997), pp.1–2.

5 See Liverpool World Heritage homepage, http://www.liverpoolworldheritage.com, p.2 (accessed March 2009).

6 *Liverpool: Maritime Mercantile City* (Liverpool: Liverpool City Council and Liverpool University Press, 2005), p.30. The source for this information was Ramsay Muir, *A History of Liverpool* (London, 1907, repr. Wakefield, 1970), pp.297–98.

7 *Liverpool: Maritime Mercantile City*, p.118.

8 C.R. Hand, *Olde Liverpoole and its Charter* (Liverpool, 1907), p.36.

9 J. Belchem, *Merseypride: Essays in Liverpool Exceptionalism* (Liverpool: Liverpool University Press, 2000), p.3.

10 See V. Vale, *The American Peril: Challenge to Britain on the North Atlantic, 1901–04* (Manchester: Manchester University Press, 1984), pp.56ff.

11 W. J. Oldham, *The Ismay Line* (Liverpool: Journal of Commerce, 1961), pp.28ff.

12 Edward Harland had bought the shipyard at Queen's Island in 1858 from Robert Hickson, a Liverpool engineer. Schwabe provided Harland with financial support for this purpose. See T. McCluskie, M. Sharpe and L. Marriott, *Titanic and her Sisters* (London: Parkgate Books, 1998), pp.26ff.

13 M. McCaughan, *The Birth of Titanic* (Belfast: Blackstaff Press, 1998), p.52.

14 Oldham, *The Ismay Line*, p.79. This service, which became the Ismay family silver, now belongs to National Museums Liverpool, ref. MMM.1983.991.

15 Oldham, *The Ismay Line*, p.81.

16 Oldham, *The Ismay Line*, p.82.

17 A. Saint, *Richard Norman Shaw* (New Haven and London: published for the Paul Mellon Centre for Studies in British Art Ltd by Yale University Press, 1976; 3rd printing, 1983), p.357. Also see P. Louden-Brown, 'White Star Building, 30 James Street, Liverpool', *TC*, vol.21, no.4 (1998), pp.4–12.

18 See R. Anderson, *White Star* (Prescot, Lancs: T. Stephenson & Sons, 1964), p.176.

19 See W.J. Oldham, 'The *Titanic* and the Chairman', *TC*, vol.11, no.1 (1987), pp.16–20.

20 'Mr. Ismay and the White Star Line', *The Times*, 1 January 1913.

21 The house was sold by Ismay in 1920, and later demolished to make way for semi-detached housing. See photograph and map on p.19.

22 *Liverpool Shipping: Who's Who?* (Liverpool: Journal of Commerce, 1911), p.121.

23 Oldham, 'The *Titanic* and the Chairman', p.30. Today's Holmefield Road in Mossley Hill is named after this estate.

24 As reported in 'Thirty-Three Years of the White Star Line – A Wonderful Record', *JoC*, 22 July 1904.

25 See 'Thirty-Three Years of the White Star Line'.

26 Oldham, *The Ismay Line*, pp.137ff.; Anderson, *White Star*, pp.89–90.

27 Vale, *The American Peril*, p.58.

28 See M. Moss and J.R. Hume, *Shipbuilders to the World: 125 Years of Harland and Wolff, Belfast, 1861–1986* (Belfast and Wolfeboro, New Hampshire: Blackstaff Press, 1986), pp.106–108.

29 Vale, *American Peril*, pp.59ff.

30 *Liverpool Daily Post*, 1 November 1902.

31 *Shipping World*, 5 November 1902. A less favourable opinion was expressed in the *Liverpool Mercury* on 28 November, 1902.

32 See P. Louden-Brown, *The White Star Line: An Illustrated History, 1869–1934* (Herne Bay, Kent: Titanic Historical Society, 2nd edn, 2001), p.19.

33 Vale, *American Peril*, p.59.

34 Oldham, *The Ismay Line*, pp.138ff. Also see W.B. Saphire, 'The White Star Line and the International Mercantile Marine Company' on the website of the Titanic Historical Society Inc., http://www.titanic1org/articles/mercantile.asp, p.6 (accessed 25 June 2008).

35 'Lancashire Today, XXVIII – Liverpool', *Daily Dispatch*, 2 December 1902. For American acquisitions in Liverpool in the recent past, including Ogden's and Bryant and May, see Vale, *The American Peril*, pp.26–27.

36 *Liverpool Daily Courier*, 30 April 1912.

37 As reported in the *Liverpool Daily Post*, 18 March 1902.

38 Pirrie was also instrumental in these arrangements, as was Albert Ballin, head of the Hamburg America Line, and Henry Wilding, head of the Liverpool firm representing the American Line in the UK. See Vale, *American Peril*, pp.78ff.

39 In July 1901 the *Deutschland* made a record eastbound crossing of the North Atlantic at an average speed of 23.51 knots. In September 1902 the *Kronprinz Wilhelm* made a record westbound crossing at an average speed of 23.09 knots. See T. Hughes, *The Blue Riband of the Atlantic* (Cambridge: Patrick Stephens, 1973), pp.96, 103.

40 *Liverpool Daily Post*, 1 October 1902.

41 Hughes, *Blue Riband*, pp.91ff.

42 See Vale, *American Peril*, pp.63ff.

43 Vale, *American Peril*, p.165.

44 Vale, *American Peril*, pp.136–38. Also see the *Liverpool Daily Post*, 1 October 1902.

45 *Liverpool Daily Courier*, 2 October 1902.

46 *Liverpool Daily Post*, 3 October 1902.

47 See 'Atlantic Transport Line History: The International Mercantile Marine Company (IMM)', http://www.geocities.com/jckinghorn/ATL/content/immc.htm, p.5 (accessed 25 June 2008).

48 'The Morgan Combine', *Fairplay*, 11 June 1903.

49 Oldham, *The Ismay Line*, p.155.

50 *The New York Times*, 24 February 1904.

51 *Daily Dispatch*, 5 July 1904.

52 *Liverpool Courier*, 5 March 1904.

53 *Manchester Guardian*, 5 March 1904.

54 *Fairplay*, 21 January 1904.

55 'Thirty-Three Years of the White Star Line'.

56 Oldham, *The Ismay Line*, p.145.

CHAPTER 2

1 Anderson, *White Star*, pp.99, 142.

2 Vale, *American Peril*, pp.81ff.

3 See Chapter 1.

4 *Liverpool Courier*, 7 January 1907.

5 *Lloyd's List and Shipping Gazette*, 5 January 1907.

6 See, for example, 'Mr. Morgan and the Position of Liverpool', *Liverpool Courier*, 2 October 1902. Also 'The Morgan Ships and Liverpool: Rumoured Abandonment of the Port', *Liverpool Daily Post*, 3 October 1902.

7 *Liverpool Courier*, 8 January 1907.

8 'The Transfer of the White Star Liners', *Liverpool Daily Post*, 8 January 1907.

9 *Daily Express*, 7 January 1907.

10 Reported in 'The Meaning of the White Star Move', *Liverpool Courier*, 8 January 1907.

11 Reported in 'Combine and Cunard: Opposing Forces', *Liverpool Courier*, 8 January 1907.

12 'Liverpool v. Southampton', *Liverpool Courier*, 10 January 1907.

13 'Transferred Steamers Will Be Replaced', *Liverpool Daily Post*, 8 January 1907.

14 'White Star and White Feather', *The Porcupine*, Saturday 12 January 1907.

15 See, for example, 'The White Star Removal', *JoC*, 8 January 1907. Also 'White Star After Continental Traffic', *The New York Times*, 8 January 1907.

16 F.E. Hyde, *Cunard and the North Atlantic, 1840–1973* (London, Humanities Press, 1975), p.103.

17 See P. Louden-Brown, 'Adriatic II – The Ship That Changed Direction', *TC*, vol.31, no.179 (2007), pp.117–29.

CHAPTER 3

1 See http://www.titanicinquiry.org (accessed 26 July 2008).

2 See the draft poster by Odin Rosenvinge p.42.

3 *Liverpool Daily Post*, 10 January 1907.

4 W.J. Oldham, 'The *Titanic* and the Chairman', *TC*, vol.11, no.2 (1987), p.47.

5 *JoC*, 4 June 1907.

6 McCaughan, *Birth of Titanic*, p.59.

7 *New York Times*, Thursday 12 September 1912; see *ET*/Articles and Stories, 'Bigger than the Lusitania' (accessed 4 May 2009).

8 Anderson, *White Star*, p.99.

9 Hyde, *Cunard and the North Atlantic*, p.148. The bank's full name was Glyn, Mills, Currie and Company.

10 Anderson, *White Star*, p.106.

11 *Who's Who & Who Was Who 2008* (Oxford: Oxford University Press, 2008), online at http://www.ukwhoswho.com.

12 He was the eighth son of the fourth Lord Lyttleton of Hagley Hall, Stourbridge. He was an MP from 1895 until his death in 1913, and Secretary of State for the Colonies from 1903 to 1905. In 1905 he lived at 16 Great College Street, Westminster. He was great-uncle of the late jazz trumpeter and broadcaster Humphrey Lyttleton.

13 D. Littler (ed.), *Guide to the Records of Merseyside Maritime Museum*, vol.II (St John's, Newfoundland: Trustees of the National Museums and Galleries on Merseyside/International Maritime Economic History Association, 1999), pp.117–18.

14 Anon., *A Short History of F.C. Danson & Company, 1879–1973* (Liverpool: privately published, c. 1973), p.3 (MMM Archives, ref. 521.DAN/PM).

15 Danson Archives, MMM, ref. D/D/V/2/35.

16 Danson Archives, MMM, ref. D/D/V/2/35.

17 Danson Archives, MMM, ref. DX/41/5/3.

18 Anon., *A Short History of F.C. Danson & Company*, p.3.

19 Littler (ed.), *Records of Merseyside Maritime Museum*, vol.II, p.117.

20 *Liverpool Customs Registers of British Ships*, Maritime Archives and Library, MMM, ref. C/EX/L/4/105, folio 23.

21 See *Liverpool Customs Registers*, ref. C/EX/L/4/105, folio 123.

22 *Liverpool Customs Registers*, ref. C/EX/L/4/109, folio 16.

23 Louden-Brown, *White Star Line*, pp.20, 22.

24 Pirrie's motto was 'An ounce of pluck is worth a ton of luck'. See Moss and Hume, *Shipbuilders to the World*, p.96.

25 Confirmed by an email from Paul Louden-Brown (July 2008) based on his earlier research in the National Archives (PRO) records at Kew, Surrey.

26 See Moss and Hume, *Shipbuilders to the World*, p.517.

27 McCaughan, *Birth of Titanic*, p.59.

28 Such as superintending engineers, marine superintendents and victualling superintendents. See the deposition of J.B. Ismay, Limitation of Liability Hearings, US District Court, Southern District of New York, May 1915, at http://www.titanicinquiry.org/lol/depositions/ismay01.php (accessed 22 April 2009).

29 Maritime Archives and Library, MMM, ref. B/CUN.

30 For Carlisle's proposal to increase lifeboat capacity on both ships see, for example, J.P. Eaton and C.A. Haas, *Titanic: Triumph and Tragedy* (Wellingborough: Patrick Stephens, 2nd impression, 1987), pp.259ff.

31 Henry Wilding retired from these posts in October 1906, and went to live in Southampton. See *JoC*, 5 October 1906. In 1905 he lived at 'Naseby' in Aigburth Drive, Liverpool 8. For Edward Wilding (1875–1939), see the *Who's Who and Who Was Who 2008* website at http://www.ukwhoswho.com.

32 Contrary to McCluskie, Sharpe and Marriott, who wrongly state (*Titanic and her Sisters*, p.82) that Wilding was summarily dismissed by Pirrie after the *Titanic* disaster.

33 *Belfast News-Letter*, 2 October 1910, quoted by McCaughan, *Birth of Titanic*, p.53.

34 McCaughan, *Birth of Titanic*, p.70.

35 McCaughan, *Birth of Titanic*, p.153.

36 See p.64.

37 See S. Mills, *RMS Olympic: The Old Reliable* (Falmouth, Cornwall: Waterfront Publications, 2nd edn, 1995), pp.32–45. D.F. Hutchings (*RMS Titanic: A Modern Legend* [Waterfront Publications, Falmouth, Cornwall, 1995], p.9) incorrectly states that *Olympic*'s courtesy call of 1 April 1911 was her 'one and only visit' to Liverpool.

38 In a talk in April 2008 for the British Titanic Society's convention in Liverpool, American *Titanic* historians John Eaton and Charles Haas stated that *Titanic*'s recovered bell, which has no ship's name upon it, has 'far too many clapper marks' for a new bell. They suggested that it might previously have been used on another ship.

39 K. Tinkler, 'Thomas Utley (1854–1927) and his Successors', in J. Shepherd (ed.), *Sixty Years of the Liverpool Nautical Research Society, 1938–1998* (Liverpool: Liverpool Nautical Research Society, 1998), p.43.

40 Ismay lived at 13 Beach Lawn. Information provided by Mr. Dick Midhage, Hon. Secretary of the Chadburn Ship's Telegraph Society, 2006.

41 See *Gore's Directory* (Liverpool, 1910), p.826. Willett Bruce lived at 4 Breeze Hill, Bootle. Merseyside Maritime Museum has a Willett-Bruce steam whistle from the White Star liner MV *Britannic* of 1930.

42 Dick Midhage of the Chadburn's Ship's Telegraph Society provided the information about Chadburn's manufacture of the steam whistles. Downie & Company exhibited the electric control apparatus at the Engineering Exhibition at Olympia, London, in late 1910 (*The Times*, 7 September 1910, p.15). Also see the Downie advertisement published in R. Lepien, '*Olympic*: The Maiden Voyage', *TC*, vol.27, no.162 (2003), p.162.

43 Lepien, '*Olympic*: The Maiden Voyage', p.162.

44 See *The White Star Liners Olympic and Titanic: Ocean Liners of the Past, No 1, Reprinted from 'The Shipbuilder', 1911* (Cambridge: Patrick Stephens, 1970, repr. 1976), pp.44–49, 63–64, 140.

45 See Eaton and Haas, *Titanic: Triumph and Tragedy*, p.33.

46 A letter and a receipt regarding this order sent by W. Jones and Son, Liverpool to *Titanic*'s Chief Officer, Henry Wilde on 11 April 1912, the day after *Titanic* left Southampton, were sold by Henry Aldridge & Son, Auctioneers, Devizes, Wiltshire on 19 April 2008 (http://www.henry-aldridge.co.uk/news.htm).

CHAPTER 4

1 'White Star Line Special Meeting, 22nd April 1912', *TC*, vol.22, no.4 (1999), p.27.

2 Liverpool Customs Registers, Maritime Archives and Library, MMM, ref. C/EX/L/4/105/123.

3 C.H. Lightoller, *Titanic and Other Ships* (London: Nicholson and Watson, 1935, repr. Hull: Historia Press, Hull, 2007), p.214.

4 McCaughan, *Birth of Titanic*, pp.128–29. She returned to Southampton on 6 March.

5 'Titanic Deck Crew: Belfast to Southampton', *ET* (accessed 7 August 2008).

6 For Murdoch see his *ET* biography and the *ET* feature 'Murdoch – the Man, the Mystery' by David Parkes (2007) (accessed 7 August 2008).

7 See his biography in *ET* (accessed 7 August 2008).

8 See his biography in *ET*, and Mark Baber's posting on the *ET* Message Board, 20 December 2002 (accessed 23 April 2009).

9 Eaton and Haas, *Titanic: Triumph and Tragedy*, p.34.

10 See his biography in *ET* (accessed 25 April 2009).

11 S. Cameron, *Titanic: Belfast's Own* (Dublin: Wolfhound Press, 1998), p.57.

12 D. Hyslop, A. Forsyth and S. Jemima, *Titanic Voices: The Story of the White Star Line, Titanic and Southampton* (Southampton City Council, Southampton, 1994), p.60.

13 See his biography in *ET* (accessed 23 April 2009).

14 *Cumberland News*, Saturday 20 April 1912 (cited in *ET*, August 2008, contributor Brian Ticehurst).

15 See the commemorative brochure, *A Tribute to the Engineering Staff: 80th Anniversary of the Sinking of R.M.S. Titanic, 1912–1992* (London: The Institute of Marine Engineers, Guild of Benevolence, 1992), p.6. See also the brief biography of Joseph Bell in *ET* (accessed 7 August 2008).

16 Eaton and Haas, *Titanic: Triumph and Tragedy*, p.34.

17 See 'Titanic Deck Crew: Belfast to Southampton', *ET* (accessed August 2008). Although listed as 'Deck Crew etc.' for *Titanic*'s delivery voyage, engineer officers and their support staff were listed as 'Engineering Crew' for her maiden voyage.

18 *Tribute to the Engineering Staff*, pp.6–17. Also see 'Titanic Deck Crew: Belfast to Southampton: Engineers', *ET* (accessed 7 August 2008). Another engineer who signed on at Southampton for the maiden voyage, Junior Second Engineer Jonathan Shepherd, had also often sailed from Liverpool. He did not survive the sinking of *Titanic*.

19 See Cameron, *Titanic: Belfast's Own*, pp.60–68.

20 See the biographies of each of these men in *ET* (accessed 12 August 2008).

21 'Titanic Victualling Crew: Belfast to Southampton', *ET* (accessed 31 July 2008).

22 See 'Titanic Deck Crew: Belfast to Southampton', *ET* (accessed 7 August 2008). For official purposes the date of his signing on was recorded as 24 March, as was that of the other deck officers.

23 *LDPM*, 17 April 1912.

24 See his biography in *ET* (accessed July 2008), and the *ET* feature by Rod Stringer, 'Titanic Town – Crosby, Merseyside's Links to the *Titanic* and Other Ships' (accessed July 2008).

25 Eaton and Haas, *Titanic: Triumph and Tragedy*, p.33.

26 On Day 1 of the US Senate Inquiry on 19 April, Charles Lightoller testified that on board during the trials were only 'about 30 of the crew and about 30 of what we call runners'. He added that some guests were also on board. This suggests that most of the crew joined the ship after the trials had been completed. See the Titanic Inquiry Project website, http://www.titanicinquiry.org/USInq (accessed 7 April 2009).

27 See his biography in *ET* (accessed July 2008).

28 Bride is listed in the Marconi examination records held in the Archives and Library at Merseyside Maritime Museum, ref. D/ROE.

29 See his biography in *ET* (accessed July 2008).

30 See Eaton and Haas, *Titanic: Triumph and Tragedy*, pp.44–47.

31 For Frank Bell, see Joseph Bell's biography in *ET* (accessed 3 December 2008) and *Tribute to the Engineering Staff*, p.6. For the three Weir's employees, see E. Kamuda's article, 'Between Belfast and Southampton: *Titanic*'s Only Complete Voyage', *TC*, vol.27, no.161 (2003), pp.5–6, 14. Also see R. Lepien, 'Olympic: The Maiden Voyage', *TC*, vol.27, no.162 (2003), p.82.

32 *The Times*, Monday 29 April 1912, cited in *ET*/Articles and Stories, 'Survivors of the Crew at Plymouth' (11 September 2008).

CHAPTER 5

1 'Special Meeting, White Star Line, 22 April, 1912', *TC*, vol.22, no.4 (1999), p.28.

2 See S. Mills, 'Captain Charles Bartlett: The Man Who Nearly Commanded Titanic?', *TC*, vol.24, no.152 (2000), pp.118–27. Also see his brief biography by Rod Stringer in *ET* (accessed August 2008).

3 See Eaton and Haas, *Titanic: Triumph and Tragedy*, pp.55–56.

4 See 'Titanic Deck Crew: Signed at Southampton', *ET* (accessed August 2008). Unlike on *Titanic*'s delivery voyage, the engineer officers and support staff were not grouped as deck crew for her maiden voyage.

5 Lightoller, *Titanic and Other Ships*, p.218.

6 See Blair's biography in *ET* (accessed 23 April 2009).

7 This letter was sold at Henry Aldridge & Son's RMS *Titanic* auction on Saturday 18 April 2009, lot number 226. Details courtesy of H. Aldridge and Son.

8 See p.55.

9 See his brief biography in *ET* (accessed May 2008).

10 *Liverpool Echo* cutting, 1958, in Maritime Archives and Library, MMM, ref. DX/1522. Also see the letter of former *Liverpool Echo* journalist Derek Whale to the editors of *Titanic Commutator*, in *TC*, vol.19, no.2 (1995), p.35. Officers Lightoller, Pitman and Moody were all ex-*Oceanic*, and Wilde, like Jones, lived in Walton, Liverpool.

11 See his biography in *ET* (accessed 2 March 2009).

12 See crew list in *ET* (accessed August 2008), and 'Southampton, Crew: Agreement and Account of Crew' (PRO Ref: BT100/259).

13 Contrary to Senan Molony in his *ET* article, 'A Last Bright Shining Lie' (*ET*/Research, dated 24 August 2004), that *Titanic*'s engineers 'were overwhelmingly Scottish'.

14 Including Liverpool-born L. Kinsella, 30, formerly of SS *Aragon*, who was one of six substitute firemen engaged on sailing day (10 April) in place of seven others who had signed on earlier, but did not sail.

15 Unless otherwise stated, all were born in Liverpool.

16 For Keegan, see pp.172-4.

17 For Hart, see pp.170-2.

18 E.L. Green, 'My Recollections of Coal-burning Ships', *Sea Breezes*, vol.68 (September 1994), p.686.

19 G. Garrett, 'The Maurie', in *The Collected George Garrett*, ed. M. Murphy (Nottingham: Trent Editions/Nottingham Trent University, 1999), p.172.

20 Lightoller, *Titanic and Other Ships*, chapter 35, p.260. This is borne out in George Garrett's very informative short story 'The Maurie', pp.170–80.

21 Lightoller, *Titanic and Other Ships*, chapter 35, p.260.

22 See pp. 170-4.

23 *ET*, 'Titanic Crew: Victualling Department' (September 2008). Note that 'B. Tucker' is wrongly included as well as B. Tucker McMicken on this *ET* list (accessed 3 November 2008).

24 The Marconi operators were employed by the Marconi company, the postal clerks by the postal authorities in the USA and Britain.

25 70 *à la carte* restaurant staff originally signed on, of whom two failed to join the ship. See *ET*, 'Titanic Discharged Crew' (accessed September 2008).

26 He was senior to Reginald Barker, who was also listed as Purser, and who, unlike McElroy, had sailed on *Titanic*'s delivery voyage from Belfast. See Barker's biography in *ET* (accessed 3 November 2008).

27 Quoted from McElroy's biography in *ET* (accessed 3 November 2008).

28 See his biography in *ET* (accessed 3 November 2008).

29 See his brief biography in *ET* (accessed 3 November 2008).

30 See the map of Crosby in Rod Stringer's very useful 'Titanic Town' website via *ET* (accessed 3 November 2008).

31 See Rice's brief biography in *ET* (accessed 3 November 2008).

32 See his biography in *ET* (accessed 26 March 2008).

33 Hyslop et al., *Titanic Voices*, p.66.

34 See his biography in *ET* (accessed 29 August 2007).

35 Benjamin also gave his age as 31 in Belfast, and Arthur apparently gave his address as 53 Suffolk Avenue in Southampton. See their respective biographies in *ET* (accessed 3 November 2008) and Brian Ticehurst's entry on the *ET* Message Board, dated 3 August 2003.

36 See Thomas Hewitt's biography in *ET* (accessed 7 May 2009). The two gold watches, donated to the Museum by Mr. Hewitt's grandson, are MMM refs. MMM.1999.882.

37 See his biography in *ET* (accessed 5 November 2008).

38 See her biography in *ET* (accessed 5 November 2008).

39 See his biography in *ET* (accessed 5 November 2008).

40 The three bell-boy stewards on *Titanic* were between 14 and 16 years of age.

41 See his biography in *ET* (accessed 5 November 2008).

42 See his biography in *ET* (accessed 12 November 2008).

43 *ET*, '*Titanic* Seamen Who Failed to Join or Deserted' (accessed September 2008).

44 See his biography in *ET* (accessed 5 November 2008).

45 See 'Titanic Victim's Funeral', *Southend Standard*, 16 May 1912 (published in *ET*, 5 November 2008), and also below, Chapter 10, p.169. The other victim buried in Liverpool was First Class passenger Alfred G. Rowe (see p.159).

46 See his biography in *ET* (accessed 6 November 2008).

47 See the biographies of both men in *ET* (accessed 6 November 2008). The information regarding Joughin's address in Everton was provided by my colleague Stephen Guy, Press Officer, National Museums Liverpool.

48 See pp.128-30.

49 See his biography in *ET* (accessed 12 November 2008).

50 Limitation of Liability Hearings, 'Testimony of Edward Wilding', Thursday 13 May 1915.

51 British Inquiry, Days 6 (Joughin), 9 (Rule), 18 and 19 (Wilding).

52 See, for example, the *ET* Message Board discussion about Scotland Road (accessed 7 December 2008).

53 See J. Belchem, *Irish, Catholic and Scouse: The History of the Liverpool-Irish, 1800–1939* (Liverpool: Liverpool University Press, 2007), pp.62–63.

54 Belchem, *Irish, Catholic and Scouse*, p.193.

55 D. Whale, *The Liners of Liverpool*, Part 1 (Birkenhead: Countyvise, 1986), p.15.

56 According to the Scottie Press Online website at http://www.scottiepressorg.uk, Scotland Road was '[a] road to which seamen from all parts of the world came during the 18th, 19th and 20th centuries and indeed a road name that was given by such seamen to the longest alleyway of many great and famous liners including the White Star Line's "Titanic"' (accessed 9 December 2008).

57 Garrett, 'The Maurie', pp.172–73.

58 Garrett, 'The Maurie', p.173.

59 Murphy (ed.), *The Collected George Garrett*, Introduction, p.ix.

60 See Lightoller, *Titanic and Other Ships*, p.226.

CHAPTER 6

1 'Special Meeting, White Star Line, Liverpool, 22nd April 1912', *TC*, vol.22, no.4 (1999), p.28.

2 See, for example, the figures published in the *JoC*, 3 April 1923, and the *Liverpool Courier*, 23 April 1923.

3 See for example D.A. Butler, *Unsinkable: The Full Story of the RMS Titanic* (Mechanicsburg, PA, USA: Stackpole Books, 1998), pp.35–37.

4 *New York Times*, 20 April 1912.

5 Maritime Archives and Library, MMM, ref. DX/1063/R. Also see J.P. Eaton, 'Cancelled Passages Aboard *Titanic*', *ET*/Research, Part 12 (accessed 2 May 2008). Eaton incorrectly states that this item is an envelope.

6 Eaton, 'Cancelled Passages Aboard *Titanic*'.

7 'Owner of Virginian in Excellent Health', Norfolk *Ledger-Dispatch*, 2 April 1909, http://en.wikisource.org/wiki/owner_of_virginian_in_excellent_health (accessed 17 November 2008).

8 See 'Passengers: Southampton to Cherbourg' in *ET* (accessed 13 November 2008).

9 See 'Passengers: Southampton to Queenstown' in *ET* (13 November 2008). One crew member also left at Queenstown, namely Fireman John Coffey, who deserted.

10 See listings of 'People who Embarked at Cherbourg' and 'People who Embarked at Queenstown' in *ET* (accessed 13 November 2008).

11 Oldham, *The Ismay Line*, p.186.

12 Oldham, *The Ismay Line*, pp.177–84.

13 Oldham, *The Ismay Line*, p.183.

14 See Ismay's testimony at the British Inquiry, Day 16, Questions 18387–97.

15 US Inquiry, Day 11 (30 April 1912). Hays died in the sinking.

16 W.J. Oldham, 'The *Titanic* and the Chairman', Part IV, *TC*, vol.11, no.4 (1987), p.27.

17 See Ismay's testimony at the US Inquiry, Day 16, 30 April 1912.

18 P. Louden-Brown, 'Ismay and the *Titanic*', *TC*, vol.24, no.149 (2000), p.26.

19 Ismay made both comments during Day 11 of the US Inquiry on 30 April 1912.

20 See Chapters 10–12.

21 Oldham, 'The *Titanic* and the Chairman', p.23.

22 See Ismay's testimony, British Inquiry, Day 16, Questions 18644–7.

23 See his brief biography in *ET* (accessed 17 November 2008).

24 Elizabeth Bonnell's details were found on the online English Census of 1901.

25 *LDPM*, 17 April 1912.

26 See the biographies of Elizabeth and Caroline Bonnell, and associated links, in *ET* (accessed 5 March 2008).

27 Eric A. Porch, 'The Wick Family and the *Titanic*', *TC*, vol.14, no.3 (1990), p.11.

28 *The Daily Northwestern*, 17 April 1912, as quoted in 'A Sad Farewell', *ET*/Articles and Stories (accessed 19 November 2008).

29 See Arrivals in UK records, http://www.ancestry.co.uk (accessed 19 November 2008).

30 See her brief biography in *ET*.

31 See Giglio's biography in *ET* (accessed 19 November 2008).

32 'Guggenheim, Dying, Sent Wife Message', *New York Times*, 20 April 1912 (in *ET*, 19 November 2008).

33 1891 England Census, http://www.ancestry.co.uk.

34 1901 England Census, http://www.ancestry.co.uk.

35 UK Incoming Passenger Lists, 1878–1960, http://www.ancestry.co.uk.

36 See their biographies in *ET* (accessed 4 September 2007).

37 This letter, with other items from the Rowe family archive, was sold by auctioneers Henry Aldridge and Son, Devizes, Wiltshire, in March 2007. See http://www.ukauctioneers.com/News (accessed 14 January 2008).

38 See his biography in *ET* (accessed 30 November 2006), including a link to the *LDPM* article about his funeral, dated 15 May 1912. Also see Chapter 10.

39 Y. Carroll, *A Hymn for Eternity: The Story of Wallace Hartley, Titanic Bandmaster* (Gloucester: Tempus Publishing, 2002), pp.33, 39.

40 Carroll, *A Hymn for Eternity*, pp.30–39.

41 Maritime Archives and Library, MMM, ref. DX/1981.

42 Carroll, *A Hymn for Eternity*, p.29.

43 Later in 1912 Black's gave union members 'the choice between leaving the Union and leaving their service on the liners'. See Carroll, *A Hymn for Eternity*, p.110.

44 This letter, written in pencil, and its torn and water-stained envelope, were found on Hartley's body after the sinking. They were included with other items relating to Hartley (lot 526) in a sale of *Titanic* memorabilia at an auction by Onslow's, London, on 15 April 1987.

45 Carroll, *A Hymn for Eternity*, p.44. Also see his biography in *ET* (accessed 8 May 2008).

46 England & Wales, FreeBMD Birth Index: 1837–1983, http://www.ancestry.co.uk (accessed 26 November 2008).

47 1891 England Census, http://www.ancestry.co.uk (accessed 26 November 2008).

48 See his biography in *ET* (accessed 21 November 2008), including the link 'An Argyle Theatre's Bandsman'.

49 See his biography in *ET* (accessed 8 May 2008), and link 'Freshfield Airman – One of the *Titanic*'s Orchestra' (contributor Inger Shiel).

50 England & Wales, FreeBMD Birth Index: 1837–1983 and 1891 England Census, http://www.ancestry.co.uk (accessed 27 November 2008). Also see his *ET* biography, which says that he lived in Liverpool. However, D. Lynch ('The Private Lives of the *Titanic*'s Passengers', *TC*, vol.19, no.2 [1995], p.32) says that he was from Manchester.

51 See Lynch, 'The Private Lives of the *Titanic*'s Passengers', p.32.

52 A similar tale was told by another English Second Class couple, the 'Marshalls', who were also not married. See Lynch, 'The Private Lives of the *Titanic*'s Passengers', p.32.

53 See their biographies in *ET* (accessed 3 October 2008).

54 A *Liverpool Echo* report of the sinking on 15 April 1912 mentions 'Messrs. Finney [sic], Gaskell and Hallas, who were taking a holiday trip', as St James parishioners travelling on *Titanic* who were not listed as saved. 'Hallas' may well refer to Thomas Palles, a crew member from nearby Upper Parliament Street, Liverpool. See Chapter 4.

55 See their biographies in *ET* (accessed 3 October 2008). Also see Chapter 10.

56 1891 and 1901 England Censuses, http://www.ancestry.co.uk (accessed 27 November 2008).

57 See his biography in *ET* (accessed 29 August 2008). Also see Chapter 9.

58 England & Wales, FreeBMD Birth Index: 1837–1983; 1901 England Census, http://www.ancestry.co.uk (accessed 1 December 2008).

59 See their biographies in *ET* (accessed 29 August 2008).

60 Storey was placed under the Liverpool Committee of the *Titanic* Relief Fund after the disaster. See Andrew Williams' comment on the *ET* Message Board, 25 April 2007 (accessed 28 November 2008).

CHAPTER 7

1 US Inquiry, Day 1, 19 April 1912.

2 Lightoller, *Titanic and Other Ships*, p.215.

3 Eaton and Haas, *Titanic: Triumph and Tragedy*, p.113.

4 See George Garrett's description of life as a member of the *Mauretania*'s 'Black Gang' in 1915 in 'The Maurie', pp.172–73.

5 Fireman John Coffey, 24, deserted the ship at Queenstown, where he was born. See his biography in *ET* (accessed 5 May 2009).

6 The two 'dog watches' were used to divide each 24 hours into seven watches instead of six, to ensure that the same watch (or group of crew) was not on duty at exactly the same times each day.

7 See the summary of Charles Lightoller's testimony on Day 2 of the legal test case, 'Ryan v. Oceanic Steam Navigation Company (Limited)' at the High Court of Justice, London, 23 June 1913, via Senan Molony, 'The Third Enquiry', *ET/Research*, p.22 (accessed 7 January 2009).

8 From IMM Rule 416, quoted by S. Halpern, 'Speed and Revolutions', *ET/Research*, 18 September 2007, p.6 (accessed 24 December 2008).

9 Eaton and Haas, *Titanic: Triumph and Tragedy*, p.113.

10 Eaton and Haas, *Titanic: Triumph and Tragedy*, p.113. Also see M. Chirnside and S. Halpern, '*Olympic* and *Titanic*: Maiden Voyage Mysteries', *ET/Research*, 29 April 2007 for updates regarding *Titanic*'s speed and daily distances travelled.

11 See J. Eaton, 'Titanic Ships: The Other Ships of the *Titanic* Story', Part 13 (2005), in *ET* (accessed 12 December 2008).

12 From 24 August to 14 January steamers followed the more northerly 'short track', which was about 110 miles shorter. See Chirnside and Halpern, '*Olympic* and *Titanic*: Maiden Voyage Mysteries', p.1.

13 Eaton and Haas, *Titanic: Triumph and Tragedy*, p.114.

14 British Inquiry, Day 16, Questions 18322–53.

15 British Inquiry, Report: 'Account of Ship's Journey across the Atlantic, Messages Received', p.2.

16 'Account of Ship's Journey across the Atlantic, Messages Received', p.2.

17 See Eaton & Haas, *Titanic: Triumph and Tragedy*, pp.114–15.

18 British Inquiry, Day 11, 'Testimony of Charles Lightoller', Question 13700.

19 See, for example, the *New York Times* article 'The Biggest Liner is Now in Port', dated 17 May 1907, which evaluates the maiden voyage of *Adriatic*, via *ET*/Articles and Stories (accessed 19 December 2008).

20 See, for example, Chirnside and Halpern, '*Olympic* and *Titanic*: Maiden Voyage Mysteries'; Eaton and Haas, *Titanic: Triumph and Tragedy*, p.114.

21 US Inquiry, Day 1, 19 April 1912.

22 See Halpern, 'Speed and Revolutions', p.78.

CHAPTER 8

1 W. Lord, *A Night To Remember* (London: Allen Lane/Penguin Books, rev. illustrated edn, 1976), p.55.

2 British Inquiry, Report, 'Account of Ship's Journey/Weather Conditions'.

3 US Inquiry, Day 4, 'Testimony of Frederick Fleet'.

4 Eaton and Haas, *Titanic: Triumph and Tragedy*, pp.137–38.

5 British Inquiry, Report, 'Description of the Damage to the Ship'.

6 British Inquiry, Report, 'Description of the Damage to the Ship'.

7 British Inquiry, Day 35, Arguments.

8 British Inquiry, Day 4, Questions 2235, 2277.

9 US Inquiry, Day 18.

10 US Inquiry, Day 18.

11 British Inquiry, Day 3, Question 1926. Hesketh did not survive the sinking. Merseyside Maritime Museum has some of his pre-disaster belongings (ref. MMM.1998.29.1-5).

12 See, for example, the testimony of Samuel Hemmings, British Inquiry, Day 15, Question 17739.

13 Senan Molony, '12.45am – A Time to Go!', *ET*/Research, 2008 (ref. 6002, accessed 16 January 2009).

14 British Inquiry, Day 13, 'Testimony of Joseph Boxhall', Question 15610.

15 See his biography in *ET* (accessed 20 January 2009). Also see Cameron, *Titanic: Belfast's Own*, pp.92–94.

16 British Inquiry, Report, 'Account of the Saving and Rescue'. Also see the biography of George Rowe in *ET* (accessed 19 January 2009).

17 See Ismay's cable to the London *Times*, published 23 April 1912.

18 British Inquiry, Day 13, Question 14995.

19 US Inquiry, Day 4, ref. HJP 528.

20 British Inquiry, Day 13, Questions 15975–83.

21 See Carter's biography in *ET* (accessed 19 January 2009).

22 US Inquiry, Day 7, 'Testimony of Edward Wheelton'.

23 British Inquiry, Day 4, Questions 2170–75. Also see John M. and Judy Y. Hennessey, *The Titanic Lifeboats Project* (2005), p.11, http://www.dweephor.com/titanic (accessed 27 February 2009).

24 US Inquiry, Day 7, 'Testimony of C.E. Andrews'.

25 See Chapter 6.

26 See their biographies in *ET* (accessed July 2008).

27 US Inquiry, Day 7, 'Testimony of C.E. Andrews'.

28 US Inquiry, Day 7, 'Testimony of Thomas Jones'.

29 US Inquiry, Day 7, 'Testimony of Thomas Jones'.

30 R.B. Bigham, 'A Matter of Course', *ET*/Research (2006), p.32 (accessed 25 February 2009).

31 From a handwritten copy in Maritime Archives and Library, MMM, ref. DX/1522.

32 See the photocopy of a postcard sent by Jones to his fiancée while he was waiting to testify at the US Senate Inquiry in Washington, held at the Maritime Archives and Library, MMM, ref. DX/1522.

33 See Chapter 6.

34 Information provided by Mr. Desmond, a descendant of John Thompson, c. 1998.

35 *The Times*, 30 May 1912.

36 Col. A. Gracie, *The Truth about the Titanic* (1913; reprinted with additional material, Riverside, CT: 7 Cs Press, 1973), pp.97–98.

37 British Inquiry, Day 6, Question 6245.

38 British Inquiry, Day 6, Questions 6237–44.

39 British Inquiry, Day 6, Question 6074.

40 British Inquiry, Day 6, Question 6255–66.

41 British Inquiry, Day 6, Question 6104.

42 British Inquiry, Day 6, Questions 6272–73.

43 See Cameron, *Titanic: Belfast's Own*, p.101 and the 1881 and 1891 England Censuses, http://www.findmypast.com (accessed 17 April 2008).

44 British Inquiry, Day 5, Question 3807.

45 According to informal evidence from Dillon, provided after his appearance at the British Inquiry. See his biography in *ET* (accessed 29 January 2009).

46 British Inquiry, Day 5, Questions 3858–3933.

47 Gracie, *The Truth about the Titanic*, p.195.

48 Information provided to the author in April 2008 by former Liverpool docker Mr. Mick Clarke, whose father was a friend of Dillon in the 1930s.

49 See Bannon's biography in *ET* (accessed 26 February 2009). Unfortunately, the source of this information is not given.

50 Information courtesy of Mr. Mick Clarke.

51 Deaths registered in January–March 1939, Liverpool North, ref. 8b, p.463, http://www.findmypast.com/bmd.

52 Eaton and Haas, *Titanic: Triumph and Tragedy*, p.178.

53 *Liverpool Echo Titanic Special*, February 1998.

54 At least 96 of *Carpathia*'s crew of 307 on that voyage were born or resident in the Liverpool area. See '*Carpathia* Passengers and Crew', *ET* (accessed 26 February 2008).

55 One of these boats, collapsible A, had already been set adrift by Fifth Officer Lowe: Eaton and Haas, *Titanic: Triumph and Tragedy*, p.179.

56 L. Harrison, *A Titanic Myth: The Californian Incident* (Hanley Swan, Worcs.: SPA Ltd, revised 2nd edn, 1992), p.39.

57 US Inquiry, Day 8.

58 Harrison, *A Titanic Myth*, pp.45–46, 52.

CHAPTER 9

1 D. Bryceson, *The Titanic Disaster: As Reported in the British National Press, April–July 1912* (Patrick Stephens Ltd., part of Hayes Publishing, Sparkford, Somerset, 1997), p.15.

2 *LDPM*, 16 April 1912.

3 Eaton and Haas, *Titanic: Triumph and Tragedy*, p.202

4 *LDPM*, 16 April 1912.

5 *LDPM*, 16 April 1912.

6 *The Times*, 17 April 1912.

7 *The Times*, 18 April 1912.

8 *LDPM*, 19 April 1912.

9 *LDPM*, 26 April 1912.

10 *LDPM*, 13 May 1912.

11 *LDPM*, 17 April 1912.

12 As told by Mr. Thompson to his shipmate John Kearon, who later worked for many years as Head of Shipkeeping, Industrial and Land Transport Conservation at National Museums Liverpool.

13 *LDPM*, 17 April 1912.

14 See Chapter 6.

15 For Palles, see Chapter 4.

16 *LDPM*, 17 April 1912.

17 *LDPM*, 17 April 1912.

18 *LDPM*, 20 April 1912.

19 *LDPM*, 18 April 1912.

20 See the 'Hybrid Solar Eclipse of 1912 April 17' pages at the 'NASA Eclipse' website, http://eclipse.gsfc.nasa.gov (accessed 10 March 2009).

21 *LDPM*, 20 April 1912.

22 *LDPM*, 20 April 1912. See the photograph of this article p. 145.

23 *LDPM*, 20 April 1912.

24 Maritime Archives and Library, MMM, ref. DX/1018/R.

25 *LDPM*, 22 April 1912.

26 See Bryceson, *The Titanic Disaster*, p.97.

27 *LDPM*, 13 May 1912.

CHAPTER 10

1 'Special Meeting, White Star Line, 22nd April, 1912', *TC*, vol.22, no.4 (1999), p.28.

2 K. Kamuda, 'The Sinking of the *Titanic* and Great Sea Disasters', *TC*, vol.24, no.149 (2000), p.21.

3 Oldham, *The Ismay Line*, p.195.

4 US Inquiry, Day 1, 'Testimony of J.B. Ismay'.

5 US Inquiry, Day 5, 'Testimony of Charles Lightoller'.

6 Contemporary copies of this and other telegrams sent by Ismay from *Carpathia* are held at the Maritime Archives and Library, MMM, ref. D/TSA.

7 Eaton and Haas, *Titanic: Triumph and Tragedy*, pp.246–47.

8 *LDPM*, 2 May 1912.

9 *LDPM*, 3 May 1912.

10 See M. Harding O'Hara, *Hands Off The Titanic! (and the Californian)* (Birkenhead: Countyvise, 1989), pp.30–38.

11 *LDPM*, 2 May 1912.

12 *LDPM*, 4 May 1912. His body was buried at sea on 3 May.

13 Maritime Archives and Library, MMM, ref. DX/1549/R.

14 See her biography in *ET* (accessed 13 March 2009).

15 *LDPM*, 15 May 1912. Also see his biography in *ET* (accessed 2 January 2009).

16 *The Syracuse Herald*, Friday 3 May 1912, via *ET* (accessed 20 February 2009).

17 *The Times*, Tuesday 23 April 1912, p.11.

18 Harrison, *A Titanic Myth*, pp.64–65.

19 Harrison, *A Titanic Myth*, p.67.

20 Harrison, *A Titanic Myth*, p.67.

21 Oldham, *The Ismay Line*, p.206.

22 See letter of Harold Sanderson to J.B. Ismay, 7 May 1912, published in W.J. Oldham, 'The *Titanic* and the Chairman', Part 7, *TC*, vol.12, no.2 (1988), p.58.

23 *LDPM*, 13 May 1912.

24 *LDPM*, 13 May 1912.

25 *LDPM*, 13 May 1912.

26 *LDPM*, 13 May 1912.

27 Oldham, 'The *Titanic* and the Chairman', p.59.

28 The *LDPM* (13 May 1912) reported that on 11 May she was 'only eight weeks old', but this appears to have been incorrect. Millvina was born on 2 February 1912, so would have been over ten weeks old on 15 April and 14 weeks old on 11 May. See her biography in *ET* (accessed 12 March 2009).

29 See his biography in *ET* (accessed 13 March 2009). Also see the photograph of Bertram Dean with Eva Hart at Merseyside Maritime Museum in 1988 p.158.

30 They may well have travelled *incognito* to avoid press attention, as they had done on *Titanic*.

31 See her biography in *ET* (accessed 20 February 2009).

32 Carroll, *A Hymn for Eternity*, p.98. Also see the *Daily Sketch*, 18 May 1912.

33 *Liverpool Echo*, 19 May 1912. Cf. the link in Lawrence's *ET* biography (accessed 17 March 2009) to 'Titanic Victim's Funeral', *Southend Standard*, Thursday 16 May 1912 (the date given to this article must be incorrect, since the *Arabic* did not arrive in Liverpool with the body until 17 May).

34 *Daily Sketch*, 18 May 1912.

35 Carroll, *A Hymn for Eternity*, pp.95–98.

36 *Daily Sketch*, 15 May 1912.

37 See Hart's biography in *ET*, and the link to 'Remarkable Statement: Cork Examiner (1912)', posted by Dennis Ahern, USA (accessed 19 March 2009).

38 J.P. Eaton, 'Cancelled Passages Aboard Titanic: Highlights from Voyage, Part 12', *ET*/Research, p.2 (accessed 19 March 2009).

39 See *The 'Titanic' Relief Fund: Scheme of Administration, 19th March 1913* (repr. Indian Orchard, MA: Titanic Historical Society, 2000), p.76. Also see Lester J. Mitcham, 'Titanic Relief Fund – Crew "Master List Case" Numbers' (2006), p.4, in *ET* (accessed 19 March 2008).

40 See 'T. Casey: A Family Mystery', on the *ET* Message Board, posted 22 April 2007 (accessed 24 October 2008).

41 See 'Particulars of Engagement: Titanic Engine Crew: Signed at Southampton: Book 3', ref. 10, in *ET* (accessed 24 March 2009).

42 See *'Titanic' Relief Fund*, p.70.

43 Brian J. Ticehurst, 'Delving into the Relief Funds', *Voyage 64: The Official Journal of the Titanic International Society, Inc.*, Summer 2008, p.225.

44 From original documents held by Mr. Keegan's grandson, Mr. W. Bowe.

45 'Thomas Casey: A Family Mystery', on the *ET* Message Board, posted by J. Capildeo, 3 April 2007 (accessed 24 October 2008).

46 *'Titanic' Relief Fund*, p.75. Cf. S. Molony, *The Irish Aboard Titanic* (Dublin: Wolfhound Press, 2000), pp.211-12.

47 See the link to 'Port Sunlight: Progress' in Clarke's biography in *ET* (accessed 24 March 2009).

48 *The New York Times*, Tuesday 23 April 1912 (via *ET*/item/3508) (accessed 26 February 2008).

49 Eaton and Haas, *Titanic: Triumph and Tragedy*, p.201.

50 See Rostron's biography in *ET* (accessed 26 February 2008).

51 'Liverpool Awards to Carpathia Crew', *The Times*, Monday 16 December 1912, p.3 (via *ET*/item/2635, accessed 26 March 2008).

CHAPTER 11

1 'Special Meeting, White Star Line, 22nd April, 1912', *TC*, vol.22, no.4 (1999), p.27.

2 See *'Titanic' Relief Fund*, p.76. Also Mitcham, 'Titanic Relief Fund – Crew "Master List Case" Numbers' (2006), p.4, *ET* website (accessed 19 March 2008).

3 *LDPM*, Monday 13 May 1912.

4 *LDPM*, Friday 10 May 1912.

5 *ET* Message Board, 'Aftermath/Titanic Relief Fund' (message accessed 2008, now apparently unavailable).

6 See, for example, the link to the *Minutes of the Titanic Relief Fund, Liverpool Area Committee, 1 December 1915*, via Norman Harrison's biography in *ET* (accessed 30 March 2009).

7 *ET* Message Board, 'Aftermath/Titanic Relief Fund' (specific message accessed 2008, now apparently unavailable).

8 'Minute Book of the Titanic Disaster Fund Committee, etc.', from the National Archives website, http://www.nationalarchives.gov.uk (accessed 12 June 2008).

9 See D. Gittins, 'Re: Sack for the Titanic Crew', http://www.titanic-titanic.com/forum/viewtopic (posted and accessed 28 July 2008).

10 Probably worth about £500,000 today.

11 See Oldham, *The Ismay Line*, pp.207–208.

12 The former address of the White Star Line.

13 E. Kamuda (ed.), 'Titanic's Loss and the Liverpool and London Steamship Protection & Indemnity Association', *TC*, vol.26, no.159 (November 2002), pp.151–55. Also see 'Insurance Companies and the Titanic', *The Times*, London, 24 April 1912, p.22.

14 Cf. Monica Harding O'Hara's interesting book *Hands Off the Titanic! (and the Californian)* (1989). The author, an experienced graphologist and journalist, analyses the handwriting of many *Titanic*-related people, including Bruce Ismay. Based on his pre-*Titanic* signature she concludes (p. 25) that he was 'a man with a mass of complexes'.

15 J.D. Gregson, *Differently Situated: The History of the Liverpool & London Steamship Protection & Indemnity Association Limited, 1882–1982* (Liverpool: Liverpool & London P. & I. Management, 1994), pp.81ff.

16 Louden-Brown, *The White Star Line*, p.30.

17 Kamuda, 'Titanic's Loss', p.154.

18 Gregson, *Differently Situated*, p.84.

19 Kamuda, 'Titanic's Loss', pp.153–54.

20 Kamuda, 'Titanic's Loss', p.151.

21 See 'Insurance Companies and the Titanic', *The Times*, London, 24 April 1912, p.22.

22 US Inquiry, Day 9 (27 April 1912). Also see Day 3 (22 April 1912), PAF344, which indicates that he meant the underwriting scheme of the IMM.

23 US Inquiry, Day 11 (30 April 1912), JB1438-40.

24 British Inquiry, Day 16 (4 June 1912), Question 18810.

25 See M. Chirnside, '*Olympic* and *Titanic* – An Analysis of the Robin Gardiner Conspiracy Theory' (BA dissertation, 2005), pp.28ff., http://www.markchirnside.co.uk/Conspiracy_Dissertation.pdf (accessed January 2009).

26 Oldham, *The Ismay Line*, p.225; Louden-Brown, *The White Star Line*, p.30.

27 See Oldham, *The Ismay Line*, pp.208–10.

28 W.J. Oldham, 'The *Titanic* and the Chairman', Part 7, *TC*, vol.12, no.2 (1988), p.60.

29 'Speech of Senator William Alden Smith', US Inquiry, Report, Tuesday 28 May 1912 (accessed 6 January 2009).

30 As was Peter Sloan, *Titanic*'s senior electrician, who did not survive the sinking. See his biography in *ET* (accessed 15 April 2009).

31 See S. Molony, 'Lord Mersey – Obiter Dicta', *ET Research*, 13 March 2005, pp.2, 7 (accessed 6 April 2009).

32 Molony, 'Lord Mersey', p.7 (accessed 10 April 2009).

33 Eaton and Haas, *Titanic: Triumph and Tragedy*, p.260.

34 British Inquiry, 'Index of Witnesses' (accessed 20 March 2009).

35 Harrison, *A Titanic Myth*, p.67.

36 Oldham, *The Ismay Line*, pp.210ff.

37 W.J. Oldham, 'The *Titanic* and the Chairman', Part 9, *TC*, vol.12, no.4 (1988), pp.41–42.

38 British Inquiry, Report, 'Account of Ship's Journey Across the Atlantic', 30 July 1912 (accessed 10 December 2008).

39 Eaton and Haas, *Titanic: Triumph and Tragedy*, p.265.

40 Lightoller, *Titanic and Other Ships*, p.237.

41 British Inquiry, Report, 'Account of the Saving and Rescue of those who Survived. Conduct of Sir Cosmo Duff Gordon and Mr. Ismay', 30 July 1912 (accessed 15 April 2009).

42 British Inquiry, Day 7, Questions 6821–22. This was the actual distance due to the ice conditions, as opposed to the 'straight line' distance shown on a chart, which Lord estimated as at least nineteen miles (Questions 6983, 6985).

43 British Inquiry, Day 7, Questions 6732, 6992.

44 British Inquiry, Day 7, Question 6991.

45 British Inquiry, Final Report, 'Circumstances in Connection with the SS *Californian*'.

46 Harrison, *A Titanic Myth*, p.95.

47 See Lord's biography in *ET* (accessed 20 April 2009).

48 Harrison, *A Titanic Myth*, pp.123–24.

49 See his biography in *ET* (accessed 20 April 2009).

CHAPTER 12

1 W.J. Oldham, 'Mrs. J. Bruce Ismay', *TC*, vol.12, no.1 (1988), p.25.

2 Oldham, *The Ismay Line*, pp.177–84, 221–24. Ismay remained a director of the IMM and a member of its British committee until he resigned from these positions in June 1916: see Louden-Brown, *The White Star Line*, p.28.

3 Titanic Inquiry Project/Limitation of Liability Hearings, 'Deposition of Joseph Bruce Ismay, May 1915', http://www.titanicinquiry.org./lol/lolh.php (accessed 6 January 2009).

4 F.M. Radcliffe, JP, was partner in the firm of Ayrton, Radcliffe and Wright, of the Queen Insurance Buildings, 10 Dale Street, Liverpool. The postmark on the original envelope in which these documents were contained is dated 7 July 1913, a week after Ismay's retirement from White Star.

5 Maritime Archives & Library, MMM, ref. DX/504. They were donated by Alderson Smith Solicitors, Liverpool, successors to Ayrton, Radcliffe and Wright.

6 Louden-Brown, *The White Star Line*, pp.24–26; also idem, 'Ismay and the *Titanic*', *TC*, vol.24, no.149 (2000), pp.27–28.

7 Maritime Archives and Library, MMM, refs. DX/504/12/4 and DX/504/12/1.

8 Oldham, *The Ismay Line*, p.217.

9 Louden-Brown, *The White Star Line*, p.30.

10 Oldham, *The Ismay Line*, p.227. In 1933 'Sandheys' was bought by Liverpool Corporation and demolished to make way for new semi-detached houses: Oldham, *The Ismay Line*, pp.244–45.

11 Oldham, *The Ismay Line*, pp.228–29.

12 Oldham, *The Ismay Line*, p.245.

13 *The Times*, 27 April 1912.

14 *LDPM*, 4 May 1912.

15 *Observer*, 5 May 1912, p.12.

16 *Manchester Guardian*, 27 June 1912, p.12. Both this and the previous reference are quoted by Jonathan Black, '"Noble Titans Born of the Mersey": The Image of the Worker as Hero in the Engine Room Heroes of the RMS *Titanic* Memorial (1912–1916), Liverpool, by Sir William Goscombe John', paper (as yet unpublished) presented at 'Culture and Merseyside' Conference, Liverpool John Moores University, Liverpool, 13–14 November 2008.

17 Black, '"Noble Titans"', p.4.

18 *LDPM*, 31 July 1912.

19 *Daily Mail*, 4 September 1912.

20 *Porcupine*, 13 September 1914

21 Black, '"Noble Titans"', p.5.

22 See L.J. Mitcham, 'The Statistics of the Disaster', *ET/Research*, 14 February 2001 (accessed 6 March 2007); also D. Zeni, *Forgotten Empress: The Tragedy of the Empress of Ireland* (Bebington: Avid Publications, 2001).

23 When she was sunk, *Lusitania* was carrying letters summoning British claimants against White Star after the *Titanic* disaster to appear at New York on 17 May. On the day before *Lusitania* left New York on 1 May Captain William Turner (from Crosby, near Liverpool) had been asked to give testimony at the same hearings in relation to the loss of *Titanic*. See Eaton and Haas, *Titanic: Triumph and Tragedy*, p.227.

24 Black, '"Noble Titans"', p.5.

25 J. Sharples, *Liverpool*, Pevsner Architectural Guides (New Haven and London: Yale University Press, 2004), p.72.

26 Barczewski, *Titanic: A Night Remembered*, pp.172–76.

27 See Chapter 10.

28 *LDPM*, 4 and 13 May 1912. Also see B. Ticehurst, 'John Frederick Preston Clarke', *ET/*Articles and Stories (accessed 16 April 2009).

29 See 'Titanic Town – Crosby's Links to the *Titanic* and Other Ships', *ET/*Articles and Stories (accessed 16 April 2009).

30 See Chapter 10.

31 See Chapter 9.

32 See Senan Molony, 'On the Trail of "Lucky Tower"', *ET/*Research (2004) (accessed 16 March 2009).

33 Information about Thompson was supplied by relatives still living in the Liverpool area.

34 See her biography in *ET* and follow the links to related articles (accessed 16 April 2009).

35 See L.H. Powell, *History of the Liverpool Steam Ship Owners' Association, 1858–1958* (Liverpool: Liverpool Steam Ship Owners' Association, 1958), p.24.

36 Louden-Brown, *The White Star Line*, p.30.

37 Louden-Brown, *The White Star Line*, p.41.

38 Louden-Brown, *The White Star Line*, pp.39–41.

39 'Over The Mersey Wall', *Liverpool Evening Express*, Wednesday 6 August 1958.

40 *Liverpool Echo*, Tuesday 5 August 1958 (MMM ref. DX/1522).

41 'Over The Mersey Wall', *Liverpool Evening Express*, Wednesday 6 August 1958.

42 MMM, accession number 1966.15.

43 MMM, ref. 1962.342.1-3.

44 Quoted by Harrison, *A Titanic Myth*, p.156.

45 Despite the resignation over this issue of MMSA president, Sir Ivan Thompson, in 1961.

46 Maritime Archives and Library, MMM, ref. D/LO.

47 See 'Rake Lane Cemetery, Wallasey', http://www.wallaseycemetery.co.uk (accessed 10 April 2009). *Titanic* steward George Dodd, Bruce Ismay's former butler, is remembered on his family's gravestone in this cemetery; see Chapter 5. William Turner, master of *Lusitania* when she was sunk in May 1915, is also buried there.

48 US Inquiry, Day 8 (19?–20 miles); British Inquiry, Day 8, Questions 6983, 6985 (19 miles). With these figures Lord meant the shortest distance (i.e. a straight line on a chart), as opposed to the actual distance (which he estimated at about 30 miles: British Inquiry, Day 8, Questions 6822–23), given the vast ice barrier between *Californian* and *Titanic*.

49 See, for example T.B. Williams, *Titanic and the Californian* (Gloucester: Tempus Publishing, rev. edn, 2007), pp.212ff.; S. Molony, *Titanic and the Mystery Ship* (Gloucester: Tempus Publishing, 2006).

50 From A. Clarkson, 'Professor Helps RMST', http://www.titanic-titanic.com/forum (accessed 3 March 2008).

CONCLUSION

1 See Liverpool World Heritage homepage, http://www.liverpoolworldheritage.com, p.2 (accessed March 2009).

2 See, for example, *ET/*Listings/People residing in Southampton (accessed 27 April 2009).

3 *Southern Evening Echo*, Southampton, 18 June 1961, p.4. News cutting from MMM, MAL, ref. D/LO/3/4/10.

SELECT BIBLIOGRAPHY

Anderson R., *White Star* (Prescot, Lancs.: T. Stephenson & Sons, 1964).

Anon., *A Short History of F.C. Danson & Company, 1879–1973* (Liverpool: privately published, c. 1973).

Barczewski, S., *Titanic: A Night Remembered* (London and New York: Hambledon & London/Palgrave Macmillan, 2004).

Belchem, J., *Irish, Catholic and Scouse: The History of the Liverpool-Irish, 1800–1939* (Liverpool: Liverpool University Press, 2007).

—— *Merseypride: Essays in Liverpool Exceptionalism* (Liverpool: Liverpool University Press, 2000).

—— (ed.), *Liverpool 800: Culture, Character and History* (Liverpool: Liverpool University Press, 2006).

Bryceson, D., *The Titanic Disaster: As reported in the British National Press, April–July 1912* (Sparkford, Somerset: Patrick Stephens Ltd, Part of Hayes Publishing, 1997).

Butler, D.A., *Unsinkable: The Full Story of the RMS Titanic* (Mechanicsburg, PA: Stackpole Books, 1998).

Cameron, S., *Titanic: Belfast's Own* (Dublin: Wolfhound Press, 1998).

Carroll, Y., *A Hymn for Eternity: The Story of Wallace Hartley, Titanic Bandmaster* (Gloucester: Tempus Publishing, 2002).

Eaton, J.P., and Haas, C.A, *Titanic: Triumph and Tragedy* (Wellingborough: Patrick Stephens, 2nd impression, 1987).

Gracie, Col. A., *The Truth about the Titanic* (1913; reprinted with additional material Riverside, CT: 7 C's Press, 1973).

Gregson, J.D., *Differently Situated: The History of the Liverpool & London Steamship Protection & Indemnity Association Limited, 1882–1982* (Liverpool: Liverpool & London P. & I. Management, 1994).

Harding O'Hara, M., *Hands Off the Titanic! (and the Californian)* (Birkenhead: Countyvise, 1989).

Harrison, L., *A Titanic Myth: The Californian Incident* (Hanley Swan, Worcs.: SPA, 2nd rev. edn, 1992)

Hughes, T., *The Blue Riband of the Atlantic* (Cambridge: Patrick Stephens, 1973).

Hyde, F.E., *Cunard and the North Atlantic, 1840–1973* (London: Humanities Press, 1975).

Hyslop, D., Forsyth, A., and Jemima, S., *Titanic Voices: The Story of the White Star Line, Titanic and Southampton* (Southampton: Southampton City Council, 1994).

Lane, T., *Liverpool: City of the Sea* (Liverpool: Liverpool University Press, 2nd rev. edn, 1997).

Lightoller, C.H., *Titanic and Other Ships* (London: Nicholson and Watson, 1935; repr. Hull: Historia Press, 2007).

Littler, D. (ed.), *Guide to the Records of Merseyside Maritime Museum*, vol. II (St. John's, Newfoundland: Trustees of the National Museums and Galleries on Merseyside/International Maritime Economic History Association, 1999).

Liverpool: Maritime Mercantile City (Liverpool: Liverpool City Council/Liverpool University Press, 2005).

Lord, W., *A Night to Remember* (London: Allen Lane/Penguin Books, rev. illustrated edn, 1976).

Louden-Brown, P., *The White Star Line: An Illustrated History, 1899–1934* (Herne Bay, Kent: Titanic Historical Society, 2nd edn, 2001).

McCaughan, M., *The Birth of Titanic* (Belfast: Blackstaff Press, 1998).

McCluskie, T., Sharpe, M., and Marriott, L., *Titanic and her Sisters* (London: Parkgate Books, 1998).

Mills, S., *RMS Olympic: The Old Reliable* (Falmouth, Cornwall: Waterfront Publications, 2nd edn, 1995).

Molony, S., *The Irish Aboard Titanic* (Dublin: Wolfhound Press, 2000).

Molony, S., *Titanic and the Mystery Ship* (Gloucester: Tempus Publishing, 2006).

Moss, M. and Hume, J.R., *Shipbuilders to the World: 125 Years of Harland and Wolff, Belfast, 1861–1986* (Belfast and Wolfeboro, New Hampshire: Blackstaff Press, 1986).

Murphy, M. (ed.), *The Collected George Garrett* (Nottingham: Trent Editions/Nottingham Trent University, 1999).

Oldham, W.J., *The Ismay Line* (Liverpool: Journal of Commerce, 1961).

Powell, L.H., *History of the Liverpool Steam Ship Owners' Association, 1858–1958* (Liverpool: Liverpool Steam Ship Owners' Association, 1958).

Saint, A., *Richard Norman Shaw* (New Haven and London: published for the Paul Mellon Centre for Studies in British Art Ltd by Yale University Press, 1976; 3rd printing, 1983).

Sharples, J., *Liverpool*, Pevsner Architectural Guides (New Haven and London: Yale University Press, 2004).

The 'Titanic' Relief Fund, 19 March 1913 (repr. Indian Orchard, MA: Titanic Historical Society, Inc., 2000).

A Tribute to the Engineering Staff: 80th Anniversary of the Sinking of R.M.S. Titanic, 1912–1992 (London: The Institute of Marine Engineers, Guild of Benevolence, 1992).

The White Star Liners Olympic and Titanic: Ocean Liners of the Past, No. 1, Reprinted from 'The Shipbuilder', 1911 (Cambridge: Patrick Stephens, 1972, repr. 1976).

Vale, V., *The American Peril: Challenge to Britain on the North Atlantic, 1901–04* (Manchester: Manchester University Press, 1984).

Whale, D., *The Liners of Liverpool*, Part 1 (Birkenhead: Countyvise, 1986).

Williams, T.B., *Titanic and the Californian* (Gloucester: Tempus Publishing, rev. edn, 2007).

Zeni, D., *Forgotten Empress: The Tragedy of the Empress of Ireland* (Bebington, Wirral: Avid Publications, 2001).

INDEX